# REVOLUTION

Volume 5

# THE BODY AND THE FRENCH REVOLUTION

# THE BODY AND THE FRENCH REVOLUTION

## Sex, Class and Political Culture

DORINDA OUTRAM

LONDON AND NEW YORK

First published in 1989 by Yale University Press

This edition first published in 2022
by Routledge
4 Park Square, Milton Park, Abingdon, Oxon OX14 4RN

and by Routledge
605 Third Avenue, New York, NY 10158

*Routledge is an imprint of the Taylor & Francis Group, an informa business*

© 1989 Dorinda Outram

All rights reserved. No part of this book may be reprinted or reproduced or utilised in any form or by any electronic, mechanical, or other means, now known or hereafter invented, including photocopying and recording, or in any information storage or retrieval system, without permission in writing from the publishers.

Trademark notice: Product or corporate names may be trademarks or registered trademarks, and are used only for identification and explanation without intent to infringe.

*British Library Cataloguing in Publication Data*
A catalogue record for this book is available from the British Library

ISBN: 978-1-032-12623-4 (Set)
ISBN: 978-1-003-26095-0 (Set) (ebk)
ISBN: 978-1-032-12638-8 (Volume 5) (hbk)
ISBN: 978-1-032-12649-4 (Volume 5) (pbk)
ISBN: 978-1-003-22556-0 (Volume 5) (ebk)

DOI: 10.4324/9781003225560

**Publisher's Note**
The publisher has gone to great lengths to ensure the quality of this reprint but points out that some imperfections in the original copies may be apparent.

**Disclaimer**
The publisher has made every effort to trace copyright holders and would welcome correspondence from those they have been unable to trace.

# THE BODY AND THE FRENCH REVOLUTION
## Sex, Class and Political Culture

Dorinda Outram

YALE UNIVERSITY PRESS
NEW HAVEN AND LONDON 1989

Copyright © 1989 by Yale University

All rights reserved. This book may not be reproduced in whole or in part, in any form (beyond that copying permitted by Sections 107 and 108 of the U.S. Copyright Law and except by reviewers for the public press), without written permission from the publishers.

Set in Linotron Bembo by Best-set Typesetter Ltd, Hong Kong.
Printed and bound by The Bath Press, Great Britain.

Library of Congress Catalog Card Number 89-50070
ISBN 0-300-04436-4

# CONTENTS

*List of Illustrations* vi
*Acknowledgements* ix
1 The Problem of the Body in Political Culture 1
2 Modern Histories of the Body 6
3 Deconstructing the French Revolution 27
4 The Eighteenth-Century Medical Revolution: Bodies, Souls and the Social Classes 41
5 A New Public Body: Stoicism, Suffering and the Middle Class in the French Revolution 68
6 Heroic Suicide: The End of the Body and the Beginning of History 90
7 The Guillotine, the Soul and the Audience for Death 106
8 Words and Flesh: Mme Roland, the Female Body and the Search for Power 124
9 The French Revolution, Modernity and the Body Politic 153
*Notes* 165
*Index* 189

# LIST OF ILLUSTRATIONS

|   |   | Page |
|---|---|---|
| I | Ford Madox Brown, *Work* (1865). City Art Gallery, Manchester | 18 |
| II | Duane Hanson, *Tourists* (1970). Scottish National Gallery of Modern Art, Edinburgh | 24 |
| III | 'L'Homme de Village', cartoon. Bibliothèque Nationale (Cabinet des Estampes), Paris | 43 |
| IV | William Cheselden, *Osteographia* (1733). Exeter Cathedral Library, Exeter | 52 |
| V | 'Qu'un sang impur abreuve nos sillons', cartoon. Musée Carnavalet, Paris | 65 |
| VI | J.-L. David, *croquis d'après Bonaparte* (? 1799). Musée Masséna, Nice | 73 |
| VII | Albert Keller, *Humboldt and Bonpland's Expedition Camp by the Orinoco*. Staatsbibliothek, West Berlin | 77 |
| VIII | Laneuville, *Portrait of Barère de Vieuzac* (c.1792). Kunsthalle, Bremen | 82 |
| IX | J.-L. David, *Brutus* (1789). Musée du Louvre, Paris (photo Bulloz) | 86 |
| X | J.-L. David, *Death of Socrates* (1787). Metropolitan Museum of Art, New York | 94 |
| XI | J.L.A.T. Géricault, *Heads of the Executed* (? 1818). National Museum, Stockholm | 113 |
| XII | 'The Death of Robespierre', cartoon. Bibliothèque Nationale, Paris | 120 |

# LIST OF ILLUSTRATIONS

XIII    F. Bonneville, engraving of Mme Roland. Bibliothèque Nationale (Cabinet des Estampes), Paris    137

XIV    G. Lavater, 'M. and Mme Roland de la Platière with their daughter at Zurich in 1787', silhouettes. Private possession    146

# ACKNOWLEDGEMENTS

This book was begun during the tenure of a research fellowship at Girton College, Cambridge, and completed at University College Cork. I would like to thank both institutions for their support, both financial and moral, and in particular to acknowledge generous financial assistance from the Arts Faculty Research Fund and the Development Fund of the latter. Much has also been contributed to this book by conversations with friends in England, Ireland, France and America, and especially by Patricia Coughlin, Tom Dunne, Bruno Latour, Jim Livesey, Jim Secord, Judith Sklar and Simon Schaffer. I would also like to acknowledge the many insights gained into the political dimension of the human body during conversations with women campaigning on related issues in the Irish context. Naturally, none of these individuals or groups are to be held responsible for any errors contained in this account. Lastly, I would like to thank my editor, Robert Baldock, for his patient and persistently sympathetic support during a difficult and complex undertaking.

Dorinda Outram

Cambridge–Cork
1988

# 1

# THE PROBLEM OF THE BODY IN POLITICAL CULTURE

> The patriots of France have discovered in good time that rank and dignity in society must take a new ground. The old one has fallen through.
>
> Tom Paine, *The Rights of Man*[1]

The physical body is at once our most intimate experience and our most inescapable public form. Because it is at once so inalienably private and so ineluctably public, it has also formed, in most western cultures, the most basic political resource. It has been used as an image of the order of state and society: the bearing, features and physical dignity – what the classical world labelled as *gravitas* – of rulers and great men has traditionally been the means, as it still is in the nations of the Third World, by which power is wielded and authority imposed. In the world of the twentieth century, the body as we experience it in western society faces us with many problems. What are our bodies for? Beyond the satisfaction of immediate biological needs for survival and of the production of pleasure, the experience of living in western societies today provides few answers to this question and none which involve the compulsive linkage to the public sphere, to structures of power, authority and order, which was commonplace in the pre-modern world. Least of all is there an awareness of any sort of sacralized picture of the body. Christianity itself was built around the transformation of the physical suffering of one particular body into the redemption of the world. Through that image, individuals were able to transform suffering, death and biological life events (the history of their own, intimately experienced body) into events of universal moral and spiritual significance. All these trends together – the conflict over the acceptance of the sacralized body, and the expulsion of the body as a symbol from the public world – mean that individuals are left with bodies whose experiences seem ineluctably private. So basic is this fact to the nature of modern political systems, that when the nature of this privacy is challenged, as for example by feminism, a new political movement is born.

Modern societies in the West are also heir to several other problems which intimately concern the body both as public symbol and as private experience. Most obviously, these societies have experienced the full force of totalitarian regimes whose political styles are characterized by an extreme focus on the public body, demeanour and physical projection of a charismatic leadership figure. Such regimes are also characterized by a very specific set of attitudes towards the human body itself, involving a total desacralization of the body; the ultimate expression of these attitudes was the concentration camp, but they were experienced also through the entire organization of mass politics, which used physical violence against opponents and massed presentation of individuals as testimony to a leader's charisma and success. Such regimes might be thought, in spite of the deep scars they have left on the twentieth century, and in spite of the fact that regimes such as those still in existence today in the military states of Latin America emulate their most salient features, to have been aberrations from an assumed norm of the 'liberal-democratic' state which, it is often assumed, gradually emerged in Europe after the French Revolution and after industrialization. It is one of the arguments of this book that the French Revolution in fact unleashed changes in the public presentation and public significance of the bodies of individuals which were crucial in the formation of public space in the nineteenth century; and that this public space was ripe for a take-over of power along the lines of the totalitarian movements in the twentieth century.

This book focuses on the period of the Revolution in France, a period which lasts, in the acute form of political conflict and change, from approximately 1787 to 1799, when fighting between various factional groups among the middle-class successors of the monarchy for control of the shape of the new republic and the definition of public space was temporarily halted by the advent of Napoleon Bonaparte. The French Revolution was important because it led to the political and cultural victory of the middle class over the monarchy and aristocracy, and this became the main pattern of development of other Western European states. But such a triumph also faced the middle class, and especially its leading edge of individuals and groups engaged in the production of political forms, symbols and practices, with huge problems. It was not only that, on the level of practical politics, the monarchical organization of government had to be replaced at virtually every level; it was also that in order for that politics to be practicable the legitimacy of its practitioners also had to be constructed, validated, and made continually visible in a newly-defined public space.

In the event, the Revolution failed to construct a 'modern state', however that is defined. Rather, what occurred was a series of transformation scenes, in which forms of government and ruling factions succeeded one another with bewildering rapidity and in which public space itself became increasingly crucial and increasingly ambiguous, as the introduction of mass political participation put new stresses on the ability to retain power. It was perhaps this very introduction of mass participation into French political life during the Revolution which has made the state forms produced by it look deceptively modern. Twentieth-century western states are, after all, distinguished by this very feature. But in fact the French Revolution failed to create coherent, stable, effective, widely accepted organs of government. It also failed to create organs of government which were easily distinguishable from the individuals and clienteles to whom their operation was entrusted. 'Objective', in the Weberian sense, the French state was not. The great retardation of industrialization in France also meant that the government of France was for most even of the nineteenth century deprived of the possibility of extracting a significant surplus from the national economy; and without that surplus, the expansive and extensive mechanism of a modern state was impossible to create. This meant, in turn, that the construction of public value systems did not transform itself as the century proceeded. The dependence of all French political groups on the rhetoric, mythology and political roles produced by the Revolution was noted by Karl Marx forty years afterwards, in 1848, and continued for many years after.

The Revolution did not create a state: rather it created a new and sensitive public space. In this public space competing discourses were produced, usually by fractions of the middle class, which attempted to legitimize one version of the new forms of government over the other. No one discourse ever obtained a decisive victory. It is this fact which is a pre-condition for the weakness and disunion of French political culture in the nineteenth and twentieth centuries and for the consequent later take-over of civil society in France by corporative fractions of the state apparatus. The collapsing into one another of state and civil society is one of the most distinctive pre-conditions for the appearance of a mass politics along the lines of twentieth-century Fascist states, and of this process the French state is, if not the most extreme example, the laboratory experiment for the rest of Europe.

Why should we be approaching this argument through a history of the body in the public sphere? One of the answers to this question is simple: that one of the most important of the tasks facing the middle class of the French Revolution was the re-creation of a public sphere which for centuries had been dominated and defined by two key concepts: by images of the *body politic* and of the *king's body*. As many historians have pointed out, much of the political culture produced by the Revolution was aimed, whether successfully or not, at redistributing various attributes of the king's body throughout the new body politic. The public space of France before 1789 had also focused on an image of heroic public dignity almost exclusively applied to monarchy and aristocracy: it was such images that the middle class had to re-create. The new public bodies which they created and filled with attributes of heroic dignity were in turn inconceivable without, and were created for, the audiences that mass politics made possible. They possessed the power, which the competing linguistic discourses obviously did not, to focus dignity and legitimacy in incontestable, because non-verbal, ways on the bodies of known individuals who acted as personifications of value systems. In creating audiences for bodies of heroic dignity, the middle class were also creating the audiences without which their own actions, in public space, and hence public space itself, would have been inconceivable. So from the beginning, the creation of a public body was possibly the most important project in that still hotly debated area, which is the meaning of middle-class political dominance of the state.

It is also the case that the history of the body allows us to explore and to challenge some of the most powerful paradigms which dominate the analysis of history and of society today: in other words, some of the most persuasive attempts made to tell us who we in the West actually are – or are not. Both Marxism and 'liberalism', the two most available ideologies of identity for the political class, have come under severe challenge in post-war thinking in Western Europe. Increasingly, philosophers such as Michel Foucault have challenged, firstly, the key liberal idea that history is about the actions and reactions of 'subjects' – separately acting individuals searching for identities based on personal autonomy. After proclaiming the famous 'death of the subject', Foucault and others have also gone on to contest the Marxist idea of a hierarchy of different levels of historical causality among different levels of the economy and society. Following Foucault's lead, it is currently fashionable to treat the way we explain our social predicaments in terms of an 'ecology' of causes, whereby it becomes difficult to privilege any one area of explanation over any other.

But there are great problems with this account. Firstly, it produces a counter-intuitive history from which individuals and their subjectivity have been peremptorily removed; while yet each one of us still experiences him or herself as irreducibly individual. Such a history, while performing the service of reminding us that history cannot be totally constructed out of the histories of individuals, also colludes with the mass politics of the twentieth century, with its devaluation of the individual historical actor and its remorseless devaluation of the human body, rather than showing any way forward to mount a challenge to it. Foucault's analysis of the authority relationships built into the control of the body in the modern world is itself as authoritarian and as dismissive of individuals as the political system it aspires to criticize. A history, to be non-collusive with current political/social trends, on the other hand, should and must focus on the body, in a quite different way from that adopted by Foucault, because the body is the only space in which intentionality can be restored to the historical subject and, at the same time, come together with that subject's connection with, transformation of, and manifestation of, current cultural paradigms.

Like a prism, the body has a unique capacity to concentrate together in the same space different rays from the surrounding world, and to re-emit light re-charged and differentiated. Intentionality and *episteme* come together, and subjective experience can be assessed as something other than simply a personalized anarchy. We can thus escape from the false dichotomies between forms of history from which individuals have been banished, and forms in which they are the *only* subject matter, and enter a history of inter-subjectivity, in which the structural forms of interlocking private experiences become the text. Such a viewpoint also enables us, finally, to assess ways of making bodies again important in modern civil society: bodies are important because the only experiences which cannot be co-opted by political systems are the inevitably personal bodily experiences of individuals. They are thus also one of the few resources through which genuinely new political systems might be created.

By assessing the success and failures of the French revolutionaries in a similar project, we learn much about the potentialities of our own political future. It will be the argument of this book that it was precisely the failure of the Revolution, in spite of many attempts, to produce enduring and practical models for the dignified public body which led ultimately to the paradoxes of nineteenth- and twentieth-century politics: that individuals deprived of public worth or visibility for their physicality, came increasingly to focus on the manifest public bodies of individual charismatic leaders; and that this allowed such leaders, playing on the frailty of the public roles of the majority of individuals, to construct a political ideology based on the construction of super-heroes who would destroy mysterious others, possessed of different bodies, such as Jews or gypsies, who threatened the frail public body itself.

# 2

# MODERN HISTORIES OF THE BODY

> Children like to touch clothes and other things that please them with their hands. This urge must be corrected and they must be taught to touch all that they see only with their eyes.
>
> J. de La Salle, *Civilité*[1]

In a famous catch-phrase, Barthes observes that it is the nature of myth to turn historical event into natural object.[2] It should thus follow that histories of the body cannot be mythological. But in fact, historians of the body have perpetrated as many myths as any inhabitant of the *Tristes tropiques* or editor of *Marie-Claire*. Current historical focus on 'the history of the body' has itself to be critically examined if we are to gain understanding of what is involved in writing about the body in a historical way, and if we are to be able to define freshly the scope of a book which dares to integrate two such extensively – and very differently – invested areas as the history of the French Revolution and the history of the body.

Since the reception of Michel Foucault's work in the Anglo-Saxon intellectual world, the 'history of the body' has achieved widespread acceptance as a distinct area of historical interest.[3] In fact, so much has it, in spite of the initially highly critical reaction to Foucault in many quarters, become a tolerated part of the intellectual landscape that it also seems to have become curiously exempt – as all good Barthean myths are – from enquiries into its origins and into its political implications and directions. But the attempt to situate historiographically these current histories of the body cannot be avoided if they are truly to become part of a generally applicable repertoire of explanatory tools for large historical developments, rather than remaining, as they are now, an accepted, but none the less isolated part of historical practice. To demonstrate that 'histories of the body' and 'big history' can be integrated is one of the purposes of this book.

Foucault, of course, is not the only contributor to this field. Very different, and important, histories have been constructed in the twentieth century by individuals such as Norbert Elias.[4] At the same time, for example, feminist historians have, in spite of their differences, also produced a specific history of the (female) body, as have the medical historians and, by implication, the family historians likewise,[5] to set against the gender-blind histories of Elias and Foucault. All these accounts have in common, at least in the Anglo-Saxon historical world, their association with fractional history, 'history of...', rather than general history. Though well known and prestigious, they are not absorbed and integrated. Standard histories of the 'classical age', or of the growth of state power, manage their accounts with no more than token nods in the directions of Foucault or Elias; in other words, history of the body is associated with the fractionalization of history, rather than its integration. Few indeed are the attempts made to integrate histories of the body with *histoire événementielle*. These 'histories' also of course themselves fractionalize far older genres in the history of the body, genres which were far more closely integrated into a general historical outlook: this would go for both classical and Christian histories.[6]

Part of the problem lies in the fact that histories of the body are not neutral, ideologically, in the way that some, though not all, general history, claims to be. It is not only that they all involve specific claims about the nature of power, but also that their historical analyses of the body are made in relation to specific philosophies and specific external ideological predicaments which are often not explicitly acknowledged. To gain a real understanding of the ways these different histories of the body are presented, and to re-fashion them, we have to find out where they come from. To do anything else is to treat them either as accidents or as Barthean myths.

Modern histories of the body originated during the same era as the high point of European Fascism. The 1930s and 1940s saw an intense focus in many of the social sciences which fed into historical enquiry on the social functions of the human body.[7] In anthropology, studies by Margaret Mead and Gregory Bateson tackled the problem of the relationship between cultures and physical expression; social psychologists began to map the gestures of aggression and inferiority; the publication of Sigmund Freud's *Civilization and Its Discontents* as well as other works produced a shift of attention to ideas that might integrate physical control and physical self-image with prevailing social forms.[8] And the factors which highlighted the body, its social representations and its political role, were not merely internal to academic discourse: they accurately mirrored an external reality. The politics of the Fascist era in Europe were nothing if not physical. The deliberate use of physical violence as a political instrument, the genocidal policies which depended on racial theories of physical characteristics, the creation of a mass political audience through relentless projection of the national leaders' appearance, voice and gestures in mass rallies, were the hallmarks of the era, which marked it out as different from any which had gone before.

Nor was this heightened body-awareness confined to the political arena, spectacular and terrifying though that was; insistent exploitation of representations of the body was an integral part both of the popular and of the official culture of the era, even outside the Fascist states. The era of mass party gymnastic displays was also that of the musicals featuring complex dance routines involving hundreds of dancers, which gained their impact, as much as did any Nuremberg rally, from the mass display of disciplined bodies making complex gestures. The body had become the prime area of public gesture, as well as the prime location where the exercise of political control was demonstrated. At the same time increased state intervention in nutrition, in medical provision, in food planning, and in population planning of all kinds also emphasized an idea of the body as an area where spiritual values were absent and the conjunction of political and physical management was dominant.[9] Very visibly, emphasis shifted from the body as the arena of *self*-control, which the nineteenth century had stressed, to the body as an arena where the sovereignty either of a mass politics or a mass culture was made manifest.

Not surprisingly, this was also the time when the issue of sovereignty itself, in the political sense, was under continuous challenge from the theory and practice of the totalitarian states, in their onslaught on the liberal parliamentary democracies which they replaced. The societies of the 1940s only intensified these trends. More and more, governments managed bodies *en masse*. And while, in wartime, this was a development which affected practically all states, the Fascist states – those in Europe, Nazi Germany and its collaborator regimes particularly – took it to its ultimate conclusion. The *univers concentrationnaire* ensured that all bodies became disposable, the rationale for their disappearance a fantasy of the state. It was against this ideological and political background that the first of the major histories of the body with which we are concerned, that by Norbert Elias, a German Jew, was written and published.

Because of the timing and circumstances of its publication, Elias's work remained virtually unknown in the English-speaking world, and had little resonance in Germany. In the 1970s, however, all this changed. Books on bodies, their representation and their decoding started to proliferate again, Elias's work was finally translated, Michel Foucault came to prominence. At the same time, organized feminism began to produce histories of its own. A new historical focus seemed to have been created. The appearance in translation of Mikhail Bakhtin's *Rabelais and His World* – again, like the works of Elias and Marcel Mauss, long after its original publication – meant that there existed simultaneously, by the 1970s, several syntheses of great power, all focusing on the historical transformations of the body.[10]

It is easy to draw links between the explosion of interest in the body in history and in social theory, and the wider culture's interest in that same area from the late 1960s onward. Physical culture, diet and appearance become culturally dominant and commercially crucial at precisely the same time as the work of Foucault, and the republication of Elias and Bakhtin, and the women's movement in history started to home in on the history of the body.[11] Nor has this interest diminished, as, just as in the 1930s, political polarization between left and right has sharpened. But I would also wish to argue that the historical synthesis which has emerged is to a large extent illusory. Foucault and Elias, in particular, on whose work we will most fruitfully focus to inform the entire body of this work, do not write out of the same concerns, in spite of the superficial convergence of their work on the question of the discipline and repression of the body, and its relationship with the formation of the state. They are, also, problematic writers, and to understand the degree of that problematic character is also to come to an understanding of the purposes and implications of their work.

Norbert Elias dedicates the first volume of the translation of his work, *On the Civilizing Process*, to the memory of his mother and father, Jews who died, respectively, in Auschwitz in 1942, and in Breslau in 1940. This dedication is the key to the book. Elias's work cannot be understood except as a hostile response to many aspects of the official philosophy of the regime which came to power in January 1933. Let us begin by giving in brief outline, which will do no justice either to the rigour of Elias's argument or to the complexity of his information, a summary of that argument. He asks: why are modern men and women less violent in daily life, more delicate in their eating habits, more secretive about such bodily functions as spitting, nose-blowing, urinating, defecating and copulating, more anxious about covering or exposing their bodies, than their medieval counterparts were? What do these alterations in 'manners' in particular and behaviour in general, in fact in the entire relation of individuals to their bodies, and to the socially acceptable relationships between bodies, have to do with the political and economic changes which created modern society, and in particular the modern state? Elias argues that the great change in physical behaviour is part of a general process of repression of immediate urges and reactions, which has ultimately affected not just physical functions and table manners, but the intimate self-consciousness of individuals as well. People begin to be separated from each other not only because it gradually becomes first uncouth, and then positively improper, to eat from a common dish, or share a bed with a stranger of either sex, or urinate in public, but also because this 'rising threshold of shame and embarrassment' means that their whole behaviour towards one another becomes more restrained, and is characterized by the absence of immediate contact and by the repression of immediate impulses. In these circumstances, individuals begin to feel sharp boundaries between themselves and others, between the inner world of the 'real me', and the outer world of 'the other'. What Elias calls the *homo clausus* of the nineteenth and twentieth centuries is thus created:

> The firmer, more comprehensive, and uniform restraint of the affects characteristic of this civilizational shift, together with the increased internal compulsions that, more implacably than before, prevent all spontaneous impulses from manifesting themselves directly and motorically in action, without the intervention of control mechanisms – these are what is experienced as the capsule, the invisible wall dividing the 'inner world' of the individual from the external world, or...the subject of cognition from its object, the 'ego' from the other, the 'individual' from 'society'. What is encapsulated are the restrained instinctual and affective impulses denied direct access to the motor apparatus. They appear in self-perception as what is hidden from all others, and often as the true self, the core of individuality.[12]

Elias acknowledges that this 'civilizing process' is not one simply to be condemned. One of the themes of his work is that suppression of immediate reaction-based urges goes hand in hand with an increasing respect for the physical sanctity of other people's bodies, because the aggressive urges are part of what is repressed. Similarly, he argues, the modern idea of equality between the sexes could appear only when people could imagine 'transcending' their bodies, and women and men could see each other in terms apart from biological functions. But he also, at other points, condemns the end product of increasing restraint, the ideal of the *homo clausus*:

> ...there is no structural feature of man that justifies our calling one thing the core of man and another the shell. Strictly speaking, the whole complex of tensions, such as feeling and thought, or spontaneous behaviour, consists of human activities.... On this

level, there is nothing that resembles a container, nothing that could justify metaphors like that of the 'inside' of a human being. The intuition of a wall, of something 'inside' man separated from the 'outside' world, ... corresponds to nothing in man having the character of a real wall. One recalls that Goethe once expressed the idea that nature has neither core nor shell, and that in her there is neither inside nor outside. This is true of human beings as well.[13]

Elias announced one of the main aims of his work, indeed, as being '...to dislodge this experience [of isolated egocentrism] and the image of man corresponding to it, from its self-evident acceptance in research in the human sciences',[14] an agenda that is still relevant today.

Elias's second major contention is that the formation of *homo clausus* and the formation of the modern state go hand in hand. He shows that in late medieval times, self-control was first linked to social status. Self-control was courtly behaviour. In the Renaissance and early modern periods, the court and the bourgeoisie began to mix; the bourgeoisie sought to win acceptance by practising the courtesies and delicacies of court life. Again, shame was the central emotion at stake. If the bourgeois could not control himself, he would be exposed as the vulgar person he secretly feared himself to be; ashamed of his origins, he paid for social ascent with the repression of his body. As medieval life waned, codes of self-control, originally the distinguishing marks of the aristocracy, spread out to become the mores of society as a whole; each new social group which aspired to upward mobility, or acceptance by the 'court society', joined the desire with anxiety about being able to control itself.

The hallmark of the modern state, de Tocqueville wrote, is the combination of individualism and nationalism. Elias goes on to show why these two terms have come to be linked. He shows that as the nation rather than the caste or hereditary station has become the unit of culture, the process of becoming cultured is now something each person does internally and alone, for the nature of becoming 'civilized' is to make biological control of oneself a private matter: *homo clausus* is born. Elias's achievement in linking physical consciousness, individual identity and state formation is a major one, and provides the basic approach of the present work. But in other ways, Elias's account of the relation between state formation and individual circumstances poses as many problems as it solves. These problems, I believe, are related not so much to defects in Elias's historical understanding as to the specific circumstances in which his work was produced.

The first problem lies in the fact that although Elias announces his theme as the relationship between the 'civilization' of shame and bodily repression and the growth of the modern state, in fact his historical analysis ceases at the end of the eighteenth century, and stops short of the period of the French Revolution. This raises a problem in Elias's own terms, since the Revolution is now regarded, by historians of many different political complexions, as the point at which the paradigmatic modern definition of the state was first made manifest.[15] This book intends to take the argument of the political theorists one stage further and connects the disappearance of the sacral state with the disappearance of a sacral notion of the human body. So Elias's account really relates only to a state formation *in potenza*. Precisely the transition from the 'court society' to the modern state, which the French Revolution encapsulates and which would at once provide a summary and a test case of Elias's arguments, is missing. It is one of the main purposes of this book to apply Elias's account of the erection of the culture of shame and its connection with the modern state to precisely that era, and in doing so to test the so-called 'modernity' of the French Revolution.

A second problematic area in Elias's history is provoked by his decision to define, after prolonged discussion of the history of the concept, 'civilization' as the increasing restraint of violence. This is a definition which is belied by the very events which were to overwhelm the author and his family so soon after the publication of his book. A possible way to resolve this very real problem is the argument – not one put forward by Elias himself – that the modern state is also distinguished from Renaissance and court societies by the fact that not only is it a national state, but that it controls a monopoly of violence, and punishes all those who try to infringe that monopoly. In a sense, the modern state has gathered up all the violence and immediacy of reaction to threat once freely exercised by individuals on their own account. But although this attempt at resolution is superficially plausible, it raises its own problems. It is not, for a start, an answer on the same level as Elias's own enquiries, and so could not plausibly be generated by his own argument as it stands. It also would not explain why some eras – given the persistence of violence in all – have been notably more violent, exhibiting less of that restraint of affect with which Elias is concerned, than are others. The period from 1933 to 1945 is one such era of extreme violence, and so is, by eighteenth-century standards, the French Revolution.

One could also attempt to resolve the problems in Elias's account by making some liberal 'act of faith', encouraged by such passages as the quotation from Goethe reproduced above, that the horrors of modern times, founded on abusive exhibition and manipulation of the body, would prove less enduring than the civilization built upon repressing instinctive reactions and controlling the bodily functions.

But this option remains only an act of faith, not an answer to the real problem, which is precisely the relationship between the growth of individual physical control and the simultaneous growth of physical violence by the state. The only real answer to the discrepancy between Elias's firmly 'liberal' history and the events among which he lived, is another history of 'civilization' to explain the coming of these horrors and their persistence. The crucial question, unaddressed by Elias but which lies at the centre of the present work, is whether through the very ways in which modern people have learned self-control there have also been implanted the seeds of self-destructiveness: whether in fact *homo clausus*, whose appearance we shall mark again and again in this account of the French Revolution and its political culture of the body, is in fact not the antithesis, but instead a necessary condition of the exhibition of physical violence as part of a revolutionary process.

These are the obvious difficulties in Elias's account – difficulties which may prove as fruitful for the present work as are Elias's more consolidated achievements. But where do these difficulties come from, and why do they persist, in a work which is otherwise characterized by an unusual degree of logical rigour? The sources of Elias's philosophy are not difficult to define. Apart from the commitment to 'humanist' values mentioned above, the most obvious influence is that of Freud's *Civilization and Its Discontents*, published in German only nine years before the first appearance of Elias's own work, and with a similar emphasis on 'civilization' as a repressive mechanism.[16] Both these sources, however, are positive inputs: by an extension of his argument to the modern state, they may contribute to what is actually present in Elias's work, not what is absent from it. The problem of omission is a far greater one; yet one which becomes more easily understandable in the context of historical writing in Germany after 1933, especially in the case of a Jewish author. There are obvious reasons why a writer so situated should not have wished to push forward into the nineteenth and twentieth centuries with his analysis of the relations between the state and the control of physical violence. On a deeper level, though, Elias in the 1930s confronted a whole genealogy of the state which had become the favourite ground of political theorists sympathetic to National Socialism.

Such a theorist was Carl Schmitt, whose book *The Crisis of Parliamentary Democracy* (1923) and *Leviathan: Significance and Failure of a Political Symbol* (1938) were published contemporaneously with Elias's.[17] Schmitt's idea of the state is profoundly different from that put forward by Elias; it might even be argued that it is Schmitt, and others like him, who is the hidden opponent against whom Elias's argument is directed. Elias's commitment to 'liberal values' is obvious; but so too is his profoundly ambivalent attitude towards the *homo clausus*. Other liberal commentators, writing without Elias's constraints, have seen the emergence of this *homo clausus* as the precondition for response to a demagogic Fascist political style, where 'the leader' exemplifies all the energies which individuals are no longer allowed to display.[18]

Schmitt's entire theory of the state is of course one which could without problems be merged with National Socialist practice. In contrast to liberal pluralistic definitions, he sees the state as manifested in collectively organized self-assertion and self-defence against external and internal enemies. Politics thus becomes essentially foreign affairs. Domestically, the state remains in being only as long as it suppresses revolutionary resistance. Far from being based on the continuous extension of *individual* self-control, the state's dynamic, for Schmitt, is the continuous containment of the chaos which is inherent in the evil nature of individuals. Far from being *neutralized* as *homines clausi*, individuals seek their own autonomy in a positively destructive way, and would perish in the terrors of their own emancipation, were they not rescued by the sovereign power. Far from being their own sovereigns, enclosed and self-possessed, individuals, through their desires and their subjectivity, present a positive threat which the state must ward off. Thus in many ways Schmitt's account, with its emphasis on the dynamic, undying evil in individuals, and their irreducible solitude, is the absent 'dark history' which Elias's own account both needs for completion, and at the same time is in passionate rebellion against.

Both Schmitt and Elias were in reaction to the situation in political theory in the 1920s. A void had been left behind, by that date, by the demise of Hegelianism, and after Weber's sociology stripped the authority of the state of any aura of kinship with reason and religion. At the time, people wanted to put behind them the loss of this aura, brought so close to home in East-Central Europe after 1919 by the final collapse of historic monarchies, but at the same time could not reconcile themselves to the banality which had come to mark the business of the bureaucratic state governed by a party democracy. It was this conflict which lay behind the disagreements between Revisionists and Luxemburgists in the Marxist parties; it was also into this void that Elias sought to infiltrate a dynamic view of the relations between society, state and individual as a perpetually changing system of accommodation, an 'enormous dance configuration', to use his words, where the state both makes individual self-consciousness through control of physical identity, and is itself made possible by that change in individual behaviour which comes from the greater control of affects and impulses. For Schmitt, the state exists precisely to *impose* such control. Elias's progressive overcoming of the disorder of individual impulse interacting *with* the formation of the state can be contrasted with Schmitt's more pessimistic account of individuals as inherently chaotic, awaiting rescue by the state.

Against this confrontation with Schmitt, Elias's refusal to carry his historical analysis forward into the classical era of modern state formation in Europe, that of the French Revolution, becomes more comprehensible, even if it still does not strengthen his argument. It was essential to counter Schmitt's association – the association of all Fascist theory and practice – between the formation of the state and the use of violence, with a theory which explicitly linked the formation of the state and the *repression* of violence. Had Elias pressed his analysis forward to the era of the French Revolution, he would have found himself unable to sustain any such thesis. The history of the body, the history of violence and the history of state formation, long before the Fascist era, were already inextricably linked. This is why, as has been pointed out, Elias's theory is in fact a far more ambivalent one than his liberal commitments would lead us to expect. In the last analysis, Schmitt's political theory addressed the problems of his age far more directly: the core of the Fascist era, the use of physical violence in a political context, is written out of Elias's history by the very success of his theory in some directions, notably the explanation of undoubted and massive changes in acceptable physical behaviour over a long period of time. It was left to the dark shadow-history produced by Carl Schmitt to complete the task: Elias's account, precisely because of its stand for a liberal, optimistic, almost progressivist view of the state and hence of human behaviour, was unable to deal with the reality of the world around it at the time of its publication.

Schmitt's analysis also engaged directly with the fact of Elias's Jewishness when at many points in his *Leviathan* he tries to construct an anti-Semitic genealogy of the enemies of the total state, beginning with Spinoza, continuing with Moses Mendelssohn and other restless Jews who undermined the power of the state with a 'sure instinct...to emancipate their own Jewish nation', and leading eventually to such subversives as Marx and Heine. No wonder that Elias drew back, so confusingly and also so thought-provokingly, from direct confrontation with the modern state. In the context of 1939, to have so engaged would have been dismissed as mere 'Jewishness'.

The republication and translation of Elias's work into English in the 1970s coincided, firstly, with the republication of Mikhail Bakhtin's *Rabelais and His World*, which may usefully be compared with the approach of Elias and Schmitt. Far from repeating Elias's emphasis on the links between the growth of 'civilization', the effective state, and the controlled personal body, Bakhtin is concerned to privilege the notion of 'carnival' in the early modern period. By 'carnival', he means acts of release of emotion, of kicking over the traces, of challenging and inverting authority relations through ritualized social forms like the charivari, the communal dance. To make such 'carnivals' happen, the bodies of those involved in them become subject to *less* restraint than is usual in the context of normal social relations, and invade the 'non-carnivalesque' areas of society, which Bakhtin sees as pervaded by coldness, abstraction, control and restraint. Bakhtin's picture of the early modern world may be seen as in many ways another unacknowledged obverse of that of Elias, showing both the limits and the perpetual challenge endured by *homo clausus*.

It is an important theme, for as we shall see, the Revolution and the period which immediately preceded it saw a struggle between the 'closed body' of the bourgeoisie and the 'carnivalesque' body of the lower orders. As eighteenth-century élite medicine began to denigrate and control the bodily practices and medical resources of the lower orders, so in the Revolution the lower orders retaliated by the production of a popular revolutionary politics based on violence towards the bodies of their social superiors. The mob destruction in 1789 of the intendant Flesselles, of the Princesse de Lamballe and the Duc de la Rochefoucauld in 1792, of the deputy Féraud in 1795, are only some of the better-known incidents among many others. In the Revolution, superiors and inferiors, the world of carnival and the world of *homo clausus*, directly contested for supremacy and in the forcefield of violence which this contest created was generated the very high levels of violence and trauma with which the Revolution is associated; a level of violence against the body was one of the preconditions for the creation of the symbolic politics of the Revolution, where each side encountered in mythical form the physical symbolism of its adversaries.

It is the importance of Bakhtin's work to keep before us, in its continual difference from that of Elias, the idea that *homo clausus* did not grow solely out of the smooth evolution from the 'court society' to the 'civilization' of the middle classes, but was equally made in contestation and challenge. The victory of the *homo clausus*, it is argued in this book, was not complete until, through the French Revolution, a representative bourgeois culture of public dominance could be constructed which functioned not only through institutionalized support in the new state, but also, as we shall see, through the creation of a new political culture defined precisely as that victory of *homo clausus* over both the feminine and the carnivalesque.

Elias's work also coincided with the major impact of the work of Michel Foucault. This chronological coincidence and superficial similarity of focus in the work of the two writers on the relations between the history of bodies and the history of the state has led to the assumption that Foucault's and Elias's projects are the same. The foregoing account of Elias's work should have made it very clear how specific are the roots of that work to the situation of the 1930s in Germany, and how much his concerns result from the challenge posed by National Socialism not only to a vaguely defined liberal humanism, but also, more specifically, to the definition of the state, of individual behaviour, and the control of violence. Foucault's origins are very different; hence his intentions and the meaning of his history as a whole are also very different.

Foucault's main arguments are well known. Here I propose to examine at some length a single work, his *Surveillir et punir*, as the most relevant to the subject of this book, because its treatment of relations between bodies and the state is the most explicit.[19] In this work, Foucault argues that the disappearance of torture as a public spectacle, and therefore of the body as a major target of penal repression, which occurred in France at the end of the eighteenth century, is linked to major shifts in the relations between individuals and the state power. This period saw the disappearance of the notion that crime was an offence to the body politic, often seen as equivalent to the king's mystical, political body, and hence that reparation to the body politic should be carried out by the infliction and exhibition of pain and death on the actual body of the criminal.[20] In turn, this is related to Foucault's theory about the relations between the body of the 'political'. It is interesting to note that Foucault writes as though his own perception of this relationship marked a profound innovation in historical thinking:

> Historians long ago began to write the history of the body. They have studied the body in the field of historical demography or pathology; they have considered it as the seat of needs and appetites, as the focus of physiological processes and metabolisms, as a target for the attacks of germs and viruses; they have shown to what extent historical processes were involved in what might seem to be the purely biological bases of existence.... But the body is also directly involved in a political field; power relations have an immediate hold on it; they invest it, mark it, train it, torture it, force it to carry out tasks, to perform ceremonies, to emit signs. This political investment of the body is bound up, in accordance with complex reciprocal relations, with its economic use; it is largely as a force of production that the body is invested with relations of power and domination; but, on the other hand, its constitution as labour power is possible only if it is caught up in a system of subjection...the body becomes a useful force only if it is both a productive body and a subjected body.[21]

1 The nineteenth-century view: the body performs economic tasks, ceases to carry the weight of political representation. Ford Madox Brown, *Work* (1865).

It will be seen at once that Foucault's idea of 'the political' is more wide-ranging and less precisely defined than that employed by Elias, who talks specifically in terms of the relationship between court and middle class at defined epochs. We may also note that Foucault's idea of 'the political' veers sharply at certain points to take in economic relations of production which are largely absent from Elias's account. There are even more fundamental differences at stake, however: Elias is concerned above all to show that the relationship between the development of the modern state and patterns of physical behaviour is mediated through the development of specific forms of self-consciousness that go to make the *homo clausus* whom he identified as particularly modern. Self-consciousness, however, is the least of Foucault's concerns. His 'political bodies' act as symbols of social and political orders, exhibition sites for displays of state force. The body is seen, in his account, from outside; the individual's *construction* of self-consciousness does not appear as an issue. This also allows him to treat, as Elias does not, the human body as a unified concrete aspect of human history, which in spite of his disclaimers can be viewed as continuous across epochs. Such a position is clearly at variance with his views expressed in other works, such as *Les Mots et les choses*,[22] on the great discontinuities in history, as well as with his insistence, in *Histoire de la sexualité*, that bodies are constructed by discourse. So, if Elias's account is not without its problems, neither is Foucault's. The point is, that Foucault's problems are very different from Elias's.

The explanation for this may well lie in the very different philosophical, not to say political, situation which underlies Foucault's work. His history must be seen against the background of specifically French postwar developments in philosophy. Both structuralism and existentialism, while neither is totally adopted by Foucault, have contributed their share.[23] Structuralism contributes to the debate on the body by rejecting the presuppositions of rationalism, which were grounded in Cartesian splits between mind and body. This rejection of a mind-body split characterized almost the whole of French postwar philosophy. Existentialism, one of the main currents of that philosophy, contributed the idea that a person is essentially what he chooses to know and to be. Structuralism contributed the analysis, which equally rejected the mind-body dualism, of the body as a metaphor in discourse, a concern which has been prominently exploited by Foucault.[24] Although neither existentialism or structuralism is wholly incorporated into Foucault's account of the history of the body, both allowed the appearance of the essential pre-condition for his approach, which is that the body cannot simply be seen as a problem in epistemology or phenomenology, but can also become a theoretical location for debates about power, ideology and economics. It can thus also be seen as the bearer of a metaphorical history.

Many difficulties and problems in Foucault's history can be traced specifically to its relationship with structuralism. That history, with its argument that bodies are constructed objects in knowledge as much as, if not more than, 'natural' entities, has a strong epistemological bias. It argues that objects are not things-in-themselves but discursive objects, which are the product of rules of discourse. This is where the problems begin. Analysis of discourse often runs the risk of reducing the individual agent or speaker to the level of a socialized parrot, which must speak or perform in a determinate manner in accordance with the rules of language. Foucault's account tends to assume without analysis that discourse is singular and has general social effects. Despite his alleged historical enterprise, Foucault frequently extracts this discourse of the body from its social context, and seems to assume that discourse operates almost independently of the social groups which are its carriers.

Foucault's major fault, in fact, is to conflate the question of the logic of discourse with the issue of its social effects. But discourses are never uniform in their effects or unified in context. There is in any case, as later chapters in this book will establish, a plurality of discourses on competing regimens and images of the body; neither discourses nor disciplines are free-floating or autonomous, but are deeply embedded features of a particular social group, modified according to the range of options available and the perceived nature of the situations in which that group finds itself. But in Foucault's account, human agency is either minimized or ignored; in exactly the same way the structuralist tradition itself, though highly critical of reductionism, has often been involved in a kind of discursive reductionism, where individual voices are subordinated to 'text' and 'discourse'. Structuralism, for example, allows no theoretical space, just as there is none in Foucault's work, for human resistance to discourse, since, it is alleged, we are determined by what we are permitted to know.

Secondly, despite the references to pleasure and desire which distinguish structuralist analyses of discourse, such analyses of the body ignore the phenomenology of embodiment – precisely the problem at issue in the present work. The immediacy of sensuous experience which is involved in the notion of having a personal body receives scant attention. Such immediate personal experience of the body is minimized in favour of an emphasis on the regulatory controls which are exercised from outside the entities, labelled 'discourse' or 'knowledge'. In Foucault's own words, the knowledge relations that invest human bodies 'subjugate them in turning them into objects of knowledge'.[25] To see bodies as symbols, metaphors and locations for the exhibition of power, and to ignore the extent to which they afford lived experiences to their possessors, or are indeed *created by* those possessors, in other words, represents a profoundly coercive understanding of physical experience. This is an emphasis that this book, while not denying the importance of the body as a symbol and a metaphor, will aim to undermine, by approaching it from the subjective viewpoint of its possessors and creators, and simultaneously by treating that subjectivity and that creation as acts linking the body to the political as strongly as does its existence as metaphor and symbol.

It is also clear that a Foucaultian account of the body actively *prevents* crucial questions being raised, questions which are going to be vital to our account. The simple question thus ruled out of court is 'Whose body?': Foucault's account makes it difficult to talk about the separate physical experiences of rich and poor, men and women, to take only some of the most obvious categories. In spite of its historical claims, his account thus rapidly becomes ahistorical. It is also anachronistic in a deeper sense, in that it is indifferent to contemporary dualities in the approach to bodies in the eighteenth century. No eighteenth-century observer would have denied the symbolic content of the body, although he might not have used Foucault's terminology to describe it; but contemporaries also veiwed the body as a *producer* of knowledge for its owner. Knowledge was not simply that which subjugated the body into conformity with the social and political order; it was also produced by the body itself in its function as the primary decoder of sense impressions, which in turn were transformed into abstractions and hence into self-consciousness.[26] Contemporaries were perfectly aware that bodies and selves could create themselves by modifications in discourse on the part of their individual owners.

A further problem is posed by the level of event which Foucault chooses to describe as the 'political'. Typically, his interests lie either in the delineation of massive change in thought structures (as in *Mots et choses*), or in the analysis of micro-events, such as executions, incarcerations, military drills and so on. It is difficult indeed to find in Foucault's account – just as it is, for entirely different reasons, in Elias's history – a confrontation with events which take place at the centre of the political space, however that is defined, and which, archetypally, occurred during the French Revolution. Indeed, although the Revolution is often mentioned in Foucault's history, and some of its by-products examined in the account of changing penal systems in *Surveillir et punir*, yet typically it remains off-stage. Foucault, in other words, is not concerned to make links between a global conception of 'the revolution', and changes in the nature of the history of bodies. Nor, as has often been pointed out before, is he concerned with the actual complex *process* of change. Thus though Foucault may offer us many insights, his philosophical base and historical practice have produced results which may not be the most helpful for our purposes.

We have before us the task of trying to understand the history of bodies as political symbols, as vehicles and transmitters of political actions and intentions, and as essential media for the construction of new forms of self-consciousness at a time of rapid and complex revolutionary change. In this task, as we have seen, the two major historians of the history of the body in modern times each, for very different reasons, avoid a confrontation with the French Revolution itself. Both Foucault and Elias have held to the insight that the history of bodies and the history of political structures cannot be separated. They have not answered the question of how that relationship works at a time of rapid revolutionary re-formulation of political structures and ideology. And in that failure is much of the explanation of the marginalization of the history of the body from *histoire événementelle*.

Historians of the Revolution have, however, devoted a great deal of time recently to areas of direct relevance to our topic. There is, first, a growing shift away from a view of the Revolution as a history of social problems and mass political mobilization to one where political culture and discourse are held themselves to have provided the motor for the revolutionary phenomenon. This view came to prominence with the well-known work by François Furet, *Penser la Révolution*, published in English in 1981 as *Interpreting the French Revolution*.[27] For Furet, to summarize a complex argument, the French Revolution appeared as a struggle between sets of competing discourses for control of the verbal symbols of legitimacy that guaranteed the power to embody the general will, and thus for control of the new political order. Furet's emphasis on discourse clearly owes much to the input of Foucault and of structuralism, though Furet acknowledges none of the theoretical underpinnings of either. His approach has been accompanied by more specific research into the linguistics of the Revolutionary discourse, by such historians as Régine Robin, or into the Revolution's visual symbolism, by Lynn Hunt, among many others. Furet's view of the Revolution itself as the phenomenon to be explained, and the role assigned to political culture in that explanation, have clearly been valuable and refreshing innovations in a field previously dominated by accounts of discrete, usually social and economic, events, and mediated through a Marxist historiography embodied in Furet's opponent Albert Soboul.

What we have to take issue with is the definition of political culture offered by Furet and his followers. Primarily this is conceived in purely verbal terms. There is little attempt to incorporate the findings earlier in this century of linguisticians such as Leonard Bloomfield and Edward Sapir, following the lead of Ferdinand de Saussure and the early Sanskrit grammarians, who insisted that language could not be understood until adequate descriptions of spoken language *behaviour* were developed.[28] We can make use of a definition of behaviour as the much wider field of coherent, socially recognized practices, expressed through the use of the body, and having and being perceived to have a public resonance. In other words, the actual untangling of *behaviour*, not just of verbal statements, should be an important part of thinking about the political culture of the Revolution. To think about that culture in terms of behaviour expressed concurrently both physically and verbally allows us to profit theoretically from much of the anthropological and sociological work of this century on precisely this topic, and opens up pioneering vistas on to the political culture of the Revolution. It also allows us to explore some problems in the historiography of the Revolution.

Usually the precise, specific behaviour of the actors who brought about this world-historical, paradigmatic event is not discussed in any detail (Furet), or is relegated to a historical version of the *faits divers* column (Cobb). When such detailed behavioural studies *are* conducted (Soboul, Lucas), they are, precisely, seen as non-paradigmatic, specific to the Revolutionary time and place.[29] While the French Revolution might be seen, in other words, as the heroic-originator paradigm for the modern state, neither 'revolutionaries' nor their behaviour are seen as paradigms for *individual* action for modern individuals.

I believe that the present book will have little more than antiquarian value, however, unless it is situated not only in relation to the history of the French Revolution but also to the history of the twentieth century. The book argues on a double front: firstly, that attitudes towards the body actively created the new public world of the Revolution, and hence influenced the sort of state it created; and, secondly, that the physical behaviour and public physical projection of the participants in the French Revolution may well have paradigmatic lessons for patterns of political behaviour today. It is from this basis that a major political and moral criticism of Foucault's position may be made, one criticism which does not apply to Elias's work: Foucault's willingness to see bodies only as objects or symbols through which existing power relations are acted out, prevents him from writing a history in which, on the contrary, bodies are active creators of new power relations, and sustain individuals in their confrontations with and against systems of power.[30] This is a valuable point to make in a world where the major political divisions are no longer really between 'left-wing' and 'right-wing' states, or whatever other labels one cares to use, but between those states which exact physical penalties for dissent and those which do not.[31] Successful withstanding of privation, illness and torture are the pre-conditions of the attainment of political hero status in our time, as the careers of such 'heroes of our time' as Nathan Scharansky are there to show. Conversely, one of the marks of a growing neo-conservatism is the effort made to undercut such 'heroes' by denying their physical fortitude, or asserting that they somehow 'provoked' or deserved to be tortured. A prime example here is the reception given by the American 'New Right' to the story of the Argentine Jewish journalist Jacobo Timerman.[32] Even in western states it is increasingly true that the politics even of legal protest is becoming differentiated from establishment politics by its large-scale use of the human body: one thinks here of the tactics of CND and Greenpeace groups, of large-scale mass demonstrations, of human chains linking hands across Scotland, and of mass passive resistance. The construction and use of a dignified individual body which can be employed as a source of authority in conflicts in the public realm can thus be seen as a hallmark of late twentieth-century political change as it has involved thousands of individuals. States do not only, as fashionable sociology would have us believe, manipulate individuals in late capitalist society through the creation and manipulation of desires; they also do so in the challenges they produce to individual physical dignity.[33]

II Twentieth-century trivialized bodies. Duane Hanson, *Tourists* (1970).

Thus, one of the major arguments of this book will be that the French revolutionaries' concern about the public roles of the body are still an important concern for us today. In thinking about the similarities and the differences in their reactions and responses, we learn more about both their and our public worlds, and the challenges they posed and pose to individuals who confront them with the idea of causing change. It is not only the French revolutionary *state* which should assume a paradigmatic importance for political historians and theorists; the actions of those involved in its creation can, far from seeming remote and historical, have messages for the far more numerous individuals locked in confrontations with state power today.

It is particularly important for us to resurrect the conflicts and ideas that went into the making of a dignified public body for individuals because modern societies make it very difficult for individuals to do just that. Body image firstly has been 'medicated', given a scientific aura, and thus related to the 'objective sphere' away from the contentious area of politics. There is the general point, made by very many sociologists today, that the self, and the presentation of the self, have become dependent on style and fashion rather than on fixed symbols or the acting out of roles which are widely accepted in the society as carrying public weight. No longer lodged in formal roles, the self has to be continuously revalidated through a competitive public sphere.[34] Behaviour is no longer seen as the carrier of public authority lodged in the individual. The opportunity to achieve heroic public personification is precisely what 'style' and 'fashion' and continuous revalidation seem to take away from us. It is the opposite of the response of the French Revolution, which was to attempt to achieve validation by the adoption of defined roles. What happened to those roles, how they changed political action, and were changed and challenged by it, is one of the ways of writing the history of the French Revolution. It is also one of the ways of understanding the history of individual political response to the extreme challenges of the twentieth century.

This book's own political ground must also, therefore, be made clear. In validating, as I do above, an account of a political crisis where selves were created by adherence to roles and to symbolic physical behaviour, I seem to be approaching that interesting and dangerous area where conservatism and the left join each other. This is the characteristic and most dangerous area of the twentieth century, and as we have seen, also the one which produced in the 1930s the first histories and anthropologies of the body. Political embodiment as a subject for consideration was the most obvious child of the Fascist era, and was produced by both left and right wing. The history of the body does not have an unambiguous political genealogy. Even histories of the body which claim, like Foucault's, to lean to the left, tend to be histories not of embodiment but of discourses imposed coercively on bodies, at the expense of exploring the individual's construction of embodiment. They are in fact often authoritarian histories which, unlike Carl Schmitt's political theory, do not have the merit of admitting that they are such. We have also seen how even in the case of Elias's explicitly liberal history, the continuing interest of his account comes just as much from the internal conflict between the 'dark history' which it needs for its completion, and the committedly liberal account to which it is explicitly tied.

The plain fact is that it is impossible to write about the body without also writing about power. It is also very difficult, though not strictly speaking impossible, to write about the body without imposing one's own relationship to power at the time of writing on to the history of embodiment. It is also impossible to write such a history as a *single* history. Every history of the body is accompanied by its shadow, or 'dark history', of unresolved problems which tug at the author's account, however much his or her pre-commitments refuse them a place in the analysis explicitly presented. This is why it is important to relate our enquiry specifically to a task connected with the politics of the present, one which, unlike much of the theorizing which occurs at Foucault's level of 'knowledge–power–discourse', is actually concerned with the problem of how individuals are to react when faced with a situation where authority in the confrontation with the state can only be gained by the construction of heroic physical dignity.

What tools do we need to carry out the double task of this book, of enlarging our understanding of the political culture of the French Revolution, and of obtaining a new grasp of one of the characteristic problems of the twentieth century? My strategy is to return, firstly, to the roots of the social study of the body in the 1930s, and to utilize the insights gained in that field by social scientists and social psychologists who also worked at a time when the study of the social uses of the body, political criticism and the creation of new political forms, had all become connected.[35] It is however important to note that I do not conceive this book as cultural anthropology, a 'thick description', to use Geertz's phrase, of the French Revolution.[36] We are, in fact, focused more on Elias's problem of the relationship between self-consciousness, political change and internalized and externalized presentations of the body.

Histories of the body also have a complex ancestry, in that they originate in both left-wing and right-wing versions. This is an important point to make if one accepts the argument that histories of the body are also histories of the state; because then, conversely, the historians' attitudes towards the state have to be acknowledged as forming part of this other history. Otherwise, the history of the body does indeed become a Barthean 'mythology'. Let us say at the outset then that this book is conceived almost as a 'Jewish history', in Carl Schmitt's sense: a history written at an ironic, critical distance from the modern state.

The French Revolution saw conflicts over the manifold public embodiments of political authority carried to an extreme point. Successive answers to this problem were challenged by the increasing momentum of the Revolution itself. The reactions of the actors in the Revolution highlight some of the consequences of the effects of rapid change in available public roles, changes which both put individuals' public authority at a high premium and made it more difficult to achieve. The men and women of the Revolution were engaged in a search for public dignity which both enhanced and distorted the revolution which began with such high hopes in 1789. They have much to teach us.

# 3

# DECONSTRUCTING THE FRENCH REVOLUTION

> Il ne faut pas que je sois entièrement en équilibre avec le présent
>
> Paul Valéry[1]

The French Revolution is probably the most heavily trampled field in the collective farm of history. Adopted by the French themselves as, for good or evil, from left or right, the founding event of their modern world, the historians of the Revolution have suffused their accounts of its events with ideas, attitudes and emphases drawn from their own very varied political commitments. Both inside and outside France, socialist and Marxist historians have traditionally taken the Revolution, as Marx did, to be that bourgeois triumph which was the essential pre-condition for the victory of the proletariat. Not only did the Revolution form an essential object of reflection by Marx himself, but it has also been the focus of the search for meanings as models for action even in strands of the radical tradition such as anarchism, which would today disavow any affiliation with orthodox Marxist-Leninism. On the right of the political spectrum, immense historical energy has been expended in finding out where the Revolution 'went wrong', which is usually seen as the equivalent of condemning the fall of the monarchy in 1792 and the use of governmental terror from 1793–4.[2]

In spite of the enormous academic industry which has been devoted to the Revolution, it has always remained within the popular imagination, as possibly no other historical event has. This is not only because of the way in which images drawn from its more heroic or more violent moments stalked the nineteenth-century novel and hence the twentieth-century film; it is also the doing of the nineteenth-century historians themselves. Writing before the academic professionalization of history, such historians as Michelet and Taine, or, later in the century, the socialist leader Jean Jaurès or the anarchist Peter Kropotkin, wrote histories of the Revolution which were best-selling texts. Their immensely detailed, passionately felt accounts contained reflections on the real significance of the Revolution which were carried forward by means of heroic anecdote and moral reflection. It is this strand in the historiography of the Revolution which, outside the readership of academic history, is the most firmly alive today. Its modern reincarnations are to be found in the endless reissues and new commissions of popularizing accounts of the heroic figures of the nineteenth-century historical canon, figures such as Charlotte Corday, Marat's assassin, and Mme Roland ('Liberty what crimes are committed in your name!'), and in the emphasis in the many popular history journals on the heroic mode of the Revolution.[3]

But in spite of all this intense and varied historical and ideological focus on the Revolution, now prolonged over the better part of two centuries, it has failed to generate any history of the body in relation to its political culture. This is a failure whose causes we will study more closely in this chapter. In particular, we will be contrasting twentieth-century approaches to the Revolution with those of the nineteenth, and be calling for a re-evaluation of the now discounted heroic mythology which dominated the nineteenth-century historians before the advent of a professionalized socialist history of the Revolution. In doing so we will be establishing the body not only as a central part of the history of the Revolution itself, but also as a medium through which the Revolution may be opened up for the understanding of the problems of modern public culture.

Two major and connected historical controversies have marked the historiography of the Revolution since the 1950s. The first of these was opened by the English historian, Alfred Cobban, in direct challenge to the Marxist historians of the Revolution who had dominated its interpretation since the closing years of the nineteenth century, and who included historical giants such as Mathiez and Albert Soboul. Cobban demonstrated that the empirical data gathered by such historians had in fact exploded the Marxist theory which purported to explain the Revolution as the point at which in France the feudal order passed away and the rule of the bourgeoisie took its place. In the Marxist interpretation it was understood, if rarely precisely stated, that by 'bourgeoisie' was meant the class of modern capitalists, owners of the means of production and employers of wage labour. Class conflict, so the theory had it, was thus the key to understanding the Revolution. The Revolution was thus also seen as a bloc defined wholly in terms of the 'rise of the bourgeoisie'; and all its events, such as working-class political participation, the peasant revolutions, and the struggles between various factions of the middle classes themselves, represented by 'Girondins' and 'Jacobins', were all encased in an interpretation which overwhelmingly privileged the seizure of power by the middle class. Cobban pointed out however that no modernized capitalistic economic system followed in the wake of the Revolution: France did not fully industrialize until late in the nineteenth century and some would argue for an even later date. Furthermore, 'feudalism' itself, whatever it had been, did not exist in eighteenth-century France, except in the sense of vestigial seigneurial rights. And it was the peasantry, not the revolutionary bourgeoisie, which acted first against what they termed feudalism. The 'revolutionary bourgeoisie' as a class concept, Cobban found, dissolves under close analysis. What remains is a congeries of socially and economically disparate middle classes.[4]

Cobban's rejection of the 'orthodox interpretation' quickly found acceptance in the English-speaking world. Its most striking endorsement came however from François Furet and Denis Richet in their 1965 synthetic interpretation, *La Révolution française*, which was carried even further by Furet alone in his more recent *Interpreting the French Revolution*.[5] Gone here is any attempt to make the Revolution fit the mould of orthodox theory, and it is no accident that the latter book was published in French at a time (1978) when the political hold of the French Communist Party was seen to be rapidly decreasing; this in turn undermined the hegemony of the Marxist approach to the Revolution. What Furet offers to take the place of that approach is an idea of political discourse as the motor for a revolutionary phenomenon which has to be studied in its own right rather than subsumed into a more general theory about the stages of social evolution necessary to bring about the dictatorship of the proletariat. In spite of a considerable challenge from Albert Soboul and other more orthodox historians in France, where Marxist inputs into the history of the Revolution have achieved a unique degree of institutionalized power, Furet's interpretation has gradually gained ground.[6] His argument is that the Revolution was a competition for legitimacy among various sections of the French middle class through the appropriation of a validating political discourse and its embodiment.

The nature of revolutionary politics, in other words, was to make political discourse central, and political discourse shaped the very motor of revolution itself. The Revolution was the first point in French history at which persuasion of a mass audience was crucial and an integral part of the political phenomenon. Words, as Furet argues, were power. At the same time, the collapse of the institutions and ideological legitimation of the old regime meant that a desperate need existed to create a new discourse of validation for the new state and for the groups which competed for its control. Control of the discourse of the Revolution gave access to opinion, to the discourse of 'general will', and conferred the power which came from successful representation of that general will to itself.[7]

We need to explain further why the discourse was capable of playing this role. The answer comes from the Revolution's rejecting and contorted attitude to power. Within the discourse of the Revolution, power was seen as evil and contaminating. It was approached, that is, almost entirely in moral terms, and politics and morality were almost completely conflated. Thus, claims to power could only come from the denunciation of power in the name of a pure and undivided general will.[8] Thus the discourse of the Revolution contained no means of admitting that political morality might be variable, and it contained no way of negotiating conflicting sectional interests which undermined its ideal of the endless unbroken harmony of the general will, from which all revolutionary legitimacy stemmed. And it was not only that 'Bourgeois political theories...evacuated concrete social relations...[and] could not be adapted to the needs of a political struggle';[9] it was also the case that the discourse produced maximum discrepancies between fact and value, a discrepancy which only a non-verbal mechanism, like that of the public embodiment of values, could overcome, and hence infuse the discourse with a true dynamic.

How is this Revolutionary discourse to be recognized? Firstly by its ritualized invocation of absolutes, such as 'virtue', or the 'general will'. These absolutes are not capable of achieving real embodiment, for if the nation is as one in its general will, sectional interests have no legitimate existence and there are therefore no descriptive terms for them in the discourse. At best, they are identified with what is hidden or unseen: conspiracy. This is also a discourse which proceeds by the ritual invocation of polarities: vice/virtue, aristocrat/people, open/hidden, transparent/opaque. This is the reason that the exclusionary power of the discourse is so strong, because of the absence from it of a middle ground which can claim legitimacy. He who is not with us is against us. This is also why struggle for the appropriation of this discourse could take on a literally life-and-death character. Furet is surely correct to see this form of political discourse as one of the explanations of the high turnover of ruling groups in Revolutionary politics.

That this dynamic cannot, however, really be comprehended by verbal analysis alone is one of the theses of this book. Furet's work did open the way for a flood of subsequent studies which departed from the traditional Marxist emphasis on the history of the popular movement and on the economic history of the Revolution, the '*foules et subsistances*', and concentrated instead on the political culture of the Revolution conceived as a dynamic phenomenon in its own right. Along with this, the emphasis has swung away from the traditional social explanations of the Revolution, towards a revaluation of its political history. Instead of being seen as an epiphenomenon of the class struggle which contained the true significance of the Revolution, the political conflicts are seen as the heart of the 'Revolutionary phenomenon': they have become the real *explicandum*.

This change has had several important and beneficial consequences. Firstly, it has allowed historians to look at the Revolution as a phenomenon on its own, without links which were created, through Marxism, to other socialist revolutions of the twentieth century, of which the French Revolution has often been seen as the paradigm. It has also allowed historians to explore the '*mentalités*' of the participants, free from the strait-jacket of the class struggle. The widespread abandonment of the Marxist interpretation of the Revolution has also allowed it to be transfused with a different set of interpretations from outside historical scholarship. In particular, political scientists such as Theda Skocpol have seized upon the Revolution as paradigmatic not of the history of the class struggle, but of the rise of the modern state. In their work, which in many respects replicates the theories of Alexis de Tocqueville, the French Revolution becomes a revolution of state and bureaucracy: still paradigmatic, it has merely changed the paradigm it is attached to.[10]

But Furet's liberation of the writing of the history of the Revolution from the Marxist line has not been sufficient, by itself, to create a new, positive history of the Revolution. Furet's entirely healthy insistence, for example, that the French Revolution must be detached from the history of the Russian Revolution of October 1917, has not opened the way for real discussion of the legacy of the former in the nineteenth and twentieth centuries as a whole, let alone, most importantly, of its bearing on the predominantly right-wing revolutions of the post-1930s period in Europe.[11] It has also left in abeyance, for the attention of the political theorists alone, the question of the extent to which the Revolution *was* a paradigmatic event, in terms of the history of modern states, of modern revolutions and of modern individual self-consciousness. Yet this is a question which must be answered, for otherwise it is impossible to explain or to justify the still-insistent focus of French historical writing, and of French national awareness, on the events of 1789 to 1799.

At first sight, another legacy of the post-Furet era does however liberate the Revolution from 'paradigm' status. This is a new focus on the Revolution as a problem in 'political culture'. It is important to examine this tendency critically and differentiate it from the approach adopted in this book.

Serious problems cluster, firstly, around the very concept of political culture, which has never really been well defined by or sat very easily within, political science. As used by the historians of the French Revolution, this concept also poses problems. The majority of those approaching the Revolution through the perspective of 'political culture' have produced studies which focus almost entirely on verbal utterances produced within highly formalized contexts, although some historians attempt to broaden their account of political culture, as does Lynn Hunt, by trying to link public and political artistic images to the verbal rhetoric.[12] Too often such a verbal definition of political culture, which arises logically from Furet's emphasis on the Revolution as a competition for control of a legitimating political discourse, ends up by implying that this culture as well as the Revolution itself was somehow monolithic; even though Furet's expressed intention was to confine his assessment to the republican, direct democratic strand of the Revolution. In thus limiting their assessments, historians of the Revolution deprive themselves of ways to account for conflict and confusion within the Revolution. Just as Furet's view is class-blind (to distinguish itself from the class-obsessed Marxist line), so too it is gender-blind and pays little attention to the way 'the discourse' might be differently received, used and experienced by different groups.

Above all, emphasis on this verbal definition of political culture runs the risk of producing the (surely unintended) implication that the actors of the Revolution, imprisoned within a monolithic discourse which shaped their political fate, were devoid of intention and volition. Thus, curiously, the 'political culture' approach to the Revolution appears to have great similarities with the 'political science' approach, which likewise has little patience with questions of intentionality. For Skocpol, revolutions 'occur'; they are not *made*. Partly, this difficulty with intentionality occurs because of the strong influence of modern linguistic philosophy, whose major proponents, such as Derrida, have attacked any attempts to make intention, let alone the speaker's behaviour, part of the *explicandum* of speech acts. We thus emerge with the curious fact that the new line on the French Revolution refuses, as much as do the political theorists, and as did the Marxists, to approach the question of the intentions and hence the self-consciousness of those who took part in the events which they are describing.

The account of aspects of the Revolution given in the present work is thus as clearly at odds with the new, post-Furet orthodoxy as it is with the older Marxist line. It also rejects the Foucaultian orthodoxy which posits the death of the historical subject. We can say, too, that it is the shared deficiencies of both Furet and his predecessors which make a history of political embodiment, which is perforce also a history written in terms of individual self-consciousness, a necessary contribution to the history of the Revolution and also a necessary contribution to our whole thinking on the way in which individuals contribute to the making of a political style.

We have thus abandoned a uniquely verbal definition of 'political culture'. But will whatever we put in its place be anything more than a 'thick description', to use Geertz's term, of the micro-history of the Revolution? Rather than attempt immediately the impossible task of constructing a new definition of the notoriously undefinable 'political culture', which would also imply a churlish rejection of the considerable achievements involved in Furet's refocusing of the topic, let us try to redefine our task by expanding outwards from that very 'political-culture-as-speech-acts' approach. Ferdinand de Saussure remarked long ago, and linguistic philosophers such as John Searle have recently reaffirmed, that speech is impossible to 'understand' without the behaviour which accompanies it.[13]

The absence of this perception is a major defect even in the work of such highly praised writers as Lynn Hunt. Confining her account to a highly selective appraisal of the 'Jacobin' style of political discourse isolated by Furet, and of isolated 'symbols' such as the Hercules images produced by Revolutionary public art, she fails either to explore the construction of a fully worked-out linguistic universe, or to produce one for the visual symbols. Hampered too by an insufficiently thought-out adherence to an overall concept of the Revolution as a 'modernization process', which is inappropriate to a political contest so divorced from real economic and social change as was the French Revolution, she is unable to link up the Revolution itself with the problems of public identity already encountered by the middle class in pre-revolutionary France. She is also self-deprived of an analytic resource, the exploration of body-politics, which, as noted in our first chapter, is valuable precisely because it enables us to unite many different levels of understanding of events as well as to isolate a crucial 'pocket', the body itself, which mediates between the individual's own subjectivity, and the creation of a public world of symbols and meanings possessed by that very same physical body. Hunt, also obviously in refusing to address the question of physicality, produces another account of Revolutionary political culture which is very nearly gender-blind, an astonishing omission in relation to a political culture which, as we shall see, used the physical aspects of gender as a crucial set of legitimating and delegitimating devices in the construction of the new public identity of the middle class. This, far more than any consciously articulated ideas of 'modernization', was at the heart of the struggles of the Revolution, and in that struggle, physicality was central.

Attention to physical behaviour also provides us with a way towards a problem which Furet's own analysis of the Revolution as competition for the legitimating discourse of the 'general will' explicitly raises, but does not solve: the problem of embodiment. As Furet says, success in the contest for the control of the discourse of the Revolution ultimately rested on the capacity of individuals to embody or personify that discourse: to make the maximum congruence between the rhetoric and an actual individual. But Furet does not develop this point further, into a full-blown theory of embodiment, seeing the discourse *on its own* as a successful device to 'account' for the violence and turmoil of Revolutionary politics. Neither had such an approach, at a conceptualized level, been produced by the nineteenth-century historians of the Revolution.[14] Why has the Revolution so far failed to link itself to, or to generate, a history of the body as embodiment?

Part of the answer must lie in the traditional reluctance of Marxism itself to consider questions of embodiment which involve the consideration of individual self-consciousness in the class struggle.[15] For different reasons, the major influence tending nowadays to transfuse the history of the Revolution, political science, with its concern for systems and structures rather than intention and self-consciousness, has also refused to see the absence of the body as a problem at all. Another reason is the abiding preconception of 'the body' as a 'natural' object by definition outside the historian's purview, a view which persists in spite of Foucault's and Elias's contributions to the subject – or more precisely because of their lack of integration with mainstream history. There is too the prevailing tendency in discussing historiography to think in terms of polarities such as structure-v.-event, or *histoire événementielle* v. *histoire de longue durée*. Into these dichotomies, the body fits very badly and is thus usually relegated, when treated at all, to analysis as a system or symbol of something else, as Foucault does in the majority of his works.

But the problem does not simply lie with the body. It lies in the historians' difficulties in coming to terms with the idea of *behaviour* rather than with *words*. Obviously, I am not arguing here that bodies can somehow create 'political culture' in the absence of words. Indeed words play a vital part in the creation of individual physical self-consciousness, which is not only derived from immediate physical stimuli, but also verbalized into being in ways which are almost as immediate and as directly internalized.[16] What I am arguing is that words do not give up their full meaning without an account of the physical behaviour which accompanies them. Thus we cannot deal with the history of the way in which the new political class of the Revolution approached the vital task of making a new self-image to fit with and to protect its seizure of power, without examining both verbal and physical behaviour and both verbal and physical symbolism.

Part of the explanation of the Revolution's failure to generate a history of embodiment must lie in the very peculiar position of the topic in relation to other ways into the understanding of society. While remaining very much open to some influences, such as Marxism, or political-science analyses, the Revolution has remained enormously closed to others, such as social anthropology, and has only recently been opened up to studies by methods originating in art history or socio-linguistics. As well, the history of the Revolution is still in large measure isolated from the history of the eighteenth century, particularly as the reverberations of the 'Atlantic Revolution' thesis die away. Historians either begin or end their studies at 1789. Rare indeed are those who try, in Keith Baker's words, to 'recover the competing representations of social and political existence from which the "revolutionary language" ultimately emerged'.[17] At the same time, the self-referential nature of Revolutionary historiography has also increased as it becomes, post-Furet, detached from the history of socialist revolutions, and as, at the same time, analyses such as Talmon's which unite it to right-wing revolutions of this century, remain marginalized.

Lack of critical examination of the key concepts routinely used in the analysis of the Revolution, post-Furet, has led historians not only into an essential vagueness on the definition of 'political culture', but also into the idea of culture as a purely expressive phenomenon, only symbolizing realities which themselves are already and independently in existence on a political or a social level.[18] This is the way in which Foucault has treated the history of the body, and it is thus no wonder that historians grappling with the exceptionally fast-moving and complex series of events which make up the Revolution, should have shouldered aside an approach which seems to deal only with surfaces and representations, and tried to focus their energies on the real and underlying phenomena. In this book, however, I am going to argue for a history of public embodiment which takes as its major assumption that the behaviour, attitudes, symbols and self-perceptions which we group together under the heading of a 'political culture', do themselves dynamically intervene in the political process and can challenge all previously secure understanding of its polarities. They create new public spaces, new political audiences and new political problems.

But it would be too easy to take the givens in this argument, generated within a liberal political tradition, entirely for granted. Post-Freud, post-Foucault and post-structuralism, one can no longer assume the historical importance of intentionality or subjectivity; nor can one assume in the face of two centuries of historical neglect that a history of bodies is a necessary part of the history of the Revolution. The two questions – the argument for producing an account based on intentionality and hence on self-consciousness, as well as the argument for producing a history of bodies *at all* – are, however, very closely linked. Historians who utilize the political-culture-as-political-discourse argument are in fact in danger of taking on an approach in which heavy philosophical freight, largely derived from structuralism, may pass unnoticed. Structuralist notions of discourse, as has often been noted, tend to ignore questions of intentionality. Text talks to text: not speaker to speaker. This produces the danger of a massive abstraction between the 'disclosure' as contained in the text and the conditions of its production and reception. Clearly, in an account of the Revolution which sees it implicitly but not explicitly as a competition for the control of discourse, there is little space for discussion of questions of intentionality. Such an outlook is also profoundly at odds with the historical enterprise itself, in that it considers discourse in terms of universals, while historical enquiry can only begin from specifics.

But what *is* intentionality and why do we *need* to include it in our account of the Revolution? After all, since Foucault, it has been open to us to analyse historical moments in term of epistemic relationships, of deep-level shifts which underlie moments of revolutionary change. However, there are, as is well known, serious problems in the way Foucault defines such *episteme*, including the fact that they are in the event difficult to use to account for change. These difficulties are in addition to the fact that *episteme* accounts seem unable to generate intentionality. All these points have a particularly ironic ring when applied to the Revolution, so often portrayed as an outpouring of conscious will and energy. Without an account of action at a level where intention can enter in we also possess no way of accounting for the diversity of the repertoires of political action in the Revolution, or for the rapid changes in those repertoires. Intentionality, we may say, enters in when discourse is approached as an object of use rather than of linguistic coercion. In Basil Bernstein's words, the distinction is one between intentional discourse, which is concentrated on to its context, and discourse conceived in a way which *excludes* context, and presents the speaker/user as totally bound by the codes of the discourse.[19]

Here, however, we encounter another problem: why have a history of bodies at all? The answer is that such a history, with such a focus, acts like a prism, concentrating rays of understanding from many different sources, which otherwise could never intersect. The body is the space where intentionality and *episteme* can come together: where the flux – in the Heracleitian sense – of intention and self-perception is held together by the boundaries of *episteme*. It also allows the historical enquiry itself to discard the false 'universality' conferred on it by an injection of linguistic theory, and to open itself, on many levels, to a more genuinely universalist goal of the exploration of the political consciousness of individuals. We have to realize that the blessed aura of 'objectivity' which has begun for the first time to descend on the historiography of the Revolution is also a dangerous delusion. History must be reinvested with meaning if it is to be written at all.

But how is this reinvestment to take place? The most obvious way to begin is to query the significance which has traditionally been ascribed to the Revolution and which seems to have acted, paradoxically, more and more to block off the process of historical questioning, the more universal that significance became. The Revolution, as we have said, has firstly been seen as the beginning of 'the modern state' in France. It has also traditionally been seen, by both Marxists and non-Marxists alike, as the time which marked the seizure of political power and social and cultural control by elements of the middle class. A third way in which meaning has been ascribed to the Revolution is as a paradigm for subsequent overthrows of authority, particularly those which took place in Europe and Russia up to 1917. But all these ascribed 'meanings' in fact do is to place an enormous explanatory weight on the very short period of time covered by the Revolution. They also pose far more questions than they answer: what, for example, was really involved in the bourgeois seizure of social, political and cultural control? Was it something which could be entirely achieved between 1789 and 1799, or was it composed of a set of unstable victories which had to be re-fought throughout the nineteenth century? What was the nature of the values established by the middle class: were they stable, or were they in a constant developmental process which attempted to produce dominance out of the resolution of opposing ideals? In what sense was this process in turn, as many have suggested about the preceding era of Enlightenment, connected with an era of 'modernity'?[20]

In addition, the very way in which the history of the Revolution has been written, let alone the questions asked of that history, has usually had an overdetermining effect. As François Furet has written,

> In the historians' trade, the French Revolution is the professional speciality in which the period chosen strictly determines the content of possible 'subjects' by virtue of an implicit notion of the event that filled that period. However varied, these 'subjects' are designed to describe or explain the Revolutionary break, since, that is the prior meaning ascribed to the period.[21]

One of the first strategies one must therefore adopt in relation to the Revolution is to abandon the chronological tyranny inherent both in its unchallenged status as an originating event in French history, and in the focus of historians on the cascade of datable events which constitute its history, and on its status as a 'beginning', the beginning of the middle-class world. The meaning of the Revolution has to be found in the values it produced. By focusing on the production of values one does two things: one bridges the divide between fact and value which is inherent in Revolutionary political discourse itself; and one also focuses on the struggle of historical actors to create identity and legitimacy in the face of a surrounding problematic, by utilizing the infinite capability of a combination of culturally available resources.

Among those resources, the body ranked high. But how did it become such a resource; in what context and through what means did such resources come into play at all? The question is meaningless if we stick with ideas of the Revolution as 'state formation', especially since most analysis along these lines has, following Tocqueville, equated 'state' with 'bureaucracy' and left to one side the Weberian question of the *values* which informed the state apparatus. But the making and utilizing of new public resources was not in fact taking place against the background of the foundation of a 'modern state': many different forms of state organization were to succeed one another with bewildering rapidity in France during the Revolutionary years, and it is quite clear that the informing values of such a 'modern state' were open to debate in that country for the whole of the nineteenth century, precisely because of the very failure of the men of the Revolution to construct a new and yet stable version of state and public space. What, however, the Revolution undoubtedly did construct, was a large and highly sensitized public realm which threw up a profusion of reference models such as 'heroic Stoicism', many of them concentrating on physical presentation, representation and control, to stabilize the conflict between fact and value inherent in the verbal discourse of the Revolution.

This analysis also enables us to escape from another dominant, and ultimately sterile, approach in the writing of the history of the Revolution, which is to see its political history largely in terms of conflict between more or less clearly defined groups labelled 'Girondin', 'Jacobin' for the middle class, and 'sans-culotte' for the *petit bourgeoisie* downwards. In spite of the criticism which historians have increasingly levelled against the use of these categories, and an increasing realization of their largely functional significance to contemporaries, it remains true that even such revisionist historians as François Furet still repeatedly use the categories rather than questioning the reasons for their existence in the first place. Contemporaries in fact labelled each other compulsively often, yet gave little secure content to the labels. Even central political participants such as Marat were often unsure in which group to place a specific individual. What was going on in fact was not the creation of political 'parties' or even of particularly firm factions; rather it was exactly what it seemed to be: an exercise in naming in order to find ways of discriminating between individuals. In that discriminating process, it was vital to find means of welding particular individuals into larger collectivities. Hence the obsessively universalistic political discourse, which tried but failed to provide unity in politics and in values; hence too the importance of political behaviour mediated through the body, at once the object most private to and most characteristic of the individual, and the one with the longest history of use as a reference model in large human groups. The body in fact focused, like a prism, both struggles over individuality *and* the making of new collective political values for the newly dominant male middle class.

Lastly, the Revolution has to be detached from its 'automatic' referents: the left-wing European revolutions up to 1917, and the history of France itself. Very few commentators and no widely accepted interpretation have really succeeded in either of these objectives. Recent critiques, such as Furet's and that of Alain Besançon, which have sought to weaken the link with subsequent left-wing revolutions, have none the less left unquestioned the pivotal nature of 'the revolution', conceived of as a series of events occurring between 1789 and 1799, for the future of France. Interpretations such as that of J.H. Talmon, which sought to break new ground by linking the Revolution to the origins of *right*-wing revolutions in Europe, have failed because of their insistence on the French Revolution as a monolithic entity entirely over-determined by an ideology which somehow survives unchanged and unmediated into the twentieth century.[22] The argument of this book is somewhat different, in that the Revolution is indeed seen as an origin and one that indeed produced a political culture which had great resonance in the twentieth century. But it was so in terms not of the making of states, which has proceeded continuously ever since, but in terms of the making of bourgeois society and subjectivity: in Heideggerian terms, of the 'second fall', into the world of the middle class. This approach alone attempts to come to terms with the fact that the Revolution forms the archetypal bourgeois experience, not just in France but in Western Europe as a whole.

By 1848, Marx was able to point out scornfully that the claims of revolutionaries, even in the German states, to exercise legitimate power were made by men still playing out the roles of Danton or Robespierre and re-enacting as farce what the French Revolution had produced as tragedy. The mythology and reference models of the Revolution, overwhelmingly concerned as they were with the conjunction of authority, embodiment and the politics of revolutionary violence, had made available a universal language for the legitimation of middle-class seizures of power.[23] The failure of the majority of the nineteenth-century middle-class revolutions, and the immense strengthening of the state as a force above society which was a consequence of that failure, also arose precisely out of the incongruence, by the mid-century, of the roles embodied and validated by the mythical history of the French Revolution and the actual situations in which specific groups of middle-class revolutionaries were to find themselves after the 1820s.

Even the isolated position of the middle class as a motor for change – in most states this had nothing to do with a non-existent industrialization process – is a result of that belated absorption of the Revolutionary myth during the Napoleonic occupations. Progressive middle-class groups, self-defined in terms of Enlightenment values, were prone to be most in favour of French occupation and intervention and most likely to collaborate with French social and religious policies which were often viewed as a continuation of the projects of previous enlightened rulers. On the collapse and withdrawal of the French, these groups remained isolated, their hold on power insecure, and it was almost always such groups which led successive revolutions in the first half of the nineteenth century. Crucial to the explanation of the political failure of those revolutions was the increasing disparity, inherent in the dialectical, unresolved nature of bourgeois values, between role and audience, fact and value, rhetoric and problematic – difficulties which could often only be overcome, to retain their hold on the political process, by the evolution of ideologies of nationalism.

If 'history's relation to the present is one of the ingredients of its relation to truth',[24] then the long shadow of the Revolution must also surely be assessed in relation to the twentieth century, which has seen an uneasy combination of the maintenance of bourgeois values and the growth of the supra-social state. In both those processes, the public fate of the body has played a crucial part. Increasingly defined in terms only of the categories of 'labour' or 'sexuality', the body in the nineteenth and twentieth centuries has lost both public authority and subjective intensity. Increasingly, a description of bodily behaviour has become the equivalent of a catalogue of acts, not of ranges of meaning. And yet the French Revolution, allegedly the primal political act of the modern world, produced a public space which was, as we will make clear, dominated by the authoritative public bodies of individuals. In order to measure our distance from, and our nearness to, 1789, we need to produce a history of how it created that now rare phenomenon – public space defined by the public dignity of embodied individuals.

# 4

# THE EIGHTEENTH-CENTURY MEDICAL REVOLUTION

## Bodies, Souls and the Social Classes

> ...the world about me gradually took on the attributes of fairyland, where everything that happened was a spell or a metamorphosis, where individuals, plucked from the chiaroscuro of a state of mind, were carried away by predestined loves, or were bewitched; where sudden disappearances, monstrous transformations occurred, where right had to be discerned from wrong, where paths bristling with obstacles led to a happiness held captive by dragons. Also in the lives of peoples and nations, which until now had seemed to be at a standstill, anything seemed possible: snake pits opened up and were transformed into rivers of milk; kings who had been thought kindly turned out to be brutal parents; silent, bewitched kingdoms suddenly came back to life.
>
> Italo Calvino[1]

The eighteenth century, the Revolution and the nineteenth century lived in a cacophony of competing prescriptions for body images. From this repertoire, members of the new French political class created powerful and politically central images of their own bodies, images which also carried historical and moral connotations, allowing these figures to gain a purchase not only on contemporary events but also on their own future historical presentation, to such an extent that later French historians were focused on their acts of heroic dignity.

Such myth-making, such creation of imputed bodies, also took place across the boundaries of class. Just as the creation of the heroic male public persona is impossible to understand except as a simultaneous exclusion of an imputed female body, so too it is impossible to understand the making of heroic middle-class dignity without understanding its exclusionary relationship with the bodies of its social inferiors. Not, of course, that this was in itself precisely an innovation in France. For generations the French nobility had reinforced its status by the creation and consumption of literary images which contrasted hideous or ridiculous peasant or middle-class bodies with its own tall and well-formed ones.[2] Whole literary genres, such as pastoral poetry, grew up from the sixteenth century, which devoted themselves effectively to distancing the physical realities of inferior social classes. Pictorial art, similarly, grappled only hesitantly with such portrayals, very often leaving the lower-class body assimilated into the natural landscape, rather than treated on the same terms as those of the glowing upper-class protagonists of portraiture.[3] Even such artists as the Le Nain brothers, who had in the previous century specialized in the depiction of peasant interiors, faces and bodies, had done so in fact precisely as a specific genre: caught within its confines, peasants escaped representative heroic dignity and remained thus precisely peasants. The same goes for eighteenth-century depictions of urban workers, who emerge not as individuals but as assimilated to the attributes of their calling or the actions of production.[4]

The eighteenth century thus fell heir to a long tradition of specialized, exclusionary depictions of the lower orders. At the same time, as an integral part of the claims to power of the new political class, the very act of seeing, and particularly of seeing other individuals or social groups, was being invested with enormous political connotations. *How* other social classes, and especially their bodies, were seen by the middle classes, and *that* their bodies *were* seen, became major determinants of class relationships in the Revolutionary world. This change both heralded and encapsulated the successful struggle by elements of the middle class to capture political and cultural dominance from the nobility, a struggle which was already well under way by the 1770s and reached its height during the Revolution itself, with the abolition of the juridical idea of nobility and the repeated onslaughts on the idea of an aristocracy, its economic foundations and many of its individual members. Such changes were accompanied by a complete change in the nature of the seeing which was socially privileged in France. Before its collapse, the nobility, like the monarchy, had been a centre of seeing, in the sense that the gaze of society was directed at its members. They existed *to be seen*, their lavish outward display focusing the sight of others, and contrasting sharply with the dull, unostentatious, typically black costume of the professional middle classes.

For the middle-class ethic, however, this calculated ostentation, this focusing of the eyes of others, was also an index of aristocratic

III The body-image of the peasant: very different from that of the middle classes.

social dysfunction. Middle-class claims to authority rested on double-pronged attacks on this claim to monopolize vision through the body, to be '*the* public body'. Firstly, they devoted great effort, especially under the Revolution, to constructing new public bodies which focused audiences and prolonged the lifetime of their acts and poses forward into subsequent historical narrative. They too were to *be* looked at. But secondly, they also began to construct those areas which privileged their allegedly superior capacity to look *into* the bodies of others, and by such looking *into*, to control those others as surely as had done the aristocrats and monarchs who were the previous focus of all looking *at*. The act of seeing became an act of power. This was also one which it was essential for the middle class to capture under the Revolution, because that act of sight had been, since Louis XIV, the archetypal one by which monarchical power over individuals was expressed. To be put out of the king's sight, into exile, was the ultimate image of political failure: to remove oneself from the king's sight was an act otherwise so incomprehensible as to be capable of only one construction, that of treason. In this sphere, as in so many others, the middle classes attempted to create a culture which should still reproduce the major boundaries of the aristocratic-monarchical world which, under the Revolution, they ostensibly aimed to replace.

In this struggle to re-position the focus of control over the crucial area of power-creation involved in seeing and being seen, two events stand out with special clarity. The first is the creation in the eighteenth century of a philosophy of mind and understanding which privileged the out-of-sight as the more or less remote generator of all abstractions, and hence of rationality itself.[5] It thus underlay the whole making of the notion of real 'self-possession', which was the ideal so strongly privileged by the revolution of the *homo clausus*.

Second, was the creation of a new medicine. Changes in medical theory, practice and institutional structure in this period have provoked considerable interest in recent years. Historians such as J.P. Goubert, Toby Gelfand and, most notoriously, Michel Foucault have emphasized changes at the end of the old regime and in the Revolution itself, leading to the increasing tendency, especially in the larger towns, and most dramatically in Paris, to emphasize provision of medical care through the removal of the sick, and overwhelmingly the sick poor, to ever-larger hospitals.[6] Hospitals, it has been argued, were multifunctional. They allowed the development of a new type of medicine by bringing together for the first time large groups of patients exhibiting similar disease patterns, making possible a diagnostic practice which privileged the collection of symptom patterns rather than of information from scattered individual patients about his or her experiences of *malaise*.[7] Such hospitals also made possible the collection of large numbers of corpses for autopsy, and were thus an essential pre-condition for the formation of pathological science which, even more, privileged the visual interrogation of the *insides* of dead bodies, rather than the taking of verbal details from the living.

Medical men argued that objectification and diagnosis of illness as disease in the hospital, populated by the poor and needy, was essential to the advancement of medicine. Thus the poor were seen chiefly as bearers of disease, while doctors saw themselves as bearers of an improved semiotics and nosology of the body. The medical profession's capture of hospitals and their conversion from hospices for the indigent and vagrant, by the late 1790s, into instruments for research and teaching gave medicine something it had never had before, except perhaps in a military setting: a specific, controlled environment as a work place.[8] Poor patients, once viewed by ordinary practitioners as clients, or by the Church as souls deserving charity, became clinical material while alive and objects for anatomical study after death.

The way the new hospital medicine functioned as a mechanism of power has been classically described by Michel Foucault.[9] He argues that in the new hospital medicine, by the end of the eighteenth century, older ways of seeing the body disappeared. In their place came a penetrating medical gaze that used the new techniques of observation, palpation, auscultation and percussion, and made the deepest recesses of the body transparent to the medical eye. Gone is the idea dominant in the bedside practice of the eighteenth century, that symptom complexes have an independent existence. Disease entities begin to be identified for the first time, and episodes of illness cease to be described in terms of long and minutely detailed 'unsorted' symptom lists. This analysis of the way the body is seen, described and constructed, Foucault suggests, might be called a 'political anatomy'. It is political because the changes in the way the body is described are not the consequences of some random efforts, or of progressive 'enlightenment', but are based on certain mechanisms of power. In the hospital, patients' bodies were subjected to new techniques of surveillance. The individual body, target and effect of a ubiquitous and calculating gaze, became docile, analysable, through pathology: passive, desacralized, depersonalized, because the patient's personal history was relegated from its primary position as the key to diagnosis and was instead subject to evaluation in the central domain of the hospital.

Foucault also sees such medical developments as only one example of the extension of a disciplinary apparatus throughout society by the end of the eighteenth century, an extension which marked the emergence of a new power, a new knowledge of and a new conception of the body:

> The moment that saw the transition from historico-ritual mechanisms for the formation of individuality to the scientific-disciplinary mechanism, thus substituting for the individuality of the memorable man: the calculable man, that moment when the sciences of man became possible, is the moment when a new technology of power and a new political anatomy of the body were implemented.[10]

The new hospital medicine also focused internal developments on the organization of the medical profession, which placed it in a stronger position to make socio-political claims than it had ever been before. The Revolution ended the old dichotomy in the profession between surgeons and physicians organized in separate corporations. It also instituted a simplification in the numerous grades of practitioners of all kinds – midwives, dentists, practical surgeons and others whose training and qualifications were inferior to those of the 'licensed' surgeons and physicians, with qualifications from the Paris Medical Faculty, and who practised in large numbers especially in the countryside.[11] Along with the unification of medicine and surgery, which helped to produce a profession of recognizably modern appearance, uniform training institutions under state control were introduced for the first time. These institutions in turn exercised far greater control over medical personnel of inferior qualifications and experience, the *officiers de santé*, who were reduced in number and subject to stricter surveillance by the licensed practitioners.

At the same time, other auxiliaries such as nursing sisters were increasingly deprived of their privileged positions in relation to patients. Medicine became firmly about saving bodies, not ministering to souls. In turn, this was the condition for the rapid growth from the Revolutionary period onwards of an esoteric technical medicine, virtually impossible for a lay person to understand. The emergence of a professionalized esoteric medicine, claiming higher social prestige and stronger control over patients, with all that this implied, took place, however, without any objective increase in the period in real therapeutic efficiency, except possibly in the control by military surgeons of a limited range of traumatic conditions.[12]

And if there is little correlation between the therapeutic effectiveness of medicine and its increasing social visibility, there are many other qualifications which must be introduced into any account which seems to present a picture of the triumphant rise and progress of professional medicine. For all the attention which has been focused on the idea that the eighteenth century was the time when France was 'medicalized', its population increasingly within the purview of official medicine, it is also clear that old regime and Revolutionary

France possessed many other sorts of medicine, many other sorts of 'medical' practitioners, and many other sorts of ideas about the body and its behaviour than those sanctioned by official middle-class medicine.[13] It is also clear that changes in medical theory and organization by the end of the old regime were having as profound, if not more profound, an impact on the middle class as they were on the lower classes.

Some of the reasons for this are obvious. The fees charged by most licensed practitioners placed their assistance in any case far beyond the reach of all but the prosperous middle class or those even more highly placed. As the century progressed, medical knowledge itself became more esoteric, less available for the comprehension of those without some degree of formal education. Most important was the fact that in spite of the claims to control and inspection of the lower classes which it voiced with increasing frequency during the closing years of the old regime, medicine was rarely concerned to speak *to* that sector of society.[14] Its direct engagement was with the middle class itself.

In its prescriptions for health, the medical profession increasingly aimed at a specifically middle-class clientele, for which it produced a medical philosophy and a therapeutic regime totally distinct from that which it advised in the treatment of the lower classes. As William Coleman has pointed out, during the eighteenth century both conception and action with regard to the health of the individual were identified with the use of the Galenic-Arabic 'six things non-natural'.[15] The concept of the non-naturals was peculiarly suited to the social realities of the period, and above all to the confidence, self-assertion and wealth of the new economic and social élite which had seized intellectual leadership and aspired to political leadership in eighteenth-century France. The 'non-naturals' were factors external to man which inevitably and continuously influenced his physical well-being: air, food and drink, motion, rest, sleep and waking, evacuation and retention. Therapeutic advice to the middle classes, contained in an increasing number of health-care manuals, absorbed by a widening reading public, emphasized the idea of health as a product of individual practice and control over the non-naturals.[16] For the first time, 'health' was erected into an ideal to strive for.

In this drive towards 'health' through the understanding of the non-naturals, 'hygiene' became the principal ally. The emphasis on hygiene was twofold: to avoid potential causes of disease and to ensure, through a knowledge of the nature of life and health, the strength and proper functioning of the organism. Such an emphasis on health/hygiene was symptomatic of the emergence and popularization of new ideas of the body itself and of disease and health in the middle classes generally. The concept of the non-naturals was treated as embracing the full range of influences bearing upon them. The idea of direct divine intervention in human affairs, which included the venerable conception of disease as the price of sin, was viewed suspiciously in an increasingly secular society where health was viewed more and more as one of the responsibilities allotted to the individual, rather than a gift from God. The emergence of the concept of 'health', let alone that of its subsidiary adjunct 'hygiene', involved the externalization of the individual body as a subject of discourse, whose physical fortunes its owner became responsible for. Instead of being one of the accidents of life, 'health' became a good, even a right, to be actively striven for.[17]

The concept of 'health' was also used to link the individual sharply to his individual body: he and no one else was the manager of that body. The individual's life became more than a set of physical responses and experiences, amongst which episodes of disease and well-being would figure along with other bodily experiences: life was more than experienced, it became an experiment. Experience forced attention to the present and the past; experiment required an idea of the future, just as much as did the dominant desire of Revolutionary heroes to overcome death and to engrave the heroism of the body on to the future historical pantheon.[18]

The pursuit of 'health' thereupon dissolved into a potentially endless calculus, by which the individual sought to meld his previous experience and the influence and interaction of endogenous (natural) and exogenous (non-natural) factors on his bodily well-being, with a course of action which he dared not evade, which must be designed to presume current prosperity and assure for future security. His only test in the success of this search for health was himself: he was the instrument and subject of his own experiment. Thus the concept of 'health' also entailed a reflexive idea of the individual body: person, body, health and self-management were welded indissolubly together in a way which separated each body from any other body. The concomitant emphasis on hygiene, the separation at frequent intervals of the body both from unwanted accretions originating in the outside world and from the evidence of its own inner fluid secretions, also went far to create the body of *homo clausus*, with its clear separation from the external world and its firm retention of all its inner secretions in the service of the making of a firm, hard line around the public self. This was the self-image of the future political class in France: it was established as much by medical intervention *before* the Revolution as by the invention of the political style of 'heroic dignity' after it had begun.

Middle-class medicine also worked in with another tendency of the political culture of the body we have already encountered under the Revolution. One of the most salient characteristics of both medical and political culture was its tendency to desacralize the body, to remove it from any theological frame of reference. Writers on the non-naturals, while not denying the existence of a 'soul', also allotted it no specific location in the body and in discussion tended to lump it together with 'the passions' themselves. Writers on the non-naturals in the eighteenth century in fact played an important role in maintaining the idea of the functional integrity of the organism, and are part of the generalized later eighteenth-century movement away from the last vestiges of Cartesian dualism. They stressed the necessary and constant interaction of body and soul. The therapeutic writers stressed the idea that the healing power of nature must be allowed to act as much upon the discordant passions as upon other more obviously physical disruptions of bodily functions. The 'passions' were thus a non-natural: they were in the most intimate union with other organic functions, and they demanded the same careful attention for the seeker of health as did diet and exercise. Just as much as Stoicism itself, careful pursuit of health demanded management both of affect and of body. And in fact, the prescriptions for the maintenance of health given by the therapeutic writers cannot be distinguished from prescriptions for the maintenance of heroic stoic dignity: Arnulf d'Aumont, a major contributor to the *Encyclopédie* on therapeutic matters, for example, recommended the same 'constant tranquillity of the soul, the rejection of all ambition, of all powerful attachment, of every domineering aversion'.[19]

It thus appears to be the case that even before the Revolution began, the kind of therapeutic advice on offer to the middle classes was approaching the same problem of self-sovereignty, of the drawing of lines between the self and others, between 'internal' and 'external' worlds, and between one body and another, as was political culture itself. In other words, the medical philosophy and therapeutics of the eighteenth century provided one of the major conceptual pre-conditions for the emergence under the Revolution itself of the isolated figures of representative virtue around which so much of the political culture of the new political class was to coalesce.

Medicine, in fact, produced images of the human body which sensitively responded to changing ideas of the body politic itself. It should come as no surprise that as the political victory of the middle class was consolidated, after the Jacobin collapse of 1794, so the definition of bodily management and therapeutic should start to change in highly significant ways. Writing and exhortation on the 'non-naturals' starts to be replaced by their former adjunct, 'hygiene', in ways which moved 'hygiene' away from its assurance of self-sufficiency, its medical individualism. To accept the therapeutic directives of the regime involved in the search for health and hygiene had always only been available to the comfortably placed middle class, those with means enough to have available to them a range of choice in life-style, a range of choice which differentiated them from the vast majority of the population whose poverty reduced the chance of making any change of life-style to virtually nothing. The regime of 'hygiene' and the non-naturals in fact operated to point up the unbridgeable gap between peasant and bourgeois, between those confined within the world of necessity and those whose means allowed them to inhabit the world of choice. The fact that the non-naturals were exploited, perhaps exclusively, by members of a single social group, also formed part of what Robert Mandrou has called 'that delimitation of cultural traits, including the conditions and modes of life, together with their verbally expressed valuation, without which valid differentiation of social classes proves impossible'.[20]

By contrast, the medical advice purveyed even to the literate outside the middle and upper classes was of a very different order, and based on very different suppositions about the relation between individuals and their bodies. The cheap chapbooks sold by a distinctive section of the French book trade, directed to a rural or provincial, often semi-literate audience, evolved only with extreme slowness towards a systematic presentation of practical knowledge.[21] Such a literature purveyed medical lore of a most traditional kind, which generally recited a set programme of remedies and manipulations, that is, a highly simplified course of active therapeutic intervention. Such a therapy expressed little or no concern for anticipatory care of the body, a circumstance mainly related to the social and economic condition of its audience, confined inexorably within the world of necessity. In contrast, for the middle-class audience of the hygiene and therapeutic manuals, medical advice orientated on a world of *citizens* had no real meaning save 'seize possession of yourself', comprehend and master those functions which inexorably influence your bodily functions, devise a reasoned plan best suited to your own personal idiosyncrasies and exercise through your newfound mastery a programme for assuring your health.

It was thus hardly surprising that, once the middle class found itself in a consolidated position of political control after the fall of Robespierre, this bourgeois image of health which entailed the middle-class heroic body image of self-possession and self-mastery, should begin increasingly to be generalized, from prescriptions for individual mastery of bodily health to therapeutics for an entire society. We may trace the production of several such programmes by the late 1790s, showing the attempt to achieve and legitimize middle-class control of therapeutic programmes throughout society at exactly the same time as the achievement of a small measure of post-revolutionary stability allowed a reorganization of the body politic itself. We find that as the late 1790s proceeded, so, increasingly, therapeutic manuals were aimed at affecting the behaviour of *collectivities* rather than that of individuals, perceived as medically autonomous entities each responsible for his own salvation through attention to health. Such texts began to use a great variety of strategies to promote, rather, the binding together of individuals into communities formed by organic bonds of responsibility. Manuals such as *La Loi naturelle ou Catéchisme du Citoyen français* (1793), by Constantin Volney, stress the idea that any behaviour which jeopardizes the quality of life in a human body is anti-social sin, which calls the whole of the bonds between individuals into question. The well-being of citizens' bodies occupied the central space of Volney's political theory, with the equally important corollary that health is not innate but learnt, and that therefore ignorance is the true original sin. Civic responsibility, for Volney and others like him, becomes the equivalent of health-seeking behaviour. In stating this, Volney brought together the political-cum-moral abstractions of individual responsibility and social good, and mundane human existence in the form of bodily functions.[22]

He could do this because of the multiple ways in which the body had altered social meanings by his date. So much had the eighteenth century and the Revolution itself succeeded in charging the body with meaning, that it had collapsed former, previously external moral grids, such as ideas of moral vice and virtue, on to the body itself. The body having become for the middle class the total image of the internal and the external worlds, and having pushed out all theological imputations from itself, to replace them with political ones, it was logical for Volney and the rest of the writers on public-hygiene questions to deny that virtue and vice are directed towards spiritual ends: they are, on the contrary, always referable to the destruction or preservation of the body. This fits in perfectly with the tendency within the political culture of the Revolution itself to home in on the body and to envisage bodily behaviour and demeanour as guarantors of virtue and indicators of vice. The body, in fact, in the political culture of the Revolution, becomes self-referential. In the absence of external validating points, body and political symbols collapse into each other. It is this which produces such rapport between prescriptions for individual and collective physical bodies and for the social body as such.

Volney extended the Stoic ideas of physical 'self-possession' which were so powerful in Revolutionary political culture, into an argument about the relationship between physical bodies and the social fabric. For Volney and other such writers, the body was the most basic form of property, a self-possession in the most literal sense, over which the individual had total control which it was imperative to

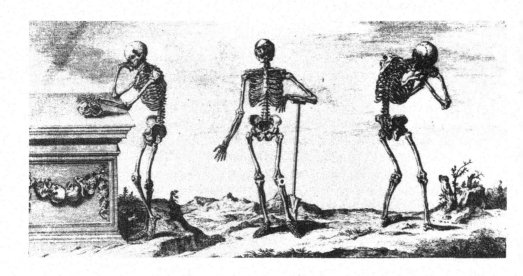

IV The skeleton adopts poses of bourgeois melancholy. It was through pictures like these that the middle classes appropriated the representation of the 'universal' human body to their own class-image. William Cheselden, *Osteographia* (1733).

exercise in the most responsible manner. Not to do so threatened the whole fabric of society. Attaching high political stakes to the quality of life was a familiar part of the medical literature on hygiene, which invariably used the language of preservation and conservation. The social order, it was held, would be sustained only by controlling the interactions between individuals and the community of citizens of which they were a part.

The literature of health produced in the 1790s also tends to place less emphasis on individuals as radically autonomous, and more on a view which treats persons as commodities, as units of exchange, as abstract constituents of a community of citizens. Bodies are thus both products and agents in the social order, which is itself not moved by the hand of God, but is entirely constructed by virtue of the powers immanent in each citizen. This view also depends greatly on the equation of life not simply with the passive ideal of 'being', but with the ideal of activity, to which physiological competence is clearly crucial. This too was a change from the passive images of the individual favoured by the political culture of the Revolution proper. But what is happening here is not a sudden re-evaluation of energy for itself, at the expense of dignity; it is much more an integration of the individual and his body into a view of society not as an arrangement of orders, but as an arrangement of production.[23]

Having captured control of the state and society, the middle class was able to release public bodies from their rigid poses of representative virtue and integrate them into a holistic model of social interaction and productivity; but, in real terms, that model could not be made to work without a positive imposition of the middle-class model on the rest of society. Volney and the other therapeutic writers thus stress education as a major vehicle of promoting acceptance of the new therapeutic ideals. In this way they, like other middle-class thinkers, were, in other words, to take over the functions of the head in the new body politic, thinking the thoughts which should direct the bodies inferior to their own. This was a task which in reality was to fail completely, in spite of the success of the middle class in seizing control of the political apparatus at the centre. The reasons for this difficulty and failure are bound up with the immense differences between middle-class and lower-class images of bodies and their insertion into the world.

The middle class itself suffered a profound change in self-perception owing to the way medicine changed in this period. In particular, this happened because élite medical science in the eighteenth century chose to grapple with precisely the issues, connected with the understanding of the nervous system, which were most immediately connected with the claims to rationality that formed so intimate a part of middle-class self-perception. Eighteenth-century physicians were led to produce a reconsideration of the nature of rationality and of the soul itself. They were also led into thinking about the origins in the nervous system of the bases of individuals' responses to the outside world and each other. From all this, one basic point emerged: which was that the springs of human physical behaviour, both voluntary and involuntary, were not to be found in external forces operating on the body, such as the will of God, or in those with only vague physicality and bodily location, such as the 'soul', but rather were to be located squarely within the body itself, and were the product of internally generated physical forces.

The body, in other words, became the ultimate sign, because things formally external to it were collapsed into its physical totality and reality. This was the pre-condition for the emergence of the body as the ultimate reservoir of signification which it became under the Revolution itself. It was also to be the pre-condition for modern views of the body as an 'economy' of physiological systems, propelled throughout by an inner dynamic, rather than by externally located forces. Such views necessarily detach the body from other levels of meaning, whether theological or moral, and lead on to the view of the body as a problem in self-management, which it has retained to this day.

Let us consider now this process of medical discourse in more detail. The eighteenth century saw the emergence of a firm challenge to the iatro-medical ideas which had dominated the medicine of the preceding century.[24] Iatro-medicine had tended to postulate the identity of biological phenomena with physical and mechanical phenomena. It explained life and the living organism as if their phenomenology and their laws would be a priori of a determinate type. Iatro-medicine's major premiss, in fact, is that whatever one identifies as 'life' can be reduced to the sort of dynamic functions exhibited by machines. By the end of the eighteenth century, however, the dominance of iatro-mechanism had begun to break down, without, however, any single dominant model of bio-anthropological phenomena being generally accepted in its place. Several schools of thought battled for predominance, among which the most famous was probably produced by the group of researchers centred on the Montpellier medical school, among them Bossier de Sauvages, Théophile de Bordeu and Paul Joseph Barthez. The Montpellier school saw the need to admit the irreducible vitality of organic bodies, to seek the source of this vitality and to analyse the most salient aspects of the manifestations, such as sensitivity, which had been ignored by the iatro-mechanists, of the interiority of the living organism. Their medicine in fact was dominated by their admission of the existence in living reality of dynamic and organic phenomena inexplicable by the physical and mechanical theories then available.

Nor did the influence of the Montpellier physicians wane after the Revolution. Bordeu's works continued to be reprinted well after his death, culminating in a two-volume collected edition as late as 1828. In the course of his research, Bordeu had been able to ascertain the existence in the living organism of functions which clearly presuppose the action of forces which are innate in living matter itself. For those who wished it to, this was also to provide a physiology which examined most of the functions traditionally associated with the notion of a soul.

Another strand of medical enquiry was provided by the work of the German, Albrecht von Haller. Working in Göttingen, Haller, whose works were widely diffused in France, distinguished through experimentation a force inherent in muscular fibre, called irritability, and in nerve fibres called sensibility.[25] Haller still tried to leave a place in his physiology for the soul, which he defined as the only centre able to perceive the sensations carried to it by the nerve fibres. For the Montpellier physicians, however, this approach was unsatisfactory. Bordeu in particular regarded Haller's distinction between sensibility and irritability as too abstract, because the two faculties were too closely linked in living beings to admit easy separation. The Montpellier physicians emphasized a much more holistic view of the organism as a self-propelling, self-regulating entity, whose 'vital force' came from within its interior, instead of as a result of receptors to stimuli applied from outside. Bordeu emphasized that organic beings seem to possess a peculiar capacity for self-control, to act in accordance with particular aims and ends, and to participate harmoniously by means of a ceaseless reciprocal interaction in that complex dynamism, not at all a 'machine', which constitutes the life of a living being. Without attributing all this to any metaphysical entity, Bordeu saw the organism as possessing something one may call a force, capable of executing functions that no blind mechanical motor could. This was the force to which Bordeu gave the name 'sensitivity', a property which he considered to be diffused by the nerves, not only to some parts of the organism, but throughout the whole of it.[26]

Such an approach had important consequences. It not only completely abandoned the mechanical approach of the iatro-mechanists, but also marked a significant departure from the age-old approach to the body which, in medicine as much as in the sphere of political imagery, considered it in terms of a hierarchy of functions. Man, writes Bordeu, is not a being who is unitarily and uniformly subject to the action of the soul, of the consciousness of the brain. He is, on the contrary, an articulate, complex and 'decentralized' being:

> Nous comparons le corps vivant pour bien sentir l'action particulière de chaque partie à un essaim d'abeilles qui se remassent en pelotons et qui se suspendent à un arbre en manière de grappe. ...elle est un tout collé à une branche d'arbre, par l'action de bien des abeilles qui doivent agir ensemble pour se bien tenir: toutes concurrent [sic] à former un corps assez solide, et chacune cependant a son action à part. L'application est aisée; les organes du corps sont liés les uns aux autres; ils ont chacun leur district et leur action; les rapports de ces actions, l'harmonie qui en résulte, font la santé. Si cette harmonie se dérange, soit qu'une partie se relâche, soit qu'une autre l'emporte sur celle qui lui sert d'antagoniste, si les actions sont renversées, si elles ne suivent pas l'ordre naturel, les changements constitueront des maladies plus ou moins graves.[27]

Bordeu and the other Montpellier physicians in fact ended by concentrating the attention of their pupils and readers – and Bordeu's friendship with Diderot ensured the implantation of himself and his idea at the heart of Enlightenment thought – on the organic interior of man. Until Bordeu's work, the 'superior' functions of the body had been attributed to a soul, or to an intellectual or conscious centre, often tacitly considered to be *sui generis*; but in Bordeu, not only does the soul appear to be cut off from any actual psychic process, but the 'monarchic' supremacy of the conscious intellectual centre is replaced by a federation of many bodily centres. The brain remains the source of ideas but is no longer autonomous or completely dominant. It is its interaction with the often autonomous ganglions which actively makes the psycho-affective life of man. After this, it was impossible for any study of the 'superior' faculties to be separated from the study of bodily activities and functions.

But such medical teachings, while they deepened the picture of man enormously, also gave the eighteenth-century middle class very little hold on the innermost centre of themselves. Rationality and response themselves, while still created in the brain, were so in an organ which had lost its autonomous and undisputed dominance over other parts of the body order. The soul itself was increasingly eased out of physiology under the ceaseless pressure of experimental work done to find reliable answers to answerable questions. Through these developments, also, the very meaning of life and especially of death were called into question.[28] Out of this insecurity came two developments: an insistence on even more self-control of body image and especially body *outline*, once the Revolution began; and an increasing desire to subject the bodies of the lower social classes to medical control, precisely at the time when widely appreciated changes in medical theory made the nature of the middle-class body, in life and in death, more difficult to define than ever before.

Indeed, as the century progressed, quite conflicting body images began to possess the educated classes. On the one hand lay the controllable body of the writers on hygiene and the 'non-naturals', one able to be managed through advice, moderation and common sense, and through physical self-knowledge; on the other, the body image revealed in different degrees by the nervous-system researches of Haller and the Montpellier physicians, in which centres of control seemed to be increasingly autonomous, scattered across the body with no clear central reference point or guiding principle. In other words, the physical foundations of what we would now call the Id were becoming confused; and the sacral part of the body, the soul, found less and less of a secure place, either in the writings of the hygienists or of the physiologists. Small wonder that as the eighteenth century wore on, 'Stoic' and 'pre-Romantic' models of being, of rationality and sensibility, battled for dominance.

In these circumstances, the enormous efforts of the eighteenth-century middle classes to secure an area of undisputed exercise for rationality, and to focus that rationality on the direction of the *bodies* of *others*, should come as no surprise.[29] But it was also here that middle-class 'enlightened' licensed medicine encountered its biggest problems. Increasingly the French medical community in the last years of the old regime and the early years of the Revolutionary period made proposals for intervention in a rural society generally hostile to its claims and suspicious of its motives. Middle-class, urban, licensed medicine became more and more eager to spread precepts of hygiene and disease control into the countryside, particularly during times of local epidemics, but also as a result of ideas of national prosperity which identified poor health amongst the lower classes as a major cause of slow economic progress, and failure to increase agricultural productivity. Yet for the middle-class medical professions, rural disease in particular presented a real problem of control. Its prevalence and its intractability, as well as its economic and social implications, provided a huge challenge to middle-class medical culture.

The encounter with rural disease emerged as a vital test case in the ability of middle-class culture to impose its own organizing codes – here meaning its own relationship to its own bodily symbols – on to the rest of society. It cannot be said that it succeeded.

The first problem lay in the nature of the contact between learned, official medicine and the peasant world. Licensed practitioners resided almost exclusively in towns.[30] Licensed medicine tended to penetrate into rural France only at times of medical crisis such as famine and epidemic disease, when licensed doctors could be paid by the state, in the person of the surgeons' and physicians' syndicate of each region, to go out and treat the sick in the villages. Physicians living in small country towns, or philanthropically running a free dispensary, or with a practice which included honorariums from a local hospital as doctor-on-call, would also come into contact with the world of lower-class disease. Yet this was always an encounter with the peasant or worker perceived as profoundly 'other'; and subject to the mystification in which all representations of the lower classes were then enveloped. In the so-called 'medical gaze', the lower-class person was the last thing that doctors were in fact able to perceive clearly. Nor were the mystifications themselves internally coherent. The peasant was commonly perceived at one and the same time as the favoured inhabitant of an unspoiled natural setting, which rendered him morally superior to the middle-class town-dweller, and as characterized by an extreme 'simplicity' which revealed his intellectual *inferiority* to the bourgeois, by a sort of moral defectiveness or obtuseness which seemed to operate in such a way as to prevent the making of 'rational' choices in the matter of health and body management.[31]

Under this barrage of contradictions, the peasant body became at once an all too real object, obviously the carrier of disease, dirt and hunger, and, at the same time, an object which threatened to fall through even the fine mesh of the new medical gaze. Unquestionably for many physicians, the peasant in health and sickness was a source of embarrassment and revulsion – emotions which, together with the increasing ambiguity of bourgeois self-perceptions, meant that nearly all were bitten by the imperative to introduce change, to reform, and to enforce their role as therapists. As body-image problems increased for the middle classes and as images of mechanical control broke down in the medical sphere as they had in the political, so did the potential threat from the peasant and his body increase. The frail self-image of the middle class, increasingly alarmed by the peasant because of his seemingly irreducible otherness, strove to reduce the *unlikeness* of the peasant body, to control it, and ultimately to strip it of all human connotations through the medium of the 'medical gaze'.[32]

For the doctors, many features of peasant life were both reprehensible *and* incomprehensible. Doctors tended to view patients as perversely intractable and resistant to medical intervention; they focused immense disapproval on such features of peasant life as periodic orgies of eating and drinking, crude sexuality and indifference to the disposal of bodily wastes. Increasingly, attention was focused on the local rural élites as part of the answer to the problem, and a large body of self-help literature was produced by licensed doctors for the use of rural landowners and their wives, clergy and professional men of benevolent disposition; the physicians also attempted to impose a peculiarly middle-class ideal of rationality and control upon the physical practices of the peasants. The essence of such roles was not only the imposition of 'health' among the peasants; it was also the reinforcement of the image of the physician as dominant through the use of a self-styled rationality. In physicians' writings, the peasant emerged as emotion/Id/child; the physician as rationality/Ego/adult. As a representative provincial doctor wrote to the Société royale de Médicine:

> The people cannot control their imaginations; they believe in the existence of everything they are told and reasoning rarely has the power to disabuse them. To enlighten them, it is necessary to take them by surprise. Thus natural suspicion will not let them hear what we are saying. If we diverge too much from their opinions, they will suspect us of contrivance, of hiding the truth from them. Let us be tender-hearted with them, let us inspire them with confidence in the resources which we offer them and we will be able then to give doctors the credit of procuring the dual advantage of consoling them and delivering them from a murderous scourge.[33]

This passage well encapsulates the simultaneous assumptions of the physician's superiority and yet the peasants' relentless insensibility to his precepts, their inaccessibility to reason, their lack of any capacity to engage themselves in the projects for their physical well-being so enthusiastically touted by the licensed physicians.

Medical discourse, in this encounter with the unmoved object of its efforts, also became distorted. Unable to engage directly with the lower classes, the so-called clear, translucent 'medical gaze' also, and necessarily, suffered from a contortion and opacity of language around the central fact of the non-engagement of the object (body) and the subject (physician) within the discourse itself. The discourse contorted itself, using ruses and subterfuge to impose an allegedly pure medical discourse. The passage above also makes very clear the extent to which the physician suspected the peasant's own version of his illness and the reality of his bodily sensations. Such suspicion made it impossible for patient and doctor to engage in real communication. What the peasant *said* he was experiencing was transformed by the physician into what the peasant *ought* to be experiencing according to the signs and symptoms of medical nosology.

Similarly discounted were not only accounts of illness experienced but also attitudes in the face of illness, most notably the fatalism with which peasants regarded physical affliction, and their adherence to religious or 'superstitious' beliefs on illness and death and divine retribution. In place of such doctrines, the physicians contributed other forms of determinism which operated effectively to reduce the peasant to the status of object. The theories of the non-naturals were used in the case of the peasants to build up a picture of a patient whose disease-aetiology was overwhelmingly the function of his physical environment. That environment could not be changed without upheavals of a magnitude which few of them were prepared to contemplate, even during the Revolutionary period itself. Peasants and other workers alike remained trapped in the world of necessity; doctors, in the middle-class world of choice, assumed the responsibilities of rationality since the peasants, weighed down with 'superstition', could not.

One of the most striking features of the 'medical gaze' which was directed from the middle class on to the peasants was its inability to come to terms with, or even admit the existence of, the other social and cultural worlds inhabited by the peasants. Peasants and physicians were literally unable to communicate within an agreed world of representations of the body and its fortunes. Part of this was due to the continuous anxieties of the licensed physicians about their lack of hold over the countryside and its inhabitants. They correctly perceived that hold to be tenuous, and their theoretical monopoly of medical practice as under continual challenge from a whole variety of unlicensed healers, almost all of whom were far closer socially, economically and above all culturally to the peasants than they were themselves. Such healers were far thicker on the ground than were the licensed MDs. Even the barber-surgeons have been calculated as numbering about 40,000 by 1789, or 1 per 1,000 inhabitants, while fully qualified medical doctors stood at under 10 per cent of that figure.[34] All those practitioners represented a threat to the monopoly of medical practice claimed by the licensed doctors. They were also viewed by the medical profession as dangerously perpetuating a brand of medicine which fed on the 'superstition' and 'ignorance' of the peasants.

In reality, such 'superstition' was a reservoir of difference. Ample ethnographical evidence exists to show that peasant views of the body could hardly have been more different from that put forward in the figure of *homo clausus* – clean, controlled, conscious of bodily outline and of physical separateness from the bodies of others, a secularized body without real physical location for the soul; a body whose outlines were characterized by the subject's manipulation of *choice* in styles of life and styles of emotions. Rationality, not 'prejudice' or 'superstition', were the guiding lines of this body. To this, the peasants opposed beliefs and practices of which we have direct evidence from contemporary observers, and from historically orientated ethnographic studies carried out in the last century.

That the peasant body was characterized by dirt and was clothed by rags which revealed that body uncontrollably should come as no surprise.[35] But, considered further, peasant ideas about such things as dirt forbid us to treat their appearance as merely a function of a life of manual labour. For them, dirt, whether composed of externals such as mud and soil, or body fluids such as sweat, urine or excrement, were seen as *part of* the body to which they adhered. As Marie-France Morel has pointed out,

> Les pratiques populaires... insistent sur les précautions nécessaires avec lesquelles on doit se débarrasser soit des excréments, soit de la saleté du corps: il ne faut pas se laver trop souvent ou n'importe où, car la *crasse fait partie du corps*, et joue d'une certaine manière un rôle protecteur, surtout chez l'enfant, plus exposé que les adultes aux mauvais esprits.[36]

In a rural milieu, in other words, dirt was seen as having a positive function, and body products were to be jealously retained and not hidden for fear of obscuring the hard outline of the body. Dirt, also, became a focal issue distinguishing urban and middle-class from peasant ideals of the body. This was a point when, as we have seen, 'hygiene' became an important part of middle-class medical therapeutic advice, at a time when 'public hygiene' was also coming increasingly to the fore, and when the cleaning of the streets from waste products of all kinds became a public priority, when public baths began to appear in the towns, and bathrooms in private houses, and where such obvious examples of physical corruption and dissolution as the cemeteries were removed wholesale from the centre of towns.[37]

The concern for the maintenance of fixed form in the middle-class body, and its contrast with the dirt-covered body of the peasant, whose unconcern over filth and excrement led to a blurring of the line between the internal and external bodies, operated as well in the case of fat, which also blurs and makes ambiguous the body outline. Writers on childhood often accused middle-class parents of underfeeding their children because 'ils ne veulent pas que leurs enfants soient gros et bien-portants, parce que l'on dit que cela ressemble trop à des paysans'.[38] The middle classes in fact, as stated before, saw the peasant as having an ineluctable *difference*. The final term of that difference was the malleability of the body outline itself. For the middle-class parent, those lines were set from birth. Peasants, on the other hand, were far from believing in such a radical autonomy of the body. For them, the shape of the body was not the result of its own inner dynamic, or vital energies, such as those isolated by the Montpellier doctors; it was the result of human intervention. Viewed as born unformed, unfinished, the peasant child was subject to swaddling, to strengthen its limbs and forbid a return to foetal postures. In many parts of France, it was also subject to radical deformation of the skull, of the hands and tongue in attempts to improve or 'finish off' the infant as it appeared at birth.[39] In other words, for the peasant, both the culture of the individual body and its radical autonomy were foreign concepts. So, it is hardly necessary to stress, would be any idea of its secular character. Lastly, the folk traditions of France still kept alive many allusions to a body conceived as a collection of detachable parts. Tales such as that of Loustoucrou, the blacksmith who made new heads for women who talked too much, of detached heads which talked, of heroes and heroines who changed body shape at will, were current, while the travelling literature of colportage kept alive older ideas of soul and body as physical entities in perpetual dialogue with one another, ideas banished from advanced élite medical physiology.[40]

The Revolution was to mix the rational and the irrational, the middle-class body and the peasant body; to confront the classical middle-class myth of the *homo clausus* with the classical peasant myth of the malleable, fluid body, each of whose parts might take on a magical significance and itself become the focus of the story. After 1789, political and hence cultural divisions began to break down. In 1790, the Legislative Assembly abolished the organized professional structures of French medicine as part of its dismantling of the institutions of the *ancien régime*. Licensing procedures, and the control of medical practice, were for a time suspended, with the result that large numbers of individuals who were denounced by the licensed practitioners as quacks and charlatans were able to offer their services to the public without restriction. In this situation, deprived of the normal means of maintaining its professional authority, and faced with competition from popular healers in an ideological environment that favoured democratic egalitarianism over corporate privilege, 'official' medicine, and its views of the 'correct' middle-class body, suffered a devastating loss of public esteem. It was this chaotic situation which led to the steps described earlier to re-establish the medical profession, and to focus it on the hospital, with the new controls, diagnostics and pathology which the hospital made possible.

But the first result of the breakdown of medical authority after 1790, like the first result of the breakdown of political authority at the same time, was to unleash a whole host of competing definitions of the body into the newly sensitive public arena. The intensity of the conflict which was thus generated, leading to traumatic incidents of mob violence and state terror, marked the political culture of France for at least the whole of the nineteenth century and, many would argue, for the twentieth century as well.

This intense violence also gives the lie to many conclusions which historians such as Robert Muchembled have drawn about the evolution of the relations between popular and élite culture by the closing years of the old regime in France. Muchembled in particular has argued that by the mid-century, versions of élite culture were available to, and consumed by, newly prosperous artisans and wealthy peasants, thus creating a cultural location where, thanks to increased literacy and the increased availability of the printed word, elements of élite and popular cultures mingled. Muchembled also argues, in his *Culture populaire et culture des élites*,[41] that the French state itself, from the sixteenth century, made a sustained onslaught on 'popular culture', that residue of beliefs and practices to be found amongst 'the people', who were thereby defined as different from the élite. By the end of the eighteenth century, the French state had established itself as the purveyor of an agreed system of élite values; and slowly, rising sections of the artisans and the peasants were being co-opted into this 'élite' cultural system.

The events of the Revolution itself indicate how fragile and incomplete both these processes were. State culture showed itself unable to withstand the force of the multiplicity of cultural prescriptions for human behaviour produced by the Enlightenment – prescriptions which became more and more crucial politically as the problem of embodiment generalized into the problem of political culture itself. Secondly, in the acute phase of the Revolutionary Terror, the middle class itself became the cultural location for the meeting of élite and popular cultures, a meeting of common concerns and images which were formed by the force-field of Revolutionary violence.

The loosing of the bonds of authority, and the increasing violence of the Revolution, violence in which peasant and artisan mobs played a great part, meant that the encounter between middle class and peasant body was no longer played out in terms of, respectively, subject and object, seer and seen. The Revolution saw not only the construction of the 'medical gaze' by which the middle classes peered into the objectified bodies of working-class patients; it was also the period when the peasant and artisan crowds subjected the actual bodies of members of the middle and upper classes to active public deconstruction. Féraud's head was brandished on a pike, like the heads of the Princesse de Lamballe, and of de Flesselles; the 1,300 executions in the prison massacres of September 1792 form merely the most immediately memorable of such incidents.[42] Part of their impact was an immediate hardening of lines between crowd and middle class, leaving a legacy of traumatic class fear for the nineteenth century and beyond. But another effect, and one which has received far less discussion, was, by such violent interactions, to produce a force-field composed of the interaction of actuality and myth, where divisions between upper and lower class, based on the imputed characteristics of each (rationality, irrationality) and their connected body images (open/closed), were blurred.

Both middle and lower classes were responsible for the enormous death count of the Revolution. They developed very similar imageries, obsessed on both sides of a seemingly irreparable social divide with cannibalism and with bodily dismemberment, and in particular with the separation of the head from the body, whether by guillotine, by citizens' justice in the case of prison massacres, or by the less formal ways favoured by the crowd.[43] We will see in successive chapters how mythologies centred on the behaviour of severed heads in general acutely reflected uncertainties about the definition of life, death and self-consciousness directly generated by middle-class medical physiology. Such confusion was also enough to allow middle-class people to lend credence to myths remarkably similar to the 'irrational' stories of the lower orders. The classical example here is that of Charlotte Corday's head, allegedly alive and responsive to the executioners' insults after its separation from the body.

The story of Charlotte Corday, in other words, widely diffused as it was, was a place where the 'medical gaze' refused to operate, and irrationality, the resolute transformation of a natural object into a mythical form, took place with the active collaboration of the middle class itself – or, as the doctors present at her execution remarked, was a 'triumph of credulity' amongst the normally rational middle class.[44] In actual form the story is also a parallel both to the classical legend beloved of the middle class (the severed head of Medusa, still active after death, causing consternation to all who see it) and to the innumerable stories of detached yet responsive heads which dot French folklore.[45] The fixation both of lower-class aggression and of middle-class fears on the severed head, also suggests, too, that at the heart of the debate centred on the body, generated by the Revolution, lay the question of rationality; precisely that posed as the ultimate issue by Cabanis and the other medical observers of the time, as that which the middle class used as its badge of social authority, yet which medicine itself had called increasingly into question.[46]

Yet other stories in the middle-class mythological canon recounted physical deeds which have a similar fairy-tale quality, and yet remained firmly focused on the world of the political élite threatened by the lower orders. A prime example here is that of Mlle de Sombreuil, who volunteered, to save her aged father's life during the September massacres, to perform the supremely cannibalistic act of drinking a cup of human blood. As late as the 1820s her heart was held up for veneration in the chapel of the Invalides, as much a detachable part of the body to be venerated as any saintly relic, or as Marat's heart, which during the Revolution was suspended from the roof of the Panthéon after his murder by Charlotte Corday.[47]

As Ronald Paulson has recently pointed out, the middle-class revolutionaries were no less obsessed by 'mythological' symbols than were the peasants and urban workers. Seeing the bourgeois mythology as preoccupied with the symbols of the redistribution of power through the redistribution of the symbolic body, he focuses on the revolutionaries' concern with myths of parricide and the consumption of the body of the slain father at the cannibal feast of his successors, the sons; myths which reflected the actual redistribution of sovereignty which the Revolution had set in motion, from the body of the king on to the bodies of everyman. In their cannibalistic concerns – a Freudian would see in the destruction of the king and queen a replaying of Oedipal struggles with the body of the mother and father – the middle classes not only generated a mythology of their own which concentrated on the dispersal and re-absorption of the human body; they also created one whose images interlocked powerfully with a pre-existing canon of French folklore, with its emphasis on the dispersal of the body and the continuous magical re-apprehension of monarchical power.[48] In spite of his suggestive insights, Paulson, however, does not link up the continuities between the 'high culture' of the revolutionaries' rhetorical allusions to themselves as 'children of Saturn', and the tales of Loustoucrou, or the common preoccupations of middle class and lower classes alike with the physical disintegration of the bodies of their opponents. Taking the autonomous nature of 'high culture' for granted, he misses the opportunity to question the uses of such imagery in the making of specific political culture.

Yet to include the 'folkloric' stories of Charlotte Corday and Mlle

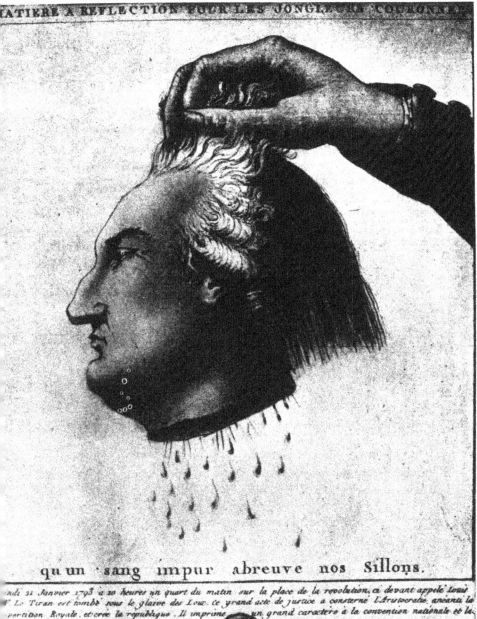

Cannibalistic metaphors were omnipresent in the popular political imagery of the Revolution.

de Sombreuil in the canon of middle-class mythology is to demonstrate the sensitivity of that canon to the central issue with which the Revolution faced the bourgeoisie: of physical trial as a means of remaking the body politic. Such recitals of trauma operate to establish end-limits to bourgeois rationality. In other words, they establish the field of negotiation in which seemingly fixed values such as 'heroic Stoicism' could be confronted with their opposites previously imputed to lower-class culture, to produce the dialectical uncertainties characteristic of middle-class culture. That confrontation left the act of seeing the bodies of others as perhaps the most important middle-class act. An inclusive or accurate act of seeing could reconcile the contradictory associations with which the body had become filled as a result of the events of the Revolution. In a political universe where language was dominated by ellipsis and periphrasis, the act provided a hold on the speaker, and a link between seer and seen. It provided a link between the natural and political worlds with difficulty re-established after the collapse of the symbolism of the king's body.

It was through such symbols and the active force-field constituted by the violent clash between middle-class and lower-class symbols of the body that the basic tensions within the value systems of the nineteenth century were to be worked out: rationality vs. sensibility, head vs. heart, man vs. woman, objectivity vs. subjectivity. In this process, the Revolution had only grouped together many trends in eighteenth-century medicine. These meanings are far from being containable in the issues of medical theory and training identified in Foucault's classic account of the new medicine in this period, *Naissance de la clinique*: they need to be filled out with the middle classes' battle for control over self and other, and transfused with political and public meanings, before they make much sense.

Eighteenth-century researchers into the workings of the brain and the nervous system had established a vision of the body in which the soul could find no clear location. Not only was the soul thus evacuated from the physical body in eighteenth-century experimental medicine; it also refused to place the images of the brain and nervous system it created at the service of the age-old hierarchy of functions in the body, which was in turn locked on to an image of the body politic as similarly organized around a hierarchy of functions. In describing the nervous system as a swarm of bees hanging off a fruit, Bordeu was doing more than being fanciful about ganglions; he was also, with pastoral calm, abandoning the idea of the brain ('containing' the soul) as unquestioned leader of the hierarchy of nervous-system functions, as the monarch or 'head' of state was the unquestioned controller of the body politic. The eighteenth century, in other words, deconstructed previously prevailing notions about the physical embodiment of rationality and the soul at the same time and in the same language as it deconstructed ideas about the hierarchical nature of political authority.

Also at the same time, paradoxically, Enlightenment thinkers in the *Encyclopédie* and the health manuals, and in the academic contests so beloved of rising bourgeois like Jean-Marie and Manon Roland, urged upon the middle class the values of rationality as the legitimation of the exercise of social authority by the middle class. *Homo clausus*, separated from his emotions and his body by 'rational' restraints, was being born. In other words, the eighteenth-century middle class was adopting a set of behaviours based on values associated with rationality and self-control, at the same time as the ideas current about the physical *motors* for these behaviours were increasingly cast into flux. The body became an object for negotiations about public authority at precisely the moment when the medical definition of its rational functions became more and more ambiguous.

In the light of this contradiction, it is easy to understand the appearance of three further contradictions: Firstly, that medical practice, both in the eighteenth century and during the Revolution itself, should increasingly have developed disciplines and institutions which aimed to help a middle-class medicine increase its hold over the peasant body perceived as profoundly other – because profoundly irrational. Secondly, that this encouraged the development of a 'medical gaze', in Foucault's term, profoundly fascinated with the inner workings of the body and concerned, in the works of pioneers such as Xavier Bichat, with disentangling the obscure interrelations of functions which now refused to fit into neat hierarchical patterns. Thirdly, that while undergoing these attempts to control medically the bodies of other social orders, while occupying itself with the exploration of structures of authority and control within the body far more complex than anything yet guessed at, the middle-class body also attempted to divert attention from these two vast areas of negotiation by producing a public body image, *homo clausus*, which was preoccupied above all else with the maintenance of the unbroken physical outline, permitting no outsider a glimpse into the untidy conflicts within. Metamorphosed into poses drawn from classical antiquity, into a revolutionary Stoicism, it sanitized the middle-class struggle for social and political control by its appeal to an eternal canon of male political virtue.

# 5

# A NEW PUBLIC BODY

## Stoicism, Suffering and the Middle Class in the French Revolution

...nouveau Robinson que j'étais...

Ramond

Calme-toi, l'empire est au flegmatique.

Saint-Just to Robespierre[1]

Tried and condemned for complicity in the popular uprisings of Prairial year III, the last popular rising of the Revolution, the Jacobin deputy Bouchotte killed himself in open court, shouting as he did so: 'O brave Cato, now it will no longer be from you alone that men will learn how free men can escape the clutches of tyranny'.[2]

What prompted men in such critical moments to identify so strongly with the heroes of a remote classical tradition of republican Stoicism? These are themes which, as we have seen, the recent historians of the Revolution have too often dismissed as bizarre aberrations of behaviour due to the heightened feelings of the revolutionary moment, or simply passed over in silence in favour of the study of mass movements or social conditions. Yet to treat such behaviour as mere hysterics, or trivial histrionics, is to display an ignorance of the ideological climate in which the men of the Revolution approached the building of their new state, and the control of their new, and often terrifying, politics. Actions and words very like Bouchotte's recur with remarkable frequency throughout the 'prime time' of the Revolution, that period stretching from August 1792 to Thermidor year II, the time when the erection of a new political order rather than compromise with the old became the definitive task of the Revolution. In that new political order, the creation of new forms of public embodiment for individuals was one of the most vital tasks.

But in describing Bouchotte's words as 'Stoic', what do I in fact mean? Clearly, the men of the Revolution cannot be visualized simply as actors-out of the complex doctrines of classical Stoicism, which in the Hellenistic period and in the late Roman republic and empire had endlessly debated the pros and cons for the virtuous man of involvement (*negotium*) in the chaos and murk of public affairs, as against a dignified withdrawal into a leisure (*otium*) occupied by scholarly reflection and the giving of good moral advice and example to others.[3] Nor were the revolutionaries likely to take on board the whole freight of the consideration which the ancient world had devoted to the control of the passions, and the maintenance of the boundaries of the virtuous self against the challenges of public life.[4] We know from H.T. Parker's classic work that the men of the Revolutionary generation in any case came across directly only a small fraction of the body of doctrine which later historians have identified as 'Stoicism', let alone encountering at first hand the Greek tradition which underlay that of Roman Stoicism.[5]

The late Roman Stoicism encountered at school or after by these men was, in fact, too complex to provide them with definite directives for responses to the challenges of public life.[6] Far more, the classical discussions within the Stoic corpus gave them not only a supply of terms and arguments, but also role-playing models through which they could organize many of their responses to the new public life of the Revolution. The following two chapters discuss in some detail the way in which two sets of responses, heroic suicide and the new philosophy of death characteristic of the new revolutionary political class, were influenced by classical models, and were crucial in creating a new political embodiment for the individuals concerned and a new audience for their politics. But whatever their alleged role-models, in fact the political actors of the Revolution were both eclectic and selective, not only in relation to classical Stoicism but also in relation to the forms of Stoicism which had become current at other earlier periods in modern history, when states had faced great challenges and evoked great creative energies in their solution.

It is often forgotten that the eighteenth century was not only aware of the classical discussions on the disciplining of the passions which went into the public intervention of the virtuous man; it was also the heir to the vigorous reworking of Stoicism which had been produced by many rulers and scholars since the mid-sixteenth century, men such as the Dutch scholar and diplomat Lipsius (1547–1606). Lipsius' work, as Gerhard Oestreich's recent discussion has made clear, not only presented an ideology of virtuous intervention in public life which, although based on classical models, was far more coherent than they were; he also produced ideas whose influence stretched far beyond the crisis and turmoil of the early modern states which had prompted his work in the first place.[7] Lipsius' work *On Politics* was translated into all the major languages, and went through 96 editions, including 7 in the eighteenth century, the last one being printed in Vienna in 1751. It was endlessly excerpted from and quoted. Lipsius' other major work of neo-Stoic philosophy, the *Constantia*, had an almost equally long life.[8]

Because Lipsius' work was, linguistically, more accessible than the classical discussions of virtuous intervention in public life, and also presented a more forceful and coherent picture of that intervention, it is worth discussing at some length in order to pinpoint the great differences between Lipsius' influential doctrines and the responses of the French revolutionaries which were clothed in the same classical drapery.

In many ways, Oestreich's discussion of Lipsius' version of Stoicism and its profound influence on the organization of early modern states and the behaviour of rulers, army leaders and bureaucrats, converges with accounts of an increasing disciplining of public life in the modern world already offered, as we have seen, by Foucault, by Elias, and also by Max Weber. While each of these writers would place the emphasis differently from Oestreich, who is the only one specifically to mention the neo-Stoic input into this development, yet his conclusions are certainly not incompatible with theirs, and have the special value, as do Elias's, of accounting for the behaviour and self-perception of individuals within a political context. Neo-Stoicism's aim was to increase the power and efficiency of the state by an acceptance of the central role of force and discipline in its existence. At the same time, the ideology demanded self-discipline, the extension of the duties of the ruler, and the education of the army, the officials and indeed the whole political nation, to a life of work, frugality, dutifulness and obedience. The result was a general enhancement of social discipline in all areas of life, and this enhancement produced, in its turn, a change in the ethos of the individual and in his self-perception. In the context of the upheavals of the late sixteenth and early seventeenth centuries, the claim to human dignity and the aspiration to freedom seemed to be guaranteed and satisfied by the demands made by neo-Stoicism for the controlling of the person, for self-inspection, self-discipline, tolerance and moderation.

These demands for individual self-control, which are very close to those defined by Elias in terms of a 'civilizing process' based on court culture, also differed radically from their classical ancestors by their unequivocal orientation towards action and involvement. Gone was the constant tension present in classical discussions between the claims of *otium* and *negotium* on the virtuous man. Gone too were the debates, so strong in Seneca especially, over whether the virtuous man should involve himself in public affairs during times of great strife and disorder. The answer for Lipsius was an unequivocal recommendation of action and involvement. In the *Constantia*, he remarks, 'Many have prevailed by fighting, not by fleeing'. Lipsius continues by remarking that, contrary to the teaching of the ancient Stoics, 'the gods do not force men's will; it is man alone who decides his own fate, and we are free to act as we choose'. In Lipsius' version of Stoicism, it is in fact action and involvement which are the main objectives. In order to achieve action by individuals, he asks for an exceedingly severe and above all controlled manliness, which owes a good deal not only to classical discussions of Stoicism but also to the classical republican tradition and its heroes, such as the elder Brutus and Cato of Utica.[9] These men had achieved decisive political action at the price of the sacrifice of personal emotions, ties and duties; they had succeeded in controllng both the affective life and the outgoing physical responses which went with it. Accordingly, for Lipsius, the ideal individual in the political world is the citizen who acts according to reason, is answerable to himself, controls his emotions, and is ready to fight, who utilizes in fact the basic concepts of the Roman Stoa: *continentia, modestia, abstentia*. It is thus a Stoic virtue given an active form, and addressed to the man of action; it is of *his* virtues and vices, strengths and weaknesses, that Lipsius speaks; and in doing so creates someone in fact very close to but more aggressive than Elias's *homo clausus*.

Commentators on sixteenth-century neo-Stoicism, when they have noticed it at all, have tended to relate it to the growth of the 'capitalist mentality', rather than to the more closely related fields to which Oestreich links it, of the behaviour and ideals which made possible the operation of modern state structures.[10] One of the reasons for this is that, as Oestreich himself points out, the neo-Stoic values as put forward by Lipsius were very different from the 'pale phantoms' which they became in the age of the Enlightenment. They were 'full-blooded, powerful and essential values, designed for the exuberant and undisciplined mercenaries of the time'.[11] This point deserves to be discussed at greater length.

The French Revolution faced, as had the sixteenth and seventeenth centuries, a crisis of state-building, and a pervasive collapse of order and discipline in society and politics. But the revolutionaries, in spite of the similarities of their problems to those faced by the men of the preceding two centuries, saw those problems differently. For Lipsius and his contemporaries, the struggle had centred around the creation of behaviour in individuals which would strengthen the state conceived as power and order, based on *vis*; the men of 1789 concentrated on problems of *consent*.[12] They thought less about what the state had to *do* than about how it was to be *made*. They faced the problem not of strengthening sovereignty (however located), but of redefining it. It was the ways in which they solved this problem which affected the sort of 'Stoicism' which they evolved as public embodiment, and the public behaviour in individuals which they validated.

It was also true that by the end of the eighteenth century, Stoicism was only one amongst a cacophony of sometimes competing, sometimes converging prescriptions available to individuals concerned about the maintenance of their dignity and authenticity. Rousseau's well-known attacks on the corruption of urban and public life had produced a whole series of ideals for the individual to aspire to in this search. The practice of pastoral solitude, the eighteenth century's version of philosophical *otium*, although condemned by Rousseau himself, was made attractive by numerous publications lauding the delights of rural retreat.[13] A new ethos of the family, to which historians have recently devoted much attention, emphasized individual validation through intimacy and the exclusion of the wider world. The cult of 'sentiment' validated individual responses to emotion through outpourings of tears, sighs and faintings, as was evidenced in the European-wide cults of 'response' which surrounded the novels of *Pamela* and *Clarissa* by Samuel Richardson, and later the *Nouvelle Héloïse* of the same Rousseau.[14]

Yet the same individuals who sighed and wept over the complicated motivations of Clarissa, Julie or Saint-Preux, might also hero-worship a canon of 'great men' which the century had elaborated: William Penn, Socrates, Voltaire, Rousseau, Homer, Newton, Franklin, Cato, all figured in this eighteenth-century pantheon.[15] These secular figures displaced for many of the middle class, especially for men, the traditional patterns of virtue previously provided by the saints. Ascribed to them was a supreme ideal, 'virtue', that meant not only that they were 'good' in some sense, but also that they were not subject to the will of others. It was no accident that the Quaker Penn, and the American republican Franklin, were so prominent in this collection of 'reference-figures.'[16] They served to provide individuals with examples of men whose inner authenticity had allowed them to achieve self-sovereignty. It is also no accident that a concern with self-modelling on such figures begins to be prominent in the eighteenth century, precisely the time marked by Elias as that when individuals were becoming, especially in the middle class, increasingly closed in upon themselves in their concern for their own physical and affective control. The 'great men' were models for this purpose, and also helped to introduce that modelling and maintain an audience for it. The cult of the great men also epitomizes a unifying feature among all the seemingly disparate cults of

VI David's sketches from life of the young general Bonaparte show the tension underlying the ideal of male heroism formed during the Revolution. J.-L. David, *croquis* (? 1799).

the self which blossomed at the end of the eighteenth century: the concern with individual self-validation through the playing of controlled public roles. Even the apparent exception to this, the cult of sentiment, became fashionable precisely because of the shock value of asserting that an individual's dignity was *not* compromised by very visible emotional and physical reaction; it thus fed upon the basic cultural assumptions of the eighteenth century, which were moving the individual squarely back into the fortress of his self.

How are we, following the general argument of this book, to relate such a movement to the history of the French state in the late eighteenth century? This is a period where, as has been noted before, Elias's arguments and models cease to provide us with much guidance, and we are forced to construct our own perspective, to take up and test, more than hitherto, Elias's notion of the *homo clausus*. At first sight, the French state at the end of the century seems to fit squarely into models current in Germanic historiography, as an 'absolute' state, capable of inserting discipline and control into society.[17] But in reality, France at the end of the eighteenth century presents the picture, paradoxical in Elias's terms, of a state under increasing challenge from its own constituted bodies (the Parlements, the Cour des Aides), weakened by an extraordinary financial pressure, and visibly losing ground as a force in international relations.

It was also the case that the 'court culture' which Elias so brilliantly describes was no longer the sole arbiter of what the 'civilized person' should be. The court culture certainly still existed. But it was challenged partly by the existence of a firm bourgeois culture, which emphasized intimacy, private virtue, financial rectitude, and the pursuit of the public good. This could not have been more different from the aristocratic values of display, conspicuous expenditure and self-glorification. At the same time, the monarchy and sections of the younger, more liberal nobility seemed themselves to be abandoning the 'court culture', to live in a more 'bourgeois' style. The breakdown of the cultural dominance of the aristocracy, and the weakening of the authority of the monarch both politically and culturally, led many contemporaries to ask the question, as Daniel Roche has put it, 'who is the real élite?'.[18] Part of the function of all these ideologies of the individual, including Stoicism, which we have described as burgeoning together in the late eighteenth century, was to attempt to answer that question. Given the breakdown of cultural sovereignty, and the slow weakening of sovereignty in the political sphere, individuals were forced increasingly into *self*-cultivation in order to validate their claims to authority in public and private roles. It became the duty of each person to make his own political body.

In this task eighteenth-century people could expect little aid from contemporary debate on political theory. The idea of sovereignty as personalized, located within the physical body of the king, which was at the same time the mystical body of the state, and where subjects acted as the organs of the body in due subordination to the head, was already greatly weakened.[19] Even the idea that sovereignty could or should lie with a particular person, rather than with an office, or indeed with the nation as a whole, was also under attack. Yet in this great reshaping of ideas on the nature of government, no firm consensus emerged before the Revolution, and certainly not during it, as to who should wield sovereign power, or with what justification. Well-known theories such as that expressed by Rousseau in his *Contrat social* hardly provided workable solutions to the problem. Rousseau's affirmation that sovereignty resides in 'the people', that it is inalienable, and that none may exercise it in the place of the people, allowed him to say that the Prince had simply an executive role, and was always dependent on the general will of the people. Nor could the Prince, or anyone else, pretend to incarnate in his own person the general will, for, as Rousseau was at pains to make clear, the general will cannot *be* incarnated or represented. Rousseau's theory completed the tendency in the eighteenth century for thought about sovereignty to become more and more abstract, to be largely divorced from the individual who wore the crown. Because of this abstraction, it was possible for the first time to think of a public interest in which individual interests are expressed, rather than denied and fused together in the king's body or 'the body politic'. In Montesquieu's almost equally influential theories, especially those contained in his work on the *Esprit des lois*, an attempt had been made to found a theory of different forms of government on different sorts of human behaviour and value systems held to be typical of each form of regime. In fact, Montesquieu went as far as to see human passions not, as earlier writers had done, as the reason for despotism, but as an essential check on it; the passions, he thought, were a continual source of centrifugal tension, an element of instability which prevents despotism from perfecting itself.[20]

Thus through Montesquieu and, very differently, through Rousseau, the eighteenth century saw the emergence of a new political figure in its repertoire of ways of approaching the problem of the interaction between individuals and the state. The passive 'subject', or member of a corporate (in all senses of the term) entity like the body politic, was joined by this new figure: the interested individual moved to express wants and needs in the political sphere and capable of effective partnership in government.[21] The creation of the new political individual also showed the tendency of the eighteenth century to disarticulate and use in different ways elements which in fact had their roots deep in the office of the absolutist king.[22] The monarchical will that represents and holds together the whole polity is for example transformed into Rousseau's sovereign general will, the 'members' of the body politic into the fused individuals who make up the general will; the king's body becomes recreated in the body of everyman, an Everyman seen as naturally sovereign in so far as he is a physical being in control of his own body: a body which, like the king's used to be, is at once physical and political.[23]

The Revolution made a repeated appeal to these ideas.[24] They were needed to confront a serious underlying problem: the location of authority, and the new ways of participation in the public sphere demanded of individuals. It was not due to success in solving these problems.[25] In spite of the increasing appeal of Rousseau's ideas, conflict raged in a prolonged manner over the problems of whether sovereignty should be dispersed amongst the people who composed the general will, or whether some centralized solution agreed by delegates of 'the nation' was preferable.[26] It was tensions like these which were to set Jacobins against federalists in the summer of 1793, and to lead directly to the explosion of the Terror in that year. Nor did the pre-existing 'individualist' ideologies of the eighteenth century offer much of a way out of the impasse created by the unsolved problems in its political theory, problems whose blank areas had consequences for the political culture of the French Revolution as important as the omissions in Marx's political economy were to be for the future history of Marxist political parties.

Very few of the 'ideal roles' validated by the eighteenth century connected individuals directly with the public realm. Among the few that did were the 'great men' cults, which meshed with the insistent harping by theorists such as Montesquieu, and to a lesser extent Rousseau, on the connection between individual virtue and the quality of public life, and hence on the nature of government. Montesquieu had argued that a monarchy was able to produce an acceptable substitute for public life, by channelling the passions; but that this should never be confused with true public life, based directly on virtue, which he associated with the classical polities of Greece and Rome.[27] To solve the problems of individual action, in the Revolution individuals at all points on the political spectrum were to turn increasingly to playing out such roles of virtue as a more effective way of unknotting the enormous problems left unsolved by the Revolution's inconclusive debate on sovereignty. For them, role-playing was to create public space anew, to create a political audience, ensure their place in history, give them secular immortality, and locate sovereignty in the only place where it could squarely be seen to exist and to be represented (in spite of Rousseau's strictures): in the virtuous, and hence sovereign, individual.

This was the paradoxical result of the theories of sovereignty which had emerged by 1789.[28] Neither royalist or Rousseauist models could produce an adequate conception of the unity and personality of the state. The fact that, as Rousseau said, sovereignty could not be represented (in either sense of the term) led to a vacuum at the heart of Revolutionary politics. That vacuum was filled by ideals of individual virtue as a constitutive element of the new state, and rooted in some elements of the ideals of individual self-cultivation which had flourished in the eighteenth century. Such role-playing acted as a vital mediator between the individual and the state apparatus which individuals were in the process of creating. Accounts of the 'political theory' of this period which, like Keohane's fine study, are conceived solely in terms of a naked encounter between hypostatized 'individual' and hypostatized 'state' are often full of insight. But, while explaining many of the problems which the state of political thought by 1789 posed to those who entered the revolutionary situation, they are also doomed to be unable to explain the *behaviour* with which the political actors of the time attempted to solve these problems.

VII An important version of *homo clausus*: the man of science in his lonely confrontation with nature; still an authority-figure today. Keller, *Humboldt and Bonpland's Expedition Camp by the Orinoco*.

How can we produce a description of this role-playing, this taking on of the identities of the heroes of virtue? First of all, we can place it in context by pointing out how very specifically French was this predilection for assimilating one's public identity to Brutus or Cato, to the men of the canon of Stoic–republican virtue. In the contemporary American republic, quite other definitions of republican virtue were in the process of elaboration, definitions which had far more concern with making republican virtue synonymous with the pursuit of private (economic) interest.[29] The French model of political virtue was thus not the only one thrown up by the age of the Atlantic revolution. It was also certainly not a literal transcription either of the neo-Stoicism of the sixteenth and seventeenth centuries, nor of any particular strand of the, in any case complex and often contradictory, body of philosophy resumed under the term 'classical Stoicism'. What was far more at stake, in the repeated classical allusions and the repeated self-identifications of public men with the sterner heroes of Rome, was the playing of the role, the taking on of the identity itself. This means that the classical reference might be a loose and inexact one, though far more insistent than recent historians in the twentieth century have allowed; the main object was not antiquarian recreation of the Roman republic in the halls of the National Convention, but the ability to personify virtue continuously and publicly.[30] The play was the thing.[31]

And it was a play which demanded, and depended upon, a certain physical demeanour, the same physical demeanour which had been demanded in times past of sovereigns themselves. It was through means like this that the revolutionaries distributed amongst themselves the physical behaviour once associated with the *auctoritas* of majesty, just as their political ideas distributed amongst the new body politic the traditional attributes of absolute kingship. Solemn demeanour, courageous words, and reserve were, just as they had been for classical emperors and for the wise captains and rulers of Justus Lipsius, the signs of the successful ability to play out a role which compelled attention, created an audience, and validated the authority of the player.[32]

The men of the Revolution in fact created such roles out of the common denominator which they found among all these varied sources: of authoritative control as the measure of public authority. It was for these reasons that the great myth-makers of the Revolution, men such as the federalist Honoré Riouffe, who wrote his major works exactly contemporary to the events he describes, should have validated his political heroes in such terms: Brissot, for example, '...grave et réfléchi, avait le maintien du sage luttant avec l'infortune'.[33] Another Girondin apologist, Dulaure, carried the emphasis on calm in the face of the ultimate test of imminent physical dissolution even further. He describes, in a near-contemporary account, the Girondins, '...après que leur arrêt de mort fut prononcé, ils passèrent la nuit à discuter sur l'immortalité de l'âme; chacun d'eux représentait Socrate au milieu de ses disciples après avoir bu la cigue'.[34]

Nor were these simply post-modern classical identities ascribed to the political actors of the Revolution by their hagiographers. We have much evidence that the men of the Revolution enjoyed manufacturing their classical identities for themselves; in doing so they passed easily from their previous practice of identifying with the heroes and heroines of novels, to identifying with the heroes of classical times. It was also a practice widespread over the whole range of the political spectrum. Thus we find Saint-Just in a private letter lamenting his 1792 failure to be elected to the Legislative Assembly: 'Dear God! Must Brutus languish far from Rome? But my decision is already taken; if Brutus cannot kill others, he will kill himself.'[35] Even more strikingly, the moderate Louvet de Coudray, who was to be proscribed in June 1793 by Saint-Just's associates, made a complete identification of himself with the same classical hero, when demanding the expulsion of the king's uncle Philippe Egalité from the National Convention: '...Ce n'est pas moi qui viens appuyer la proposition du Buzot, c'est l'immortel fondateur d'une république fameuse, c'est le père de la liberté romaine, Brutus'.[36]

Very often, such an identification was built up through reading, just as, previously, the encounters with novels had caused a tidal wave of identification with reference-figures encountered solely as verbal constructs. The royalist deputy Vaublanc, for example, sustained himself through a terrifying 18-month odyssey through France during his proscription, 1792–4, by reading a translation of Plutarch's *Lives*, full of the examples of austere heroism drawn from classical antiquity; he read, he said, '...avec avidité, et...je rapportais tout ce que je lisais à la pénible carrière que j'étais destiné à parcourir'.[37]

From quotations like these, we can also gain some idea of the functions which such role-playing, such intense identification with the heroes of austerity, principle, dignity and reserve, may have performed in the political culture of the Revolution. It is clear, first of all, that the major Revolutionary actors were the heirs of the prolonged eighteenth-century debate on the nature of dramatic experience. In particular, authors like Diderot had questioned whether dramatic illusion was produced by the actor assuming his part, like a mask, or by really becoming the part.[38] The revolutionaries themselves never resolved the question. Thus their poses and role-playing were often fraught with immense ambiguity. In the pursuit of the personal authenticity so vaunted by Rousseau, and by the ideologies of solitude and intimacy produced in the eighteenth century, they rejected the idea of putting on a mask to hide their real faces; instead they aimed to '*become* the part'. Yet, becoming the part, becoming Cato or Brutus, was also aimed at in the service of models of individual virtue and autonomy which were seen as essential constituents of the new revolutionary polity. The manipulation of roles and of body-image in these circumstances was bound to be complex and to point in more than one direction; and that is something that our final summing up of the fortunes of the 'Stoic' role during the Revolutionary period will have to take account.

But one thing all sides were agreed on: that political figures *were* actors in a theatre, not only playing to an audience, but actually creating that audience through the existence of their drama. The very definition of the public man was of one perpetually open to the gaze of others: 'L'homme publique est sur un théâtre où de tous côtés des regards curieux l'observent, et où il ne suffit pas d'être vertueux, mais où il faut le paraître', remarked one author in the magazine the *Décade philosophique*.[39] Naturally, with that visibility went a careful control of body signals. The public man, it was urged, should follow the example of Pericles, who 'réforma jusqu'à sa démarche; il prit un air pensif, marcha gravement et posément, tenant ses mains dans sa robe, et ne paraissant plus qu'à la tribune ou au Conseil'.[40] Their audience was not only in the here and now but equally in the future. As a contemporary notes, men like Danton played out their last days in talking constantly, '...et s'efforçait de donner à ses phrases une tournure précise et apophthegmatique, propre à être citée'. Nor was Danton himself any less explicit about his ultimate destination: 'Bientôt dans le néant, et mon nom au panthéon'.[41]

Just as the development of political theory in the late eighteenth century had been to scatter many attributes of the king's body amongst now sovereign individuals, so, it would seem, a similar redistribution of the divine body itself was also taking place. The intensity of the interaction between the public men of the Revolution and their audiences, both present and future, reflected a secular displacement of the desire for immortality away from a religious afterlife on to a desire for a posthumous presence in this life. It is thus no accident that many of the legends drawn from the martyrology of the Revolution place an almost New Testament emphasis on the sufferings of their subjects, on their progress to their secular Calvary. A case in point are the stories surrounding the execution of the moderate former mayor of Paris, the astronomer Jean-Sylvain Bailly.[42] Forced to stumble the length of Paris through mud and rain, and whipped by a biting wind, to his execution place on the Champ de Mars, Bailly's martyrdom was completed by a prolonged three-hour wait on arrival while his scaffold was erected before his eyes. The executioner's assistant mocked his involuntary shivers with 'Tu trembles, Bailly?'. His reply, 'Oui, du froid', administers at once a dignified rebuke to the insinuation that he was trembling with fright, and also shows how that dignity has remained intact in spite of the assault of the elements. Bailly's torments and his response to them encapsulate elements both of the Stoic control over the physical self in the interests of public dignity, and of emulation of the fate of the divine body involved in the Crucifixion. Such stories show the capture by the Stoic ethos, and the redistribution of the major images of the body circulating in the surrounding culture, the suffering body of Christ, and the king's body symbolizing the whole polity. Part, in fact, of the attraction of Stoicism was its ability to transfer to different situations, and to encapsulate many different, but validating, reference points for its users.

The image of the controlled, insulated, impermeable body, like Bailly's, was also of vital importance to its users and its audience at a time when the first use in French history of state terror on a mass scale was demonstrating how, on the contrary, in reality the body was frail, vulnerable, ultimately disposable. In the headlong galvanization of the nation for war and for virtue which marked the years 1792–4, even those individuals who survived often did so precisely by sacrificing heroic dignity, or even a consistent public identity. Many different roles might have to be played by the same man, whether openly or in the circumstances of proscription, in order to survive. As the Comte de Ségur, son of Louis XVI's war minister, and himself French ambassador in Russia until his recall in 1790, was later to explain,

> ...tout ce que j'ai vu, fait, éprouvé et souffert pendant la révolution, ces alternatives bizarres de bonheur et de malheur, de crédit et de disgrâce, de jouissances et de proscriptions, d'opulence et pauvreté, tous les états différents que le sort m'a forcé de remplir, m'ont persuadé que cette esquisse de ma vie pourrait être piquante et intéressante, puisque le hasard a voulu que je fusse successivement colonel, officier général, voyageur, navigateur, courtisan, fils de ministre, ambassadeur, négociateur, prisonnier, cultivateur, soldat, électeur, poète, auteur dramatique, collaborateur de journaux, publiciste, historien, député, conseiller d'état, sénateur, académicien, et pair de France.[43]

Similarly, the Comte de Vaublanc sustained his life on the road by playing the part of a 'buyer of national property', the National Convention deputies Pilastre and Leclerc in similar circumstances by taking the roles of cabinet-maker and carpenter; the former postmaster general, botanist and Rolandist sympathizer, Louis-Guillaume Bosc, hid in the forest, disguised in sans-culotte clothes, and performing manual labour. All these were men who had exchanged a consistent public face for disguises which were also in all cases acts of social derogation. In these circumstances the few roles available which promised permanence rather than change, dignity rather than derogation, offered a special attraction.[44]

The 'Stoicism' of the Revolution is about the definition of an autonomous self through an autonomous, impermeable, controlled body. This makes it something very different from the Stoicism of the classical world, or even from that of the seventeenth century, so different indeed that we may prefer to drop the term completely, and describe it simply as an ethos of heroic dignity. The focus of the anxieties of the men of the Revolution was not on balancing the conflicting claims of *otium* and *negotium*, for the claims of the revolutionary state made it difficult to find space for *otium* at all.[45] Nor were they trying to forge a rationale for a serenely disciplined

VIII Bertrand Barère, member of the Convention, is represented as *homo clausus*. Unadorned and alone, his black clothes maintain an unbroken body line and allow his gaze to dominate his self-projection in the public sphere. Laneuville, portrait of Barère de Vieuzac (c.1792).

intervention in the public world, nor, even, were they often concerned with the militant struggle for discipline in the public sphere which had pre-occupied the sixteenth and seventeenth centuries. Rather, their rhetoric and behaviour had quite a different focus, though it happened to use some of the drapery of classical figures who made heroic gestures of self-sovereignty and emotional austerity. They were concerned with the forging of roles of personal autonomy and personal virtue as the means by which their seizure of power from the monarchy could be validated, and the new state strengthened. It might even be argued that such autonomy was a necessary pre-condition for revolutionary action. But, sadly for them, the enormous force of the Revolutionary phenomenon itself was to deny almost all the public men of the Revolution a long span of time in which to achieve these aims. François Furet has recently and convincingly established links between the nature of the Revolution itself and the rapid turnover of ruling groups, factions and individuals which it brought with it.[46] In these circumstances, it was not surprising that rather than concentrating on an ideology of public involvement in terms of the dynamic of a lifetime, as do both classical authors and Lipsius, almost all the myths of Revolutionary heroic dignity centre on episodes of death, or imprisonment and imminent death; they centre on moments, not processes.

Because they do so, they also function to create images of individuals of heroic autonomy. Such images successfully preserve the desires of those to whom they relate, desires which were translated into a distinctive political practice. The cry of the Girondin sympathizer Boyer-Fonfrède, 'Je ne suis d'aucun parti; je ne veux appartenir à personne; je suis à mon conscience et à mon pays',[47] relates straight back to the dislike and inability of the public actors of the Revolution to form tight-knit political groupings.

The men of 1789 cannot be understood in terms of the clienteles of their British contemporaries. Here, as so often, rhetoric, individual self-perception and Revolutionary reality coincide. The men of the Revolution certainly did not form clear or persistent party or even factional groupings. Such groupings were indeed universally condemned, from all sides of the political spectrum, as productive not of stability, as the British might have argued, but, to the French mind, of *'faction'* or *'tumulte'*, by which they meant the selfish division of the General Will into short-sighted competing interest groups whose very existence would contest the feasibility of finding and locating an overall sovereignty. This is the main reason why modern historians, like the revolutionaries themselves, encounter such difficulty when they attempt to delineate Revolutionary politics as the product of encounters between 'parties' labelled 'Jacobin' or 'Girondin'.[48] This was also the reason why the turnover in political leaders and dominant groupings was so high. Such groupings were bound to be unstable because they tended to cluster around individuals who could momentarily monopolize the symbols of legitimacy, symbols which were not only the *discourse* of the General Will, but also the *bearing* and *behaviour* required by the current definition of virtue. Fonfrède's outburst, with its evident linkage between assertions of personal autonomy and the validation of a public role, makes this very clear. But, in the nature of things, personal authority based on the claim to personify 'virtue' is also uniquely open to challenge. It is therefore no wonder that the history of the Revolution should be to a large extent also the history of the rapid appearance and disappearance of figures of authority such as Marat or Roland or Robespierre, and the conflicts between their loosely associated supporters and challengers for the role of the supremely virtuous man.[49]

One further point deserves to be made. Throughout this chapter the words 'men' and 'man' have been used deliberately, not to imply that the Revolutionary version of Stoicism was generally adopted by its contemporaries, but, on the contrary, to alert the reader to the extent to which the ideal was specifically applied to and used by men rather than by women. Contemporary accounts of women's reactions to the crises of the Revolution are very different from those of the male actors-out of the creed of 'Stoic' heroic dignity. Not that they are derogatory; far from it, as tale after tale of female heroism ornaments the Revolutionary mythological canon, and these were tabulated after Thermidor into an entire hagiography.[50] What is clear is that the reactions ascribed to women in this canon of heroism are quite different from those of the men. They are different firstly simply in *being* reactions. *Homo clausus* was not accompanied by *mulier clausa*. Whereas the male heroes emphasize their non-reactivity, their remorseless control over body and emotion, women, on the contrary, perform heroic acts precisely because of their reactivity. They react with warm and generous outrage, and through maternal or married love or family affection of other kinds, perform acts of courage and sacrifice. They also invest enormous energy in the act of perception. Their emotional capacity, contemporaries held, allowed them to see into things more deeply than could men, precisely because they were held to be less concerned about the maintenance of dignity, and its concomitant, the strict line around the self which does not allow *penetration into* different scenes and problems. In other words, in the Revolutionary mythology, women react, relate, perceive, involve; men cling to the heroic *moments* and *postures* of personification.

Contemporaries were quick to provide physical explanations for this divide. It became a major subject in the debate on self-consciousness which was intensified, as the next chapters show, by the physical trials of the Revolution. As the well-known doctor Jean-Jacques Süe was to write:

> Laissons aux hommes les traits hardis et l'expression des passions fortes; mais avouons que les mouvements doux, délicats, légers, et mille détails que l'homme ne distingue pas, ou qu'il craint peut-être d'approfondir, sont reservés au sentiment aussi courageux qu'admirable et à la touche fine et ingénieux des femmes. Combien des récits touchants pourraient aujourd'hui se mêler à ses vérités! Qu'ils soient précieux à réunir, ceux qui nous rappelleroient cette foule d'actions vraiment héroique qu'ont immortalisé tant de françaises dans les funestes époques de la révolution. Les femmes ont prouvé que le courage du sentiment étoit le plus puissant de tous, qu'il n'était point d'actes de vertue dont il ne les rendît capables; et cette abandon, qui n'appartient qu'à elles, cet abandon, à qui le malheur donne tant de dignité, voilà ce qui légitime en France les droits que l'on disoit usurpés par leurs charmes.[51]

Many consequences flowed from the contemporary movement

to distinguish sharply between male and female reactivity in the Revolutionary situation. Firstly, of course, there was a heightened tendency, visible throughout the nineteenth century, for women to be defined increasingly in terms of this reactivity, and disqualified by it from participation. It was made clear that whatever the heroic value of female action, it did not carry public weight. Women's actions were portrayed as always being in the service of people, not of ideas.[52] Though it is far from true that the persons benefiting from acts of female heroism were always male, it is true that no female in the canon was portrayed as acting from devotion to an ideal, or as an autonomous individual. Their acts were in fact the converse of Fonfrède's cry: they showed that they *did* belong to other people, and that they were concerned not with *le bien publique* but with the destiny of individuals near and dear to them. It was as if women's actions had taken over all the involvement and energy so strongly present in earlier versions of Stoicism, both the classical and especially the early modern, and which had been conspicuously down-played in the male version of Revolutionary heroic dignity, only to have that energy deprived of public weight through its personalization.

This was a situation which also posed serious problems to the women of the Revolutionary period who were in politics on their own account. Put briefly, women like Charlotte Corday, or Rose Lacomb or Mme Roland, women whose political views had little in common, were all faced by the same problem, of how to achieve effective public personification when the entire realm of public dignity had been defined in a specifically male way through the use of the male body-image.[53] These topics are explored in much greater depth elsewhere in this book. But they do point to a decisive sectioning of the public realm between male controllers and personifiers, who gain status through their non-reactivity, and female feelers and doers, who cannot gain public weight and dignity: between males who are subjects alone, and women who are both subject and object. Thus, although the public space established by the Revolution, after the collapse of the monarchy and the disintegration of aristocratic cultural and political controls, was a new one, it was one which both the actions and the mythology of male public personification had quickly imperialized to the exclusion of all other challengers.

It was, too, almost as though the male definition of psychic autonomy required myths involving women and showing the rejection of the sexual peril which women posed for men as an integral part of both the male role of heroic dignity and the building of a new and specifically republican state. It is as well to remember that the association of Stoicism with republicanism was carried, not just by figures such as Cato, but also by Brutus the elder, who sacrificed his sons *against* the pleas of their mother; and even more dramatically by

IX This painting prefigures the separation of male and female public identities in the Revolutionary period. In contrast to the brightly coloured, swirling female figures registering extremes of grief and horror, Brutus sits apart, in a darker area, self-contained and rigidly separated on the canvas from his womenfolk, as the bodies of his sons, executed for plotting against the Republic, are carried past. J.-L. David, *Brutus* (1789).

the story of his avenging the rape of Lucrece by King Tarquin, which led to the expulsion of the kings from Rome and the foundation of the republic.[54] In all these stories, women's weakness or the unleashing of physical response in the male has to be repressed or avenged (equalized) before republican stability can be achieved.

What is also at stake in these stories is the physical and psychic autonomy of their male actors. And this takes us back to the point that the struggle for the new political body of the revolutionary 'Stoics' was also a struggle for psychic autonomy. This was a struggle against *sensibilité* in all its forms, and in particular against the fusion of subject and object, reaction and occasion, which was its hallmark and which women, contemporaries felt, displayed in such a high degree.[55]

What the Revolution did was decisively to force the abandonment of the *sensibilité* which had united men with women in their reactions to novels, to drama, and to real-life events in the late eighteenth century. Men and women had sighed and wept together over the novels of Rousseau, Richardson and Goethe. Now that kind of reaction was confined to one sex only. Whatever 'feminization of the public realm' had been accomplished before 1789, by these means was decisively reversed after 1789.

How are we to sum up? Although this working of Stoicism is clearly not the whole story of Revolutionary political culture, it is a very important part of it. Revolutionary republicanism was inseparable from the roles of heroic, Stoic manhood. More than that, it has exercised a decisive influence on the political, social and scientific attitudes of the nineteenth and twentieth centuries in ways that are only recently coming under real challenge. It was also, I would argue, the matrix in which crucial elements of bourgeois public identity were forged. Elias's *homo clausus* really came into being in the nineteenth century, after the end of the Revolution, but still encapsulated many of the main teachings of the creed of heroic dignity: the separation of individuals from each other, and from the surrounding social and natural world, the imputed separation, psychological and physical, between men and women, and the exclusion of women from independent participation in public life. So, as a set of agendas for male public action, 'heroic dignity' cast a very long shadow indeed.

But it would, on the other hand, be hard to disagree that as a set of *practices* including heroic suicide, invocation of an austere version of the classical past, self-identification with the Stoic and republican heroes, the Revolutionary experience was comparatively short-lived. As many historians have noted, all these practices, together with their sustaining rhetoric, became rapidly attenuated after the Jacobin collapse of 9–10 Thermidor 1794, and had died out almost completely by the time of the Napoleonic regime of 1804.[56] It is also the case that many of the 'recipes for autonomy', already present by the late eighteenth century and in competition with the creed of heroic dignity in 1789, such as the glorification of solitude, the intimate private world of the family, and pastoral retreat, lasted longer, into the nineteenth century. Part of the answer might be that these depoliticized versions of validation of autonomy remained in being while Stoicism collapsed, to surface again only in time of extreme crisis in highly politicized bodies, simply because the middle-class conquest of and redefinition of the public realm had been so complete that by 1799 there was no longer a need for roles which inexorably locked autonomy to virtue to the creation of the just state. Part of the answer was simply that the stabilization of politics after 1799 meant that individuals were no longer faced with the extreme situations in which acts of heroic dignity might seem appropriate.

But one can also point out that, although the occasions for and actual practice of heroic dignity might have disappeared from public life, the mythology it had generated, and which infiltrated the whole of the obsessional concern of nineteenth-century French history and literature with the Revolution, remained in full force, until at the turn of the century great figures such as Aulard and Mathiez both professionalized Revolutionary history, and replaced the heroic myths which centred on individuals with the study of economic conditions and mass movements. It was only with the onslaught of socialist history that the impression gained by the ordinary person that the Revolution was 'about' the forging of the nation through acts of individual heroism and dignity began to be seriously challenged. And so powerful was the hold of the mythology over the public mind that it still reigns supreme in all the very large amount of Revolutionary history which is not directed at a professional audience. Revolutionary Stoicism in fact lived on, and lives on today, as a mythology, a mythology of heroism which validates the middle-class control of the public sphere. In that sense it has in fact outlasted all the other before-mentioned ideologies of autonomy which are now, in the late twentieth century, under attack.

But the ultimate reason why 'Stoicism' collapsed at the level of practice was that there were changes in the nature of the state itself. The French Revolution was not an ending, but rather a transition point between one sort of state and another, a transition in which elements of personalized power, located in the symbolic bodies of individuals, whether monarchs or their middle-class successors, warred with elements foreshadowing the impersonal, unethical states which were to emerge in the nineteenth century. With the impersonal, utilitarian and positivist state came the end of the time when dramatic gestures of individual heroic virtue could be seen as coherent or meaningful, let alone constitutive, gestures. It is a mark of another change in the nature of states that seems to be occurring in our own time, that such gestures, in many parts of the world, have recovered precisely that significance.

Because of this it is important to end this theme with a full awareness of the profoundly ambiguous message left by the French Revolution's reworking of Stoicism. The Revolution saw a dramatic speeding up of the drive in western society as a whole towards the formation of Elias's *homo clausus*. The gestures of heroic dignity, along with all the other political tasks we have mentioned, performed the essential function of helping the revolutionaries to manage their fear of imminent death, a death which for many of them had become a totally secular event, susceptible to no promise of spiritual reward.[57] Without this management, the constitutive gestures which they made would have become impossible to sustain, and they would have left no legacy for successive generations of revolutionary martyrs and dissidents living in a secularized world.

Other legacies are not so clear-cut. In fact, so deep is the remaining ambiguity that it would be doing violence to reality to try to resolve it; it must simply be left for the reader to decide which, of the possible interpretations of the political effects of the pervasive ideology of heroic dignity, is the 'dark history' of the other. One thesis would say that however noble such gestures, they in fact brought about, or actively encouraged, government through terror. Preoccupied with personification rather than with action, with secular immortality rather the doubtful victories of actual political struggle, male political actors became passive, and this passivity may well have colluded with the government of France through terror.[58] It could also be argued that because the ethos of heroic dignity depended on the redistribution of the attributes of both regal and divine bodies, this ethos contributed to the evacuation of theological values from the political sphere of the middle class. During the French Revolution, in fact, politics became the dominant cultural sphere, that which attracted to itself, and which subsumed within itself, all other available ideologies in the surrounding society. Such a development was the pre-condition for that 'aesthetic politics', made up of all-encompassing gesture and display, which Walter Benjamin saw as the hallmark of Fascism – an aesthetic necessary to order the mythological overcrowding of the political, and thereby to produce the compellingly coherent gestures of mass mobilization. A second thesis, in direct opposition to the first, would insist that assuming a role of heroic self-possession was, and is, in fact quite a healthy reaction for individuals confronted by an increasingly aggressive and demanding state apparatus; it represents a refusal to accept the trivialization of the body, implicit in mass terror, and it also shows a willingness to stake a claim on future history in ways which, in the case of the Revolution, succeeded in denying the power of oppressors by filling that history for a century to come with the dignity of the oppressed. The reader should choose.

# 6

# HEROIC SUICIDE

## *The End of the Body and the Beginning of History*

> We are so estranged from our human essence that the direct language of man, the expression of need, strikes us as an offense against the dignity of man.
>
> Karl Marx

Between 1793 and 1797, 27 members of the National Convention committed or attempted to commit suicide. Of the 58 *conventionnels* who were guillotined in this period, 7 had attempted, often with great bravura, to kill themselves.[2] At least two ministers, Roland and Clavière, did the same, to be followed by Pétion, the former mayor of Paris, and L'Huillier, its Procureur-général-syndic. Many others, well-known figures such as Danton, Babeuf, Darthé and Lavoisier, acted in such a way as to court imprisonment and almost certain death sentence. Other examples here could include the Girondin Ducos, voluntarily joining the imprisonment of his brother-in-law Boyer-Fonfrède, or Soubrany returning to join the other 'Prairial martyrs'.[3] Nor was this behaviour pattern confined to the political élite; court records give many examples of working-class people forcing themselves on the attention of the Revolutionary Tribunal, often with fatal consequences.[4] In other words, suicide, whether active or passive, had become a predictable part of Revolutionary political culture, and was not simply confined to figures of great political visibility, although the state of the evidence will probably confine us for ever to discussion of suicide by the élite.[5] Yet this practice of suicide under the Revolution, often described simply as 'heroic' suicide, has been seen in some quarters as little more than an outcrop of the *philosophes'* discussion of heroic suicide in the classical world. The suicides, it is implied, were emulating the classical models of Senecan Stoicism, revived by the *philosophes*.[6] While such discussion of 'sources' for actions has a valuable part to play, it is also open to many qualifications. First of all, it has to be noted that such an approach also very largely fails to recognize that understanding 'heroic' suicide is not simply a matter of assessing literary 'influences', but is also assessing of attitudes to an ultimate physical event, and that it cannot, therefore, be dissociated from ideas about the body held by the suicides, and by their surrounding culture.

If we are to reassess the practice of suicide amongst the élite – that form of suicide known as 'heroic' suicide, in emulation of the historic suicides of classical antiquity, usually undertaken in public, often while imprisoned, and often in imminent proximity to a judicial death sentence following a political offence – we have to insist, firstly, on the radical change in its incidence when compared to old-regime France. During the eighteenth century, as John McManners's fine study makes clear, while suicide of all kinds was increasingly discussed and revaluated, at the same time the legal and religious penalties for it, such as confiscation of the suicide's property, humiliation of the corpse, or refusal of burial in consecrated ground, were increasingly rarely applied. Yet in spite of these two developments, actual 'heroic' suicide, as distinct from the discussion of it, was unknown. Suicide was simply not part of the repertoire of political gestures at the disposal of the political élite, let alone of other social groups. No *parlementaire* killed himself in protest against the Crown's bitter onslaught on privilege and rights of remonstrance; neither did any unsuccessful French eighteenth-century general.[7] When we come to the Revolution, the picture is reversed. Suicide amongst 'disgraced' members of the élite becomes relatively common, and is accepted as an integral part of the political repertoire. After an initial flurry of liberal legislation in 1790 and 1791, which removed legal and fiscal penalties for suicide, these were reimposed after the suicides of Generals Houchard and Gilbert, and of the financier Devoisins, taking effect on 10 March 1793 and only being repealed in 1795. The 10 March decree specifically stated that the property of those who killed themselves while awaiting judgment should be confiscated, and that the suicide itself would be taken as evidence of guilt.[8] And yet the suicides continued. 'Heroic' suicide only begins to peter out in precisely the year, 1795, when the March decrees were repealed. By the Empire, it had become rare in the extreme.[9]

So we face the paradoxical position that when 'heroic' suicide was both well publicized and all suicide relatively penalty-free in the eighteenth century, 'heroic' suicide is not practised; when re-penalized under the Revolution, its practice rises to an all-time high in French history. Clearly, we need to discuss factors other than prolonged exposure to the *philosophes'* discussion of 'heroic' suicide to account for this pattern. While we can say that the *philosophes'* re-evaluation of heroic suicide might have increased awareness of the model, we have to look elsewhere for the meaning of the act to those who actually practised it under the Revolution, meanings which had to be very powerful indeed if they were to appear to override the massive legal and fiscal penalization not only of the suicide, but also of his family, involved in the March 1793 decrees.

But first we must look at the nature of the evidence at our disposal in relation to this question. Statistically, the overall picture is problematic. Loss of prison documentation means that we will never be able to reconstruct a comprehensive statistical portrait of heroic suicide in the prisons of the Terror.[10] Problems of a different kind are raised when we come to examine literary accounts of heroic suicide. One source in particular stands out, both by its eye-witness quality, and by the extent to which it was used as a quarry for subsequent accounts: Honoré Riouffe's account of his imprisonment in Paris at the same time as the Girondins.[11] His account, which went through three editions in 1795 alone, was written in the Conciergerie prison contemporaneously with the events it describes. As he wrote his text, Riouffe states, he would read completed sections to his fellow prisoners.[12] In other words, whatever the accuracy of Riouffe's account of the last days of the Girondins, it is clear that his version of events, read to an audience whose need of heroic images of imminent death bravely faced could not have been more acute, was at the very least an acceptable portrayal of a very powerful set of symbolic actions. Riouffe's account, and this is its main value for us, has to be read as much as a collection of acceptable mythologies as it does as 'historical' narrative. The account is also valuable to us because it refuses to treat heroic suicide as an isolated symbolic act. It carries us with great ease across the whole range of attitudes not only to self-inflicted death but also to political imprisonment, and the management of the body which these reactions presupposed. Nor, as we will see, are the attitudes displayed in Riouffe's account exceptional. They recur in many other sources for this period, and add up to a consistent 'Stoic' self-presentation for the political élite.[13]

But we are still left with the question of how to account for the 'explosion' of 'heroic' suicide, and the associated reactions to imprisonment. Some of the answers to this question are very simple. Those of the political élite brought to trial for offences within the purview of the Revolutionary Tribunal, or its forerunners, were so in far greater numbers than had occurred during the old regime. Not only were the middle and upper classes the subject of legal attention as never before, but if convicted on a capital charge, they were faced with a form of execution, the guillotine, regarded both as peculiarly humiliating, and as posing the most agonizing questions about the survival of self-consciousness in the executed person. In these situations, new responses were needed to deal with a death whose incidence, publicity and physical effect were all new and terrifying. What more natural than that in this situation, the political élites should turn back to the models of 'heroic' suicide as practised in the classical antiquity they had confronted at school, and which had so recently been revitalized by the intervention of the *philosophes*.

This explanation has the advantage of simplicity. But it fails to take account accurately of the crucial question of the likely audience for the *philosophes*. Whatever the force of Montesquieu's arguments in the *Esprit des lois*, the *Lettres persanes*, or the *Grandeur et décadence des romains*, that suicide was a part of human liberty, a justified way of refusing infamy, defeat or submission, or whatever the appeal of Rousseau's portrayal of suicide as an essentially virtuous act, it still remains true that in the context of the two writers' work as a whole, discussion of suicide is of very minor importance. Nor can we guarantee how many of the busy lawyers or local administrators who formed the backbone of the Revolutionary governing class would have spared the time for such a detailed study of their *œuvre*. It is far more secure to say that every member of the Revolutionary assemblies would have been brought forcibly into contact at school with classical texts, including those containing discussions of heroic suicide for political motives. To understand such accounts as Riouffe's we have not only to consider political circumstances, and Enlightenment writings: we must also confront its other sources in classical literature.

How were these models utilized or transformed?[14] H.T. Parker long ago made it clear that few of the political nation of 1789 would have encountered Greek texts in the original in their school-days, and few indeed thereafter. For all practical purposes we can assume that classical discussions of heroic suicide would have been encountered mainly through the presentation of Stoicism in Cicero, Plutarch and Seneca.[15] Cicero's only prolonged consideration of suicide, which uses material from Greek Stoicism, occurs in a text that was also a firm favourite in the French *collège* of the old regime, the *Tusculan Disputations*. Cicero turned the story of Cato of Utica, who committed suicide at the fall of the Roman republic, into the focal point of his discussion, and it was Cato who was to emerge as the leading role-model for heroic suicide during the Revolution. Cicero praises his act, seeing it as the culmination of Cato's lifelong search for extraordinary dignity – *incredibilem gravitatem*.[16] Cicero goes on to stress the cheerfulness with which self-inflicted death should be encountered, as well as the importance of refraining from suicide for 'frivolous' reasons; he emphasizes, however, man's right to depart

X The death of the Greek philosopher was one of the most frequently cited models for heroic suicide in the Revolutionary period. J.-L. David, *Death of Socrates* (1787).

from life if 'the God within us' gives us a 'sign' of a good reason to die. There is little development of Greek Stoicism in Cicero's discussion of suicide, but he did leave to the men of the Revolution three key legacies: the 'reference-figure' of Cato of Utica which associated suicide with the defence of republicanism; the idea that suicide could be and should be chosen with joy; and the idea that it was also a proper part of '*gravitas*', that seriousness of demeanour through which the great Romans proclaimed and exercised both moral authority and political leadership,[17] and which was emulated by the new French political class.

Plutarch contributed little more than this, apart from giving his readers further material drawn from Greek Stoic sources inaccessible to them. He too fastens on the figure of Cato of Utica, and not only has Cato discuss Socrates' suicide as a model for his own, but also presents the central Stoic paradox that only the good man is free, and can therefore be allowed to commit suicide for a proper reason, while the foolish are slaves, and therefore must be prohibited from suicide. Plutarch, in other words, reinforces Cicero's association between freedom and suicide. *Liberté*, perhaps the least discussed term of the Revolutionary triumvirate, certainly took on for the would-be suicide a very specific meaning. Plutarch's arguments were also appealing in his reservation of truly rational and justified suicide to the élite.[18]

But both Plutarch and Cicero are in fact concerned, like the Greek Stoics, and like the majority of Enlightenment thinkers, with suicide as a subject of only passing interest. It was Seneca alone, of the classical 'Stoics' likely to have been encountered in the *collèges* of the eighteenth century, who gave suicide a central role in his thought.[19] Seneca is the only one of these thinkers to stress man's absolute right to commit suicide, whether he be wise or foolish, bond or free, with or without a sign from the gods. Suicide in Seneca is exalted as the exemplary act of human freedom.[20] It was also, for Seneca, an act of exemplary virtue, personified as in all classical discussions of suicide by the figure of Cato of Utica. By his death, Seneca argues, Cato kept virtue before the eyes of mankind. Most importantly for our purposes, however, Seneca seems to regard the freedom conferred by the act of suicide, not so much as the opportunity to act, as a state in which one could not be *forced to* act. In Seneca the Revolutionary élite found validation for a notion of true freedom as role-determined heroic stasis rather than action, a notion highly important in their own accounts of actual 'heroic' suicides. This is an ideal which emerges with great force in Riouffe's description of the heroic impassivity of the imprisoned Girondins.

> Gensonné, recueilli en lui-même, semblait craindre de souiller sa bouche en prononçant le nom de ses assassins. Il ne lui échappait pas un mot de sa situation, mais des réflexions générales sur le bonheur du peuple, pour lequel il faisait des voeux.... Pour Valazé, ses yeux avaient je ne sais quoi de divin. Un sourire doux et serein ne quittait point ses lèvres, il jouissait par avant-goût de sa mort glorieuse. On voyait qu'il était déjà libre et qu'il avait trouvé dans une grande résolution la garantie de la liberté.[21]

From the classical sources, main ideas emerge: suicide as connected with freedom, with republicanism, with *gravitas*, with exemplary virtue, and, importantly for our purposes, heroic status gained not through active struggle against evil, but out of an acceptance of death. Also present was the theme, summarized by Cicero, of suicide as a response to an affront to dignity or to one's public role. Epictetus, Cicero recalled, chose, for example, to commit suicide rather than shave off the beard he regarded as the mark of his vocation as sage.[22] If suicide, thanks to Seneca, was often allied to passive dignity rather than courageous resistance, it is also worth remembering that heroic suicide for the revolutionaries was rarely a solitary act. Since they connected heroic suicide with virtue at its most exemplary, it could hardly have been other than public. And not only was it public: it was also theatrical, reproducing what one modern commentator has called the 'theatricality which was both part of the legacy of Cynicism to Stoicism, and, more widely, an unexamined premiss of most ancient conceptions of nobility'.[23]

Such theatricality and publicity – for example the group suicides of 9–10 Thermidor among the Robespierrists, and of the 'Prairial martyrs' the following year, or, inevitably public, in such prison suicides as Clavière's – had distinct effects: they not only maximized the visibility of the act itself, and rendered those who witnessed them collusive with the act. They also served to create an illusory impression of solidarity among such in fact very disparate individuals as the Jacobin rump known as the 'martyrs of Prairial', or of those remaining around Robespierre. They recreated a shattered dignity by connecting the participants, not to their current circumstances of defeat and imprisonment, but to the heroic male figures of classical antiquity.[24]

We also find that 'Stoic' values were not simply confined to heroic suicide. They pervaded the demeanour of many others who did not kill themselves. For such men, the expression of emotion could only break down the theatrical *gravitas* which guaranteed their heroic status. The Stoic, as classical authors like Seneca made clear, armoured himself in the heart of his being as though besieged.[25] Riouffe, for example, presents a significant anecdote of the last days of the Girondin Boyer-Fonfrède, the brother-in-law of Ducos, and a voluntary prisoner in the Conciergerie:

> Une seule fois Fonfrède me prit à part, et, comme en cachette de son frère [i.e. Ducos], laissa couler un torrent de larmes aux noms qui brisent *les coeurs les plus stoïques*, aux noms de sa femme et de ses enfants. Son frère l'aperçoit: 'Qu'as tu donc?', lui dit-il.... Fonfrède, honteux de pleurer et *rentrant ses larmes*: 'Ce n'est rien, c'est lui qui me parle....' ...Fonfrède arrêta ses larmes qui coulaient, son frère arrêta les siennes prêtes à couler, et *tous deux redevinrint vraiment Romains*. Cette scène se passa vingt-quatre heures avant leur exécution. [*Italics mine.*][26]

Whether or not such an incident actually occurred is less important than the fact that Riouffe in this passage seeks to make the Girondins worthy of admiration by their adoption of Stoic poses in the face of imminent death, Stoic poses which are indistinguishable from the values of heroic suicide itself. Fonfrède and Ducos become 'Romans again' by control of the bodily fluids which signify emotion. Fonfrède literally puts his tears back inside himself and in doing so reabsorbs private feeling into the public role. Suicide for these men was not about 'who one was': for them it was about who one wished to *appear* to be, and how one wished to organize the appearances of one's death for others. In other words heroic suicide, and attitudes towards conduct in the face of *any* imminent death, have to be read as part of a unified ideal. Overwhelmingly, what survives the filter of revolution is a concern with theatricality, with *gravitas*, and with the achievement of a heroic status characterized by heroic dignity rather than by active reaction.[27] The important thing was the ability to remain within the confines of a role, whether by actual suicide or by the playing out of the 'Stoic' attitudes to death which went along with it.

Certain comportments, sometimes but not necessarily always orientated towards actual suicide on the Stoic model, carried high public approval, and were important to the individual because they afforded a publicly valid way of controlling his own death, and in doing so, becoming a figure of representative political virtue. The end of life could be as controlled as the dénouement of a theatrical plot. The important point to make is that actual heroic suicide was only the most extreme of a whole range of related comportments in the face of imminent or predictable death. What was important was the *display* of Stoic self-control in the face of death, whether that control was taken to the extent of suicide, or rested at the stage of Girondin calmness and joy. Such ideas placed a higher value on individual role-playing than on political combat or even survival.[28] Contemporaries from all points on the political spectrum were not slow to isolate them as one of the main factors colluding with the system of the Terror, and especially with the victory of the Montagnards over the Girondins. The moderate La Révellière-Lépaux was in no doubt that the crucial purge of Girondins from the Convention on 31 May and 2 June 1793 could have been resisted '...si les vingt-deux proscrits n'avaient eux-mêmes perdu du courage et ne s'étaient soumis à une arrestation si injuste...tandis que notre lâche soumission occasionnait un abattement général qui la [the Convention] ferait passer sous le joug de la plus hideuse des factions'.[29] On the royalist wing, the Comte de Vaublanc recounts a very similar story. Fearing arrest after the fall of the monarchy, he consulted his equally loyalist neighbours near his family estate. None, he relates, apart from himself, had any idea of either fleeing or resisting. Most stayed on their estates 'to await their fate'.[30] Most were executed. Such reactions make it permissible to wonder if, in the last analysis, the ideological issues which divided the political élite in the Revolution were as important as the public mentalities shared through the political spectrum from the extreme Jacobins like Romme and Soubrany, through to the monarchists like Vaublanc.

This is not to say, however, that the Stoic ethic did not pose great problems for its users. First of all, it placed nearly superhuman demands on individuals, demands whose cost can be measured in the struggles of Ducos and Fonfrède not just to restrain, but physically to put back inside themselves, the natural human reactions of grief and fear. Such irreconcilable discrepancies between human capacities and the demands of the role-model, were themselves an invitation to seek the only possible resolution, in death. This was noted as early as 1822, in Falret's study of political or 'heroic' suicide:

> Un grand nombre des maximes des Stoïciens étaient gigantesques, et ne dérivaient point de la nature de l'homme. Elles fomentaient une guerre continuelle entre l'homme et le philosophe, et dans les occasions critiques il ne leur restait que de couper le noeud qu'ils ne pouvaient resoudre. Comment réaliser le portrait qu'ils font du sage?[31]

Another problem lay in the ambiguity of Stoicism's relation to issues of power and freedom. Death willingly encountered, as the completion of the fated plot of an individual's life, whether through actual suicide, or through acts which had the same consequence, was important, because such a 'managed' death was one of the few surviving points of decision for individuals caught up in the mechanisms of repression of Revolutionary France. Under the Stoic umbrella the choice of death rather than resistance or flight could manage to seem like an act of freedom, which allowed the individual to retain control over his life even in a situation of imprisonment and imminent, humiliating death. The choice of suicide, or of a suicidal situation could thus look like action for freedom. Such a focus on heroic individualism, managing the last act of a life's drama, was able to obscure very satisfactorily not only the fact that suicide was ultimately about death; it also managed to present passivity and powerlessness as their opposites.

Outside the political élite, others, however, were not so convinced. Imprisoned initially with ordinary criminals in the Conciergerie, Riouffe, for example, received a sharp challenge to his ideas. His initial reaction to the shock of imprisonment was passively to await death: 'je me suis toujours arrangé comme un homme qui sait très-bien qu'il est mort...[with] une patience, une résignation que ne pouvaient me donner toutes les leçons de Sénèque et d'Épictète lui-même'.[32] But such complacency was quickly undermined by the criminals with whom he shared his captivity: 'ils méprisaient beaucoup les *révolutionnaires*, nom donné par eux aux gens arrêtés pour affaires politiques, et les regardaient comme des hommes sans industrie, sans invention, sans courage, et capables de faire manquer une entreprise'.[33] Riouffe's bourgeois revolutionaries located virtue in Stoicism, in patience, dignified resignation, and managed, individual death. For criminals, just as much as for the lower-class political militants, energy and activity, 'être toujours debout pour la Patrie', were the ideals.

In the prison context, where Riouffe's encounters must have been repeated hundreds of times over by middle-class members of the political élite, 'Stoic' comportments were an important part of the maintenance of a class identity against the fears of degradation aroused not only by the guillotine but also by imprisonment with members of the criminal classes or lower orders. During the Revolution, it should not be forgotten, the numbers of middle-class persons sentenced to more or less lengthy periods of imprisonment was even greater than the numbers of those guillotined.[34] When Rioufte also describes himself as '*glacée*' in prison, he is not simply describing a classic shock-reaction; he is also describing a rigid physical control in the face of the greatly differing comportments and expectations of the lower classes with whom he was imprisoned.[35] The adoption of 'Stoicism' cannot be understood without taking into account the whole of the prison experience of the potential 'heroic' suicide, rather than focusing on that suicide alone.

The reverberations of that experience can be assessed through another, apparently non-Stoic, part of the mythology of middle- and upper-class imprisonment under the Revolution: that of the stories of role-reversal told specifically in relation to judges and criminals. This is the point, for example, of Rioufle's story of the former judge Barré, condemned to death by the Revolutionary Tribunal on the evidence of a man whom he had himself previously condemned for forgery: 'un brigand, échappé au supplice, porta la désolation dans toute une famille honorée, patriote et paisible, et la fit disparaître de la terre'.[36] The same point is also made in the mythology of Malesherbes, Premier Président of the Cour des Aides, one of the official defenders of Louis XVI at his trial, guillotined in 1794. Much stress is laid by his biographers on the Stoic cheerfulness with which he met his coming fate. For evidence of such cheerfulness, the story is told of how Malesherbes joked about the discovery that his birthday was also the anniversary of the execution of the famous robber chief and folk hero, Cartouche. It was a joke which offered to his many hagiographers the opportunity of mediating and controlling the impact of what their reading public most feared: their assimilation to the *classes dangereuses*.[37] Malesherbes's jokes both maintained the distance between the upper classes and the criminal world which they encountered during imprisonment, and tamed the reality of that world: self-mocking jokes, after all, are usually made by those of high, and secure, status.

We have to turn not simply to exposure to classical or Enlightenment sources, but to the actual experience of imprisonment to explain the adoption of the 'Stoic' demeanour which could issue in 'heroic' suicide. By conflating the actions of the 'Stoic' with the reactions of men shocked into immobility by political, social and legal humiliation, it was also possible to minimize the reverberations of the latter. 'Stoicism' made it possible to turn the classic physical demeanour of profound shock into a willed, controlled and sanctioned imperviousness, which preserved the superiority of the wise man (the bourgeois) over the slave (the criminal). At the ultimate term of such 'prison Stoicism', suicide was the evidence that, stripped of all else, the suicide still held on to self-possession in its most literal sense. Romme, for example, in concluding his defence, exclaimed, 'J'ai fait mon devoir, mon corps est à la loi, mon âme reste indépendante et ne peut-être flétrie'.[38]

But the point sarcastically raised by the criminals in Riouffe's cell still remains. The desire to hide the rigidity of shock under the approved demeanour of a willed, Stoic death, can go only some of the way to explaining another problem. It was not, after all, with a static, heroic dignity, but with violent energies that the entire political framework of France had been altered since 1789. It is also clear that to answer this question we need to know much more about contemporary attitudes to display of energetic action. There are many instances of this becoming a major area of division. Vaublanc's discussion with his neighbours revealed, for example, their distaste for the undignified, energetic response he proposed to his situation: that of flight, in lower-class disguise. In the same sort of way, Danton's energy at his trial stands out markedly from the passive, withdrawn, 'Stoic' attitudes of his co-defendants. Exceptions, such as Danton and Vaublanc, tell us much about the way in which the majority responded to situations of threat. Partly, as we have remarked before, the Stoic role-playing, even if it fell short of 'heroic' suicide, absorbed enormous energies in the repression of the tumultuous emotions natural in situations of imprisonment and imminent death; partly also it covered, enforced, and legitimated, the paralysis which was another response to such situations. All this is fairly clear. But there is another level on which we can understand the role-playing of the 'prison Stoics', a level which will link their behaviour, and their posturing, more closely to Revolutionary political culture as a whole.

As François Furet has persuasively argued, control of the symbols of legitimacy, control of the tools of politics, came, during the Revolution, from the ability to personify the values of the Revolution.[39] This, rather than any actual governmental responsibility, was the basis of Robespierre's power. Power, in other words, came in the last analysis not from *doing* but from *being*, or appearing to be. Role-playing was the essence of the struggle for political authority. It was a role-playing which, as we have discussed in the previous chapter, was profoundly different from that of the 'classical age'. In the mid-eighteenth century, it was still possible to assume, and to commend the idea, that public role-playing was the production of appearances bearing no necessary relation to the person who produced the role.

Therein lay the art. By the 1780s, however, new trends in the theatre and in public reflection had reversed this. The more the role-playing coincided with 'real' feeling, the more it was commended.[40] The Revolution took this to an ultimate term and totally collapsed individual into role – just as, increasingly, other forms of representation were seen as copies of reality: thus the role of Stoic, by the Revolution, was seen not as a disguise, or as any other way of appearing which might presuppose a gap between player and role, but as the player *becoming* that which he copied. Thus, the Revolutionary Stoics, in spite of the passivity so mocked by Riouffe's criminals, although abandoning the search to impose power on one level, were also involved in enhancing it on another: successful personification of values was the way to supreme authority in the context of Revolutionary political culture. Heroic suicide meant that one *became* Cato.

Stoicism was successful in collapsing personality into role, and making role bear the entire meaning of a political process. It also had the advantage of placing a purchase on the future in a way that few actions in the chaos of Revolutionary real politics were able to do. Both the Stoic valorization of heroic self-control and the joyful acceptance of death, which were built into the ethos, prevented any acceptance of the finality and irrevocability of actual physical death. By encasing the progress towards death in a role indistinguishable from the person playing it, that death was itself placed outside history. The rejection of mourning so painfully self-imposed by men such as Ducos and Fonfrède, fixed their deaths as eternally present. The effect of such actions, so typical of the Revolution, was to make it impossible for the survivors either to forget, or properly refer to, the events of their immediate past.[41] In other words, it is too easy to define 'Stoicism' as an absence of energetic reaction to the present; much more, it contains an enormous deflection of energy on to the future. The entire political culture had to change before a truly introspective philosophy of individual perception re-evaluated interiority and autonomy, and could emerge, under the last years of Napoleon, in the work of Maine de Biran.

If, for the Revolutionary élite, energy in the ultimate circumstances of trial, imprisonment and death was displaced on to control of the future, in the making of actual politics it was often rhetorically displaced on to two groups outside the élite of male bourgeois politicians: on to the working-class and petit-bourgeois militants, the sans-culottes; and on to women. Both these topics are discussed in chapters 7 and 8. None the less we should not forget how prone the middle-class politicians were, even during their greatest political reliance on the sans-culottes, to label their energy, 'popular fury';

and also how that very Revolutionary middle class produced a whole literature after Thermidor praising the heroic *energies* of women,[42] while leaving to the self-image of the male politicians the emulation of Cato's *incredibilem gravitatem*. Such a division of labour held considerable advantages for the male political élite. It preserved the heroic dignity of physical and emotional containment intact from the uncertain outcomes of action or resistance. It preserved those claims to moral superiority, on which the pre-Revolutionary middle class had based its claim to be the 'real élite' of France, the moral élite which would replace the corrupt world of court politics.[43]

But whom did these ideals convince? Certainly not Rioufle's sharply critical forgers, fences and murderers. Nor were the sternly moral sans-culottes convinced either. For them, revolutionary virtue was identified not with the opaque, controlled body-image of the prison Stoics but with a complete transparency of thought, deed and word. For the sans-culottes energy was another index of revolutionary virtue, energy which placed a purchase on the present, in the recurrent crises of the Republic, rather than on the future.[44]

It seems, in conclusion, that we must be very careful not to look at 'heroic' suicide in a way which isolates it from its many contexts. Heroic suicide formed a very small part in the thinking of either the classical sources to which the Revolutionary middle class were exposed during their school-days, or of the *philosophes* whose writings they might, less certainly, have encountered in later life. Values from a wider range of Stoic teaching than that directly concerned with suicide also entered into the Revolutionary version of Stoicism, ideas such as 'fate', and the whole question of the maintenance of *gravitas*. While the work of the eighteenth century was certainly to remove theological and other penalties from suicide of all kinds, neither this fact nor a straight reading off of classical and Enlightenment texts will explain the startling increase in both the visibility and the incidence of suicide itself as part of the repertoire of political gestures during the Revolutionary period – an increase directly linked both to the violence of the Revolutionary state and its inability to find new sources of legitimacy. Nor can suicide be understood in isolation. To concentrate on active, 'heroic' suicide alone, on the Clavière model, is to disregard the problem of passive suicide on the lines of Ducos and Lavoisier, and also to disregard the fact that members of the Revolutionary élite of all shades of opinion, whether future suicides or not, acted with remarkable unanimity under the experience of imprisonment and imminent death, and that these comportments were exactly similar to those adopted by the would-be suicides themselves. 'Heroic' suicide, in other words, is only understandable as a *component* of the role of the 'Stoic'.

We thus have to enquire into the precise functions which 'Stoicism' served, both for those who practised it, and for those who enforced it as a behaviour model, by writing about it. Heroic suicide itself, unknown as an actual practice in the eighteenth-century political classes, and very rare after 1795, responded very precisely to the ambience created by the Terror, and the reversal of legal and social relationships from one moment to the next which it implied. The functions of heroic suicide were as many-layered as Stoicism itself. It operated very simply as a way to avoid the humiliation of public execution. It also operated, as did the rest of the Stoic ethic, to preserve that self-possession which was seen as an integral part of social and public authority. Stoic imperatives also permeated the demeanour of those who, like Malesherbes or Fonfrède, did not in the end actually kill themselves. The Stoic imperative is also visible, almost to the exclusion of any overtly Christian response to death, across the whole range of political opinion, and also across the whole range of the élites: from provincial manufacturers or lawyers like Ducos or Buzot, to great dignitaries of the old regime such as Malesherbes.

With this broader understanding of the Stoic role, we may also see that the adoption of Stoicism fits into many of the most crucial areas of Revolutionary political culture of this date. The playing of roles and the personification of values were crucial to political authority. The heroic suicide wills and controls his end before, usually, an audience of fellow prisoners, and plays out his part as much as an actor would. Some suicides, like Clavière, even die with lines from verse dramas on their lips.[45] It was far better to die thus, in front of a chosen audience of one's equals, than in the derisorily brief theatre and before the unpredictable, heterogeneous spectators, at the guillotine. Stoic demeanour and heroic suicide were certainly two most effective ways of creating and controlling a political audience, itself one of the fundamental innovations of Revolutionary politics. The act itself was almost always public, and the mythology which surrounded it was rapidly made and influenced an infinite future public of readers. Having become figures of symbolic virtue, the suicides and Stoics were also sheltered from the minute dissection of personality and action which would have been their fate in the rest of their public lives had they lived. Stoicism and suicide, in other words, had mythological functions: to freeze and maintain the 'meaning' of individuals.

If Stoicism had functions, it also had effects. It demanded a bodily and emotional control which concentrated the energies of the imprisoned and the proscribed. It undoubtedly made the Terror easier to operate against the political élite. Stoicism also fed into the doubts of the middle class as to the display and use of energy, and validated not only the sorts of behaviour displayed by Vaublanc's neighbours, but also a gap between sans-culottes and bourgeois political culture, a gap which was far deeper than the ideological differences among the middle classes in terms of which so much of the history of the Revolution has been written. For the middle class, the essence of Revolutionary politics was being or personifying; for the sans-culottes it was activity. To choose flight or resistance rather than Stoic dignity, as did Vaublanc, was perforce to cross a social boundary, to disguise demeanour, and to misrepresent social class affiliation, to refuse the publicity of Stoic personification.[46] Above all, the Stoic demeanour served to demarcate not only significant behaviour, but also significant solidarities. Its lack of appeal to working-class militants and women alike only served to enhance the message that the political body – the controlled dignified personification of virtue – was reserved for the male bourgeois. Energy, activity and mass action, located in women and sans-culottes, paradoxically, were culturally marginalized by the Revolution's version of Stoicism. For these men the body, with all its energy, and all its inconvenient effusions of tears and passions, had been managed, controlled and removed from view. For them, and *from* them, but perhaps for them alone, the modern historians of the body have produced their accounts.[47]

The association of heroic suicide in particular and 'Stoic' behaviour in general with the problem of solidarity, deserves to be considered further. Of course, not all such suicides took place as part of an exercise in group solidarity. But in some instances, such as the Robespierrists, the 'Prairial martyrs', and, through Stoic behaviour, the Girondins, group solidarities were formed which had not previously existed. Romme's most recent biographer makes clear how few previous links there were among members of the group who committed suicide along with Romme and Soubrany; historians' difficulty in defining 'the Girondins' have been notorious.[48] Suicide and Stoicism together gave unity in the way that the chaotic fragmentation of revolutionary politics could not. Active resistance, or even flight, such as Vaublanc's or La Révellière's, were exercises in isolation not solidarity, of enforced disguise, not personification. Even the decision *not* to commit suicide, could involve a decision for solidarity. Riouffe reports, for example, that Vergniaud had brought poison with him into prison, for the purposes of suicide, but had made a conscious decision *not* to swallow it in order to make plain his solidarity with the rest of 'the Girondins'.[49]

Such a connection with solidarity also dramatically distances the French Revolution's use of Stoicism and of 'heroic' suicide from its classical models, which are entirely concerned with the conduct of *individuals* of heroic virtue. But in another sense, the revolutionaries were acutely aware of the firm link which the classical world had established between republicanism and heroic suicide. Riouffe's insistent linkage of the Girondins with the Stoic ethos certainly has this underlying message, one particularly important in the case of the Girondins, whose fall had been precipitated by accusations of federalism, of a desire to destroy the unity of the Republic so painfully constructed. Riouffe hammers the point home in the case of Clavière, a native of Switzerland. '...né dans une république ancienne, et fils adoptif d'une république nouvelle qui lui destine la ciguë'.[50]

Suicide, Stoicism, management of the body and the emotions, and the formation of male, upper-class political solidarities were thus inextricably linked. The French Revolution brought into being the stoical male figure as the archetypal public actor, dissociated from Christian reference points, and serving to exclude the 'peripheral' political groups such as women, and sans-culottes, from access to dignified, heroic personification, which was at the heart of the struggle for the control of power in Revolutionary politics.

# 7

# THE GUILLOTINE, THE SOUL AND THE AUDIENCE FOR DEATH

> Nous prostituons la sensibilité, et nous méconnaissons le sentiment; nous ne savons pas aimer, et nous sommes idolâtres.
>
> Jean-Paul Marat[1]

A year after Thermidor, Mirabeau's physician, the *idéologue* Pierre Cabanis, described Robespierre's ascendancy as 'une tyrannie...qui semblait avoir pris la guillotine pour étendard'.[2] Yet potent as the guillotine was, and is, as a symbol of the Terror, few recent historians of the French Revolution have seriously examined the reactions it aroused or the debates which surrounded it.[3] This chapter seeks to re-examine such reactions and debates as indicators of a whole range of concerns aroused, mainly in the middle class, to the experience of revolutionary repression as a whole.

In 1791, decapitation was declared the only legal form of capital punishment in France. Its mechanization by the guillotine was thus the essential technical pre-condition for mass, state terror on the scale achieved in France. But the guillotine was more than a mere technological fact. It had the capacity, as we will see, to focus upon itself clusters of concerns arising from the relationship between the middle class and the Terror. It came to symbolize the new relationship of that class with state repression, to articulate many of its worries about lower-class attitudes to such repression; and, above all, those which seemed to threaten aspects of the middle-class struggle for social and public identity. All these were crucial issues for a middle class uncertainly wielding power for the first time, and preoccupied with forging a political identity as it simultaneously fought off the demands of other social groups to share in that power. Lastly, listening to what contemporaries said about the guillotine, about certain guillotinings, and about the crowds who came to watch them, teaches us a great deal about that most neglected of subjects, the formation of mythologies in the Revolutionary period.

The guillotine itself was not a new machine in 1791. There is much evidence that it was used in Renaissance Italy. From the 1530s onwards it even became positively cliché'd in pictorial accounts of the death of Titus Manlius Torquatus, the Roman Consul's son executed by his own father for disobeying the military dispositions of the Senate.[4] From the beginning, therefore, the representation of the guillotine is bound up with the idea of the triumph of civic virtue over 'sensibility', which was one of the main themes of the rhetoric of the Terror.[5] It was this image, as much as the lengthy and macabre experimental verification of its efficiency by Dr Antoine Louis of the Academy of Sciences in 1791–2, which lay behind its acceptance by the Legislative Assembly as the only legal method of capital punishment by decapitation, by decree of 20 March 1792.[6]

The guillotine also answered very specific needs arising out of the prolonged eighteenth-century debate on the related themes of capital punishment, and *'les peines infamantes'*: penalties, including capital punishment, which extended not only disgrace and possible confiscation of goods to convicted criminals, but to their families as well. These are debates important for our purpose of understanding the significance of the guillotine to contemporaries, because they laid down patterns of concern and perception which were carried over into the Revolutionary period, and into the post-Thermidor debates on the guillotine itself.

The eighteenth century saw a widespread attack on the administration of the death penalty in France.[7] In spite of the translation of Beccaria's work by Morellet in 1766, attacks on the death penalty itself were rare. In a society which had very few coercive forces to hand, by comparison with modern states, it was widely believed that the deterrent property of the death penalty was too valuable to be abandoned, whatever the moral objections to it. Criticisms focused far more on the cruelty with which capital punishment was carried out, forms of execution including burning, impalement and breaking on the wheel still being current. Great concern was also felt about the inequality of the application of the death penalty among different social classes, and in different regions of France. A noble convicted of the same crime for which a commoner was hanged could, for example, claim the less 'degrading' death by the headsman's axe. Lastly, it was often pointed out that the death penalty was applied to crimes of very different orders. Nearly 1,500 offences in theory carried the death penalty, and they ranged from murder, kidnapping, aggravated highway robbery, to minor domestic theft, sodomy, and the cutting down of trees. Against this background of severe and continuous criticism, Louis XVI raised hopes of a thoroughgoing reform when he abolished judicial torture by a series of decrees between 1780 and 1788. But by 1789, little else had been done. The sweeping reforms set in motion by the Legislative Assembly thus had the urgency deriving from generations of frustrated criticism.

This was all the more true, since the attacks of the jurists and the *philosophes* on the administration of capital punishment before 1789 had not simply been fuelled by a high-minded desire to abolish cruelty and inequality in the application of the law. It was also, as some contributors to the debate made clear, that the character of capital punishment before 1789 had threatened not only the indigent and criminal to whom it was most often in actual fact applied; it also contained specific features threatening to the middle classes who in fact were far less likely to fall foul of the law. In the eighteenth-century struggle to define and validate the middle classes of society, the notion of the *peine infamante* in particular struck hard at the middle-class image of itself as an élite not of birth but of virtue. Pierre-Louis Lacretelle, for example, in his 1784 prize-winning essay on this topic, even while admitting that few middle-class persons came within the purview of the criminal law in this way, nevertheless spends a disproportionate amount of time expatiating on the extreme threat which the *peines infamantes* posed to the public dignity of the middle class. Public punishment, he wrote, was humiliating even for the poor: 'Les châtiments publics mettent dans la plus humiliante évidence, le peu de cas qu'on fait du peuple, en comparaison de la classe des grands...'. But the bourgeois suffers even more:

> Un grand crime vient d'être puni par un affreux supplice; tous les esprits sont révoltés; leur aversion cherche les parents du criminel, pour les accabler de tous les témoignages de l'horreur et du mépris. Sont-ils des hommes obscurs; ils sont pour ainsi dire à nud devant elle; une bonne renommé, l'estime publique ne suffiront pas pour le défendre.... Et voilà pourquoi ces crimes déshonorent si fort, dans les classes mitoyennes; c'est qu'ils les assimilent au petit peuple; ce qu'elles détestent le plus parce qu'elles ont toujours l'ambition de s'élever vers la classe supérieure.[8]

Lacretelle's essay contains many of the concerns that would continue to lie behind reactions to the quite different situation in which the guillotine was used during the Revolution: the fear that the apparatus of capital punishment, which *seems* to exist to repress lower-class crime, will reduce any bourgeois caught up in it to the level of the *petit peuple*; and the fear of social humiliation expressed as a fear of physical intrusion so intense that shame is equalled with nudity in the face of a hostile public.

The essay also foreshadows attitudes towards the crowds which attended public executions, attitudes which survived intact into the changed circumstances of the Revolutionary period. Arguing against the cruelty of many forms of execution, Lacretelle describes how 'La foule, toujours avide de ces atroces tragédies, y court et s'y presse'.[9] The crowd as a collective monster, hungry for sensation and horror, and learning only cruelty from the cruelty of the punishments displayed before it, a favourite resource of the post-Thermidorean writer, is already present by the end of the old regime. So too is the idea of public execution as a *tragédie*, an idea of course far older than Lacretelle's essay, important because it carries the implication of an unfolding and revealing process ending in the merited punishment of great crimes.[10] It was an idea to which the actual experience of mass execution by guillotine was to deal a severe and, to contemporaries, horrifying blow, as we will see later.

Yet, once discussion of a new system of criminal law had got under way between 1789 and 1791, the reforms in the administration of the death penalty seemed to answer all the critics' demands. The multiplicity of cruel and protracted forms of execution was replaced, by decree of 3 May 1791, by the single and rapid penalty of death by decapitation.[11] Article I of the new Criminal Code of 1791 outlawed differentiation of penalty by social class; Article II abolished the *peine infamante*, and established the principle of personal responsibility for offences. The general reasoning was clear: public capital punishment must be retained, but it must be performed in as expeditious and humane a way as possible. Nor were there to be 'humiliating' forms of execution: decapitation, once reserved for the nobility, was now to be applied to all convicted of capital offences, whatever their social class. Finally, the legal codes severely restricted the number of capital offences, though many forms of theft, and aggravated robbery, as well as a number of crimes against the state, remained among them. On 20 March 1792 the Legislative Assembly finally decreed that decapitation was to be carried out by guillotine only.

But amidst all this humanitarian glow, it was the leading technician of death, Henri Samson, public executioner of Paris, who pointed out, in a famous letter to Dr Antoine Louis, how necessary the guillotine was to the new levels of repression which France had reached by 1792. Under the old regime, he began by recalling, decapitation was a rare penalty, reserved for the nobility, and administered by axe. Now, decapitation was democratized. It was the fate of all those convicted of capital offences, whether criminal or political. The old method with the axe would simply not have been adequate to the job in hand in 1792:

> ...lorsqu'il aura plusieurs condamnés qui seront exécutés au même instant, la terreur que présente cette exécution par l'immen-

sité du sang qu'elle produit et qui se trouve répandu portera l'effroi et la faiblesse dans l'âme du plus intrepide de ceux qui resterait à exécuter. Ces faiblesses produirait un obstacle invincible à l'exécution. Les sujets ne pouvant pas se soutenir, si l'on veut passer outre, l'exécution deviendra une lutte et un massacre.[12]

The heroic self-control which might be expected from a Lally-Tollendal was not to be expected from those lower-class persons executed in batches.

It was the guillotine which solved all these problems. It was quick, required little or no skill or strength on the part of the executioner, and because the convicted person was delivered bound, and tipped mechanically into place beneath the blade, it required only passivity, rather than positive fortitude, from the victim. By abolishing direct contact between executioner and victim, the guillotine eliminated the risk that deficiencies either in the skill of the one, or the self-control of the other, might turn the execution into a 'lutte et un massacre'. By the same token, however, it eliminated much of the drama that arose from that contact. For all these reasons, the guillotine profoundly altered the whole nature of what was involved in capital punishment. Most obviously, it allowed the execution of greater numbers of people. It is difficult to see how the 14,080 death sentences passed between March 1793 and August 1794, an enormous number compared with the Paris annual average of 54 pre-1789, could have been carried out without the new machine.[13] The great group executions of the Terror, of Danton and his followers, of the Hébertistes, and of Robespierre and his followers (109 people in two days) would all have been rendered more difficult, if not impossible, with the old methods, as Samson's letter makes clear.

The guillotine not only changed the *scale* on which capital punishment was possible. It also changed the nature of the experience for all involved, victim, state, and watching crowd. Firstly, it brought far closer to the middle class the fears already expressed in eighteenth-century writing on the *peines infamantes*, of the possibility of public humiliation through contact with legal process. The middle class was faced with a situation in which far more middle-class people were executed than had been in the eighteenth century, both absolutely, and proportionately to the rest of the population, forming the largest single social contingent to face the guillotine.[14] Moreover, they were executed in ways which assimilated them to the *petit peuple*, and subjected them to what was viewed as public physical humiliation even before execution itself was carried out. In an age where, in spite of the Revolution's theoretical aspirations towards legal equality, social distinctions remained highly important for a middle class, and where distinctions in dress between classes were all-important in fixing status and exacting deference, to be delivered to the guillotine head shaven, coatless, bound, and shirt open, was a deep humiliation.[15] Much as they might have protested against it in the eighteenth century, the middle class was in fact habituated to a legal system which discriminated among social classes in the award of penalties. The Revolution democratized penalties at a time when few foresaw that the middle classes, far from being virtually absent from capital proceedings, as they had been under the old regime, would in fact form the largest single social contingent to fall under the guillotine. It was also the case that death by guillotine was without that dramatic elevation so marked a feature, and so long-remembered a feature, of aristocratic execution before 1789. Execution took place in ways which seemed humiliating to a class which depended to a large degree on the tight control of body-image and emotions to validate their worth as a class and as individuals. It is these fears which were the basis of the great controversies provoked by the guillotine after Thermidor.

Let us examine here the contributions of four participants in these controversies who engaged directly with one another: the physicians J.J. Süe, P.L. Cabanis and the German Christian Soemmering, and the political writer Charles Ernest Oelsner.[16] All of these writers agree in their demand that the guillotine should be abolished. Their reasoning is based on allegations about the cruelty of execution by this means, supported by more or less convincing physiological experimentation, and on study of the effect of the use of the guillotine on the demeanour of victims and crowds.

In 1795, Oelsner published, with his own commentary, in the widely-read *Magasin encyclopédique* a letter written to him by Soemmering. The latter recounted experimentation he had undertaken, such as the irritation of the spinal cord of a decapitated head, to prove that far from being a humane form of death, death by guillotine in fact involved frightful suffering:

> la téte séparée du corps survit au supplice.... Dans la tête séparée du corps par ce supplice, le sentiment, la personalité, le moi, restent vivant pendant quelque temps, et ressent l'arrière-douleur dont le col est affecté...et je suis convaincu que si l'air circuloit encore régulièrement par les organes de la voix, qui n'auroient pas été détruits, ces têtes parleroient.[17]

The Frenchman Süe's opinion was substantially the same. Citing the well-known case of after-sensation in amputated limbs, he contended that in the same way

> la tête, quoique séparée du corps, aura aussi la conscience de la douleur, jusqu'à ce que sa vitalité, entretenue par sa chaleur lui soit enlevé...je crois entendre ceux pour qui la douleur des autres n'est qu'un songe, objecter que le temps de son supplice étant très-

court, la douleur doit être presque nulle...[Mais] quelle situation plus horrible que celle d'avoir la perception de son exécution et à la suite l'arrière-pensée de son supplice?[18]

Cabanis, however, contended that experimental verification of this point was impossible.[19] He went on to reprove Oelsner, Süe and Soemmering for their belief in a diffused unitary consciousness, a *sensorium commune*. It was in terms of this belief that it became possible to posit the survival of '*le moi*' after the separation of head from body.

So great was their investment in the union between body and spirit that their very fears for survival after execution were in fact a continuing argument for the strength of such a union. But why should these fears have been focused on death by guillotine? One searches in vain for such concerns to be raised apropos the older form of decapitation by axe. The answer must surely be in other and attendant fears raised by the guillotine, but which had little ostensibly to do with the physiological questions raised by decapitation. Soemmering, Süe and Oelsner were concerned to argue for the survival against all odds of unity of consciousness, and to see the guillotine as an attempted invasion of that unity. It was an invasion which began, as Oelsner remarked, even before execution, in the relations between the condemned man and the waiting crowd at the scaffold:

> ...on avilit l'homme avant de le frapper: les mains sont liées derrière le dos; on le dépouille de ses vêtements; on lui coupe les cheveux; on le prostitue aux regards de la populace.... Vous méconnoissiez la pudeur! Vous n'avez pas senti que chez un peuple qui porte des vêtements, c'est une brutalité abominable, que d'exposer aux regards du public le nudité d'une femme ou d'un vieillard.

Soemmering's letter harps on the same theme, denouncing 'l'appareil affreux, les liens atroces, la hideuse coupe des cheveux, les nudités indécentes...'[20] These descriptions, vivid in their descriptions of the physical humiliation of the victims of the guillotine, also make clear the origins of another contemporary fear, that such persons would simply go to the guillotine as humiliated bodies, without any opportunity to act out the heroic roles which were so great a part of the political culture of the Revolution. This, surely, is the point of the myths surrounding the execution of Jean-Sylvain Bailly, first mayor of Paris, which as we saw emphasize the prolonged misery of his journey to the scaffold, his humiliation and enforced passivity.[21] Bailly is specifically mentioned by the contemporary playwright Amaury Duval, as an example of the way the guillotine frustrated

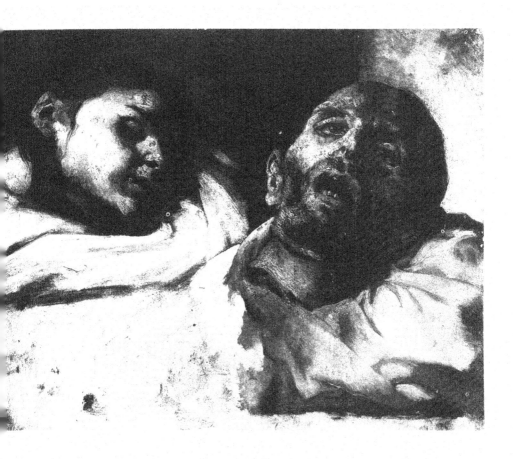

XI These portraits of heads of the guillotined exemplify some of the fears expressed by contemporaries about the use of the machine. Géricault, *Heads of the Executed*.

heroic role-playing: 'Ils n'ont pu mourir comme Socrate, ceux qui en avaient les vertus'.[22]

The last participant in this debate, Cabanis, places far less emphasis on the physically invasive preliminaries to execution in his argument against the guillotine. This is entirely consistent with his objection to the idea of the *sensorium commune*. Cabanis is concerned, to an even greater degree than were Soemmering, Süe and Oelsner, with crowd reactions to the guillotine, reactions which, he argues, are so harmful as to alone warrant its abolition. The guillotine had been much vaunted for its speed of operation. But, as Cabanis pointed out, for a crowd accustomed to the prolonged executions of the old regime, this was precisely where lay the harm. In terms which recall Morellet's earlier concerns, he pointed out that

> Quand on guillotine un homme, c'est l'affaire d'une minute: la tête disparoit, et le corps est jeté sur-le-champ dans un panier. Les spectateurs ne voient rien; il n'y a pas de tragédie pour eux; ils

n'ont pas le temps d'être émus, ils ne voient que du sang couler; et s'ils tirent quelque leçon de cette vue, ce n'est que de s'endurcir à le verser avec moins de répugnance dans l'ivresse de leurs passions furieuses.[23]

The people, he concludes, had ended by regarding executions almost with indifference.

Nor were Cabanis's arguments merely post-Thermidorean special pleading. There are strong indications that from the start, the guillotine failed to provide the crowd with the *tragédie* to which execution under the old regime had accustomed them. The *Chronique de Paris* reported in terms similar to those used by Cabanis the very first execution by guillotine, on 21 April 1792, of a criminal accused of robbery with violence:

> Le peuple d'ailleurs ne fut point satisfait; il n'avait rien vu; la chose était trop rapide; il se dispersa, désappointé, chantant, pour se consoler de sa déception, un couplet à propos:
>
> > Rendez-moi ma potence de bois,
> > Rendez-moi ma potence.[24]

Even at the height of the Terror, there were suggestions that the attention of the crowd could only be purchased by additional attractions. Prud'homme's pro-Jacobin paper, the *Révolutions de Paris*, published in 1792 a letter from the deputy Giraud to the Committee of Public Safety, in which he urged that

> il faut suppléer à la promptitude de la guillotine pour électriser le peuple en conduisant ses ennemis à l'échafaud. Il faut que cela soit une espèce de spectacle pour lui. Les chants, la danse, doivent preuver aux aristocrates que le peuple ne voit de bonheur que dans leur supplice. Il faut en outre faire en sorte qu'il y ait un grand concours de peuple pour les accompagner à l'échafaud.[25]

Thus, many different sources agree that the guillotine was a disappointment in that it failed to provide a *tragédie* of any great drawing power. The prolonged unfolding of retribution for crime in the lengthy death-throes of old-regime capital punishment had been replaced by a brief, virtually invisible passage into death, which, devoid of drama, was perilously close to losing significance altogether.

But the worries of contemporaries about the apathy with which the crowds viewed the guillotine also face us with a picture of crowd behaviour at executions which is very different from that on which the historiography of the Revolution, from 1794 on, has always insisted. The picture of the Revolutionary crowd, violent in *émeute de subsistance*, Revolutionary *journée*, or execution of enemies of the

Republic, comes both from contemporary police reports which mechanically attribute *'applaudissements'* and *'vives acclamations'* to the crowd at each fall of the blade, to the conventional post-Thermidorean reports which delighted to paint such crowds as populated by 'furies' hurling insults, through Taine's ferocious *canaille*, Dickens's Mme Defarge, and on to Cobb's, Rudé's and Soboul's violent and above all *participatory* rioters.[26] When contemporaries report, instead, a crowd which worries them by its apathy rather than its violence, then we are confronted with an enlargement of our understanding of the nature of collective assembly in the Revolution.

We can say first of all that crowd demeanour at executions by guillotine *did* differ from that of old-regime execution crowds, in the sense that we have no record of expressions of crowd sympathy with the victim, or even of crowd efforts to help prisoners escape, such as were a feature of the old regime, at executions of both political *and* common-law criminals.[27] Otherwise, eye-witness, participant accounts of execution crowds from 1792 are disappointingly, and significantly, meagre. Those few that we do possess often emphasize crowd apathy.[28] We possess no account of the guillotining of an ordinary criminal in this period, and no account by any of the *menu peuple* present at the execution of a 'political' criminal. Discounting stereotyped police descriptions of crowd joy at the execution of traitors, we are forced to fall back on the comments of observers such as Cabanis. I would argue that their depictions of 'passive' crowds are more likely to approach the truth. The image of the ghoulish execution crowd, *'avide de ces atroces tragédies'*, as Lacretelle had put it, had a long history even before 1792, and was ready to hand for the obvious purposes of post-Thermidorean writers.[29] Equally obvious is the investment of official sources, during the Terror itself, in descriptions of crowd pleasure at executions. It is less easy to see why Cabanis should have any investment in describing the crowd as passive if it was not, especially as he could have made his point about the brutalizing effects of the guillotine on the crowd far more dramatically by describing conventionally bloodthirsty and demonstrative behaviour. There is, finally, the pictorial evidence.

Contemporary engravings all make it clear that the crowd would indeed have had grave difficulties in seeing anything of the execution. Even apart from the rapidity of the operation, the guillotine itself was small, and although mounted on a platform about six feet high, is also shown in most prints as surrounded by at least one, if not several, rows of troops or police, often mounted. This is very different from prints of old-regime executions, where such a 'screen' is far smaller, if not altogether absent. Since most spectators would be standing, it is clear that the majority of them would have seen very little, if anything at all. This very simple fact goes far to explain their relative apathy. As well, picture after picture shows a mounted officer placed directly in front of, and facing, the victim at the moment of execution. Since such a position could have served no purpose of crowd-control, one can assume that it was taken up precisely in order so that the crowd should *not* be able to see the face of the victim. Admittedly, the executioner by law had to display the severed head; but who among the crowd, behind perhaps a double row of mounted men, could have made it out?

Pictorial evidence takes care that in a real sense, nothing will be seen of the *tragédie*. It may well be that, not at the scaffold itself but on the long *trajet* from prison to the guillotine, where there was no impersonal machine to interpose itself, the crowd was far less passive. It was only on the *trajet*, which could last for anything up to an hour, that the crowd was given *time* to establish a relationship with the condemned. Given time to react, naturally its behaviour was far less apathetic. It is of course amply demonstrated that militant sans-culottes held the guillotine to be the solution to most of the economic problems of the Revolution, and were given to panegyrics of the machine.[30] None the less, we should still distinguish between the *propos* of the militants in the Section assemblies and the bread queues, and the behaviour of a crowd facing the guillotine itself.

We should also, to conclude this argument, note that crowd apathy at the scaffold, created by all the foregoing reasons, could only have been increased by the fact that the Paris guillotine itself was repeatedly moved during the Revolutionary period, whereas old-regime execution had been concentrated in the Place de Grève. Times of execution were also highly variable; sometimes they were held late at night, by torchlight, sometimes in the middle of the working day. The execution site for ordinary criminals was also different from that for those processed through the Revolutionary Tribunal. Uncertain hours, changing places, and a rival attraction: all very simple reasons which help to explain, even apart from factors relating to the very nature of execution by guillotine, the comparative sparsity of crowds.[31]

Contemporaries also discussed yet another reason for crowd apathy. It was, they asserted, also a direct reflection of the demeanour of the victims themselves. This very assertion is based on the expectation that crowds and victims *would* normally be responsive to each other, and that the guillotine was causing them not to be. As Cabanis wrote:

> Une circonstance dont l'histoire se servira pour caractériser avec plus de force l'atrocité de tant de massacres a contribué cependant à

l'indifférence avec laquelle le peuple avoit fini par les contempler: c'est le courage tranquille de presque tous ceux qui marchaient à la mort. Les cris aigus, les supplications, les sanglots de Mme du Barry touchèrent profondément ceux qui l'accompagnaient dans les rues; et sur la Place de la Révolution, presque tout le monde s'enfuit, les larmes aux yeux. Mais les hommes de coeur ne peuvent pas s'abaisser à ce lâche désespoir, pour rendre des entrailles au peuple: la vertu ne va point jusque-là.[32]

Perceived by the victims as withdrawal into a heroic kind of Stoicism, this demeanour meshed all too well, for the spectators, with the impersonality of the guillotine itself.

It is also important to note, however, that such demeanour, which does indeed seem to have been general, had effects which were far less innocent than the provision of a therapeutic shield for persons faced with an intolerable ordeal. Such passivity, such lack of outward emotion, also made it easier to execute them without guilt. The majority of the victims made no appeal whatever to that *sensibilité* which modern commentators have seen as increasingly a part of middle-class reactions to physical suffering in this period.[33] They would not *allow* others to feel sympathy with them, if, as Cabanis ironically remarks, that sympathy had to come from a lower social class. The issue posed by the guillotine for the middle class was not only the relation of that class to an increasingly coercive state, which had overthrown all the class barriers to its operation that the old regime had so insisted on; it was also that of maintaining a class definition in the face both of potential lower-class sympathy, and of physical humiliation in front of a lower-class audience. No wonder Mme du Barry's reactions on the way to execution surprise us with their 'naturalness'. The rest of the accused had abandoned the exhibiting of 'sensibility' for the more important task of attempting a demeanour of rigid self-control at their supreme moment of exposure before a lower-class audience. In doing so, they depersonalized themselves, and made it fatally easy for executioners and terrorists to approach what modern sociologists have called the 'conditions for guilt-free massacre'.[34]

Two other points deserve to be made here: Firstly, that we have no eye-witness account of the execution of an ordinary criminal by guillotine, and very little indication even of the behaviour of any of the *petit peuple* who were executed for 'political' offences in increasing numbers towards Thermidor itself.[35] This significant lack of evidence shows us how much the debate about the guillotine and its impact on crowd reactions is in fact a debate about middle-class sensibilities towards middle-class victims. The famous *'sensibilité'* of the late eighteenth century had still to cross class boundaries. The second point is that, unlike old-regime execution, that by guillotine contained no visible religious element. One searches in vain for evidence of the priesthood assisting at executions, except in prints portraying the death of Louis XVI. The absence of religious consolation on the way to the scaffold further evacuated emotional content from the scene. It also evacuated from the executions any relationships other than those between the victim and the state. Many of the victims also refused the attentions of a priest even when these were available to them in the prisons.[36] Many committed suicide, as we have seen, rather than submit to the indignities of public execution. Such a withdrawal of religious attention by the state, and its simultaneous rejection by many of the accused themselves, could do nothing but further empty the new form of execution of symbolic and emotional content. On the guillotine death was reduced to its bare physical fact, no longer either *tragédie*, nor battlefield for a soul. The guillotine, in spite of the efforts of the Revolutionary authorities, was certainly no longer a theatre of vice punished; it was not even a theatre of cruelty; it became perilously near to being a *théâtre du néant*.

But however disappointing as spectacle, the guillotine, the place where the utmost stress was placed on physical dignity as part of the definition of class, did show a unique capacity to gather myths around itself, some of which have already been mentioned. It was after all hardly surprising that in this political world where persons and ideologies were so inextricably linked, the fate of the bodies of specific human beings should have assumed symbolic importance.[37] Possibly the most significant of these myths is involved with the execution of Marat's assassin, Charlotte Corday. It is a pre-Thermidorean mythology whose formation we can trace with unusual chronological precision, and in whose content appear many of the concerns we have already noted in the controversy of 1795. The process of the myth's accretion in fact began on the day after the execution, when the deputy Sergeant Marceau wrote to the Président of the Revolutionary Tribunal, to make the following accusation against the public executioner: 'Hier, celui qui est chargé de la douloureuse fonction d'exécuter vos jugements, se livra, en présence du peuple, à des excès répréhensibles sur les restes du monstre qui a arraché la vie à un des représentants de la nation française'.[38] Samson, he alleged, had held up Charlotte Corday's severed head, and struck one of its cheeks. A blush of shame and indignation had appeared on the other. The story was quickly repeated in the next issue of the *Révolutions de Paris*, that of 13–19 July. Henri Samson then protested to the Tribunal that it was not he, but his carpenter, Legros, who was guilty of this excess of revolutionary zeal. His protest to that effect was also published in the *Chronique de Paris*, together with a report of legal penalties to be inflicted on Legros.[39]

Yet both Marceau's original accusation, and Samson's blame of Legros, are thrown into doubt by other sources. Cabanis remarked in 1795 that several of his friends who had attended Charlotte Corday's execution specifically in order to test theories on the survival of the head after decapitation, had seen neither Samson *nor* his assistant offer any violence to the head. Why then has the story achieved such credence that the legend has become enshrined in prints and in popular history from 1793 virtually to the present day? An acute comment by Cabanis may offer some solution to the problem: 'Je sais trop avec quelle facilité l'on voit des merveilles dans le temps d'agitation et de malheur. Quand les lumières publiques ne permettent plus de voir des miracles, on veut du moins trouver de nouveaux phénomènes dans la nature'.[40]

It is not surprising that the place, both where the displacement of religion was at its most visible, and where the question of bodily dignity was faced most painfully, should also be the place to produce a miracle located in the physical body. The story of Charlotte Corday was also ready ammunition for those who wished to make the case for a resistant, unitary consciousness out of the survival of the decapitated heads. This is why it was accepted by Oelsner, and by Süe, while Cabanis, without such investments, could subject the 'miracle' to a 'sociological' explanation. Miracles centred on execution by guillotine also had the advantage, acutely realized by Cabanis, that they could easily be made 'convincing' to the enlightened wishing to cling to a rationalist world view, in the sense that they occurred in front of an audience, the waiting crowd – and it is worthwhile remembering in this context the degree to which eighteenth-century ideas about experimental verification turned on validation by an eye-witness audience.[41] Supporters of the Corday myth thus make frequent attempts to drum up the crowd as a verifying witness: '...tous les spectateurs furent frappés par le changement de couleur et demandèrent aussitôt par de bruyants murmures vengeance de cette lâche et atroce barbarie'.[42]

This transfer of the miraculous on to the physical plane, which so facilitated the adoption of the Corday myth by the 'enlightened' section of society, was also encouraged by the very vocabulary of physiology itself. Just as the crucial Revolutionary word *'vertu'* referred both to a moral attitude and, in woman, to physical intactness, so the word *'sensibilité'* signified both the sensitivity of an organism to stimuli and, in the moral sphere, a feeling of universal sympathy with the feelings of others.[43] The 'fact' that Charlotte Corday's head reacted after decapitation showed both *sensibilité* in the physiological sense, and that moral *sensibilité* was so intrinsic to the human organism that it continued, even after 'death', to register indignation and shame. The whole myth of Charlotte Corday

XII This cartoon of the death of Robespierre clearly shows the mechanism of the guillotine.

exemplifies all the fears of the middle class for the preservation of that intact, controlled, unitary body-image, a body-image which differentiated that social class from others, and allowed it to validate its claims to revolutionary control as against the disordered dress and wild 'passions' and 'energies' of the lower-class political movements.[44] Bodily dignity, as well as political and moral virtue, gave the right to rule. It is no accident that the embodiment of virtue, Maximilien Robespierre, should also have been the embodiment of order and control in his physical person.

The extent of this concern in large part explains why, in defiance of all obstacles, the Corday myth rushed into being, and stayed alive. It overcame the eyewitness medical men who said that no blow had ever been given to the head, and that even if it had, the 'blush' could not have happened. It overcame the fact that very few in the crowd would have been in any position to see it if it had happened. It survived all these common-sense obstacles, because of the intensity of the need generated by terror and execution to externalize concerns such as the survival of a unitary experience of mind and body, and of the possibility of physical dignity, both of which seemed under extreme threat. Above all, it survived because it asserted that in spite of the guillotine's capacity to evacuate all significance both from death and from the body itself, an individual reaction to these outrages could survive even execution itself.

It is of course no accident that such needs clustered around a myth about a young girl, and play no part in the mythology of any male figure. The stories, discussed earlier, of Bailly's execution simply insisted on the extent of his physical misery *before* execution; they give no account of any defiant reaction *after* death. Such concerns also conspicuously fail to appear in the mythologies of older married women also executed by guillotine, such as Marie-Antoinette, or Mme Roland. The other figure around whom similar concerns *do* cluster is that of Mme Elizabeth, Louis XVI's unmarried sister, who just before execution pleaded with the executioner to replace the scarf covering her neck and shoulders, 'Au nom de la pudeur'.[45] It is hardly surprising that two presumed virgins should have borne the weight of all the concern which the guillotine aroused in the middle class about physical invasion and shame. Nor that the authorities should have tried to discredit at least Corday's claim to virginity in an attempt to destroy her capacity to represent these concerns.[46]

To sum up: The guillotine made possible the execution of large numbers of people within a relatively short space of time; it was the technological pre-condition for state terror. In doing so, it also changed what was involved in public execution in ways which contemporaries found profoundly disturbing. Execution by guillotine produced no drama of vice punished, and had generally little holding power for the crowd. Middle-class contemporaries found this crowd apathy almost as disturbing as the crowd violence of the Revolutionary *journées* and the *émeutes de subsistance*. As Mona Ozouf has observed, such passive crowds tend to be less receptive to the spectacle which they are ostensibly gathered together to see, than to the very experience of being in such a mass situation.[47] Turned inwards on to themselves, they enforce the sense of mass consciousness which Albert Soboul has defined as one of the characteristics of the popular movement.[48]

But above all, the guillotine placed the self-image of the middle class under threat. Lacretelle makes it plain how vulnerable the middle class's sense of social worth was to any elements of the legal system which broke down barriers between itself and the *'petit peuple'*: how much more so was this the case in a revolutionary situation, where the middle class had seized power for the first time, in which it equated political worth and moral virtue, and was simultaneously having to beat off the political demands of the *petit peuple* themselves.

Middle-class reaction to the guillotine had not much to do with that increasing 'sensibility' to physical suffering which some recent historians have seen as the hallmark of changing attitudes to public punishment in the late eighteenth century.[49] Although some appeal is made, in the post-Thermidor arguments for the abolition of the guillotine, to the presumed sensibility of the reader,[50] the main area of concern is always with the nature of the interaction between middle-class victims and lower-class crowd. For the middle class this was where the *tragédie* lay under the new system of capital punishment. It was not a drama of the unfolding of human sympathies between individuals, on which the rhetoric of sensibility turns. The problem for the middle class, as Cabanis ironically pointed out, was precisely the reverse: they were afraid to release the human emotions of fear and regret in front of a crowd which custom had long taught them to regard as *avide*. *Sensibilité* was part of an *intra*-class language; a rigid self-control was the only proper attitude in the face of *inter*-class relations.

These reactions reveal some basic contradictions in the notion of state terror itself. Such a policy is meaningless without an audience, just as the great Revolutionary fêtes would have been. Yet that audience, like many of the manifestations of the popular movement, was disliked and feared by the middle class. In the case of the guillotine crowds, their invasive scrutiny was perceived as bearing the power to intrude upon the very physical self-possession of the middle class, that very factor which was seen as separating it decisively from the *petit peuple*. For the bourgeois, typified by

Robespierre himself, a self-controlled, opaque body-image was an essential part of public identity. The ideas of the sans-culottes, on the other hand, extolled the virtues of energetic action and transparency, openness to scrutiny by the eye of virtue, as the supreme sign of revolutionary worth.[51] Contemporary reactions to the guillotine, in other words, should heighten our awareness of the extent to which body-image was seen by the middle class as a political resource and as social validation. Threats to middle-class control of that image could do nothing but add to the chaotic and violent relations between the classes with which the Revolution is marked.

It has also recently been argued that public capital punishment is the classic sign of the weak, pre-industrial state.[52] This is difficult to reconcile with the usual interpretation of Revolutionary Terror in France as an essential part of the creation of strong central government. It seems more likely that the use of the guillotine in this period shows a state in transition. Execution is indeed still public, but gone is the prolonged *tragédie* which was supposed to demonstrate the power of the state to repair the order of the body politic, or the king's peace, by punishing the bodies of wrongdoers. It was replaced by a machine whose use made visible the extension of state punishment to classes never before routinely in the purview of legal process. Yet in so doing the very nature of the machine itself empties death of significance.

For this development, however, the middle class had none but themselves to blame. Michel Vovelle has made it clear how the late eighteenth century had already systematically worked to evacuate dread from death, and in so doing, made it lose a great deal of its religious and moral significance.[53] Public execution by guillotine had the features that it did not only because of the real failure of the movement of *'sensibilité'* to measure up to political and public threat, but because of the previous work to change the significance of death. The guillotine even prevented the middle class from playing out the new dramas of death which it had invented to replace the old. It was not possible, as Amaury Duval had remarked, to *'mourir en philosophe'* on the scaffold of the guillotine. It is hardly surprising that many chose to act out that drama while they still could, by committing suicide in prison.

The guillotine provoked such doubts, confusions, disturbance and anguish that it produced, even as it worked, countervailing myths to the fragility of life and status revealed by Terror and the guillotine. Self-possession, the union of the experience of the self and the conduct of the body, the myths asserted, were not so frail; they could survive even decapitation. As Cabanis had hinted, the guillotine had helped to make the physical body become both the area of doubt and of miracle.

# 8

# WORDS AND FLESH

## Mme Roland, the Female Body and the Search for Power

> Fût-on un Caton, on doit craindre les Circés.
>
> Hébert, 1793

> En lisant les *Mémoires* de Mme Roland, on aperçoit l'actrice qui travaille pour la scène et qui noie dans une foule de puérilités l'apologie de ses amis et la satire de ses enemies; toutes les figures y sont peintes en buste, et le plus souvent par le pinceau des passions. J'ai connu personnellement cette femme dont la mort héroïque a expié l'égarement, dont l'âme ardente et la tête ambitieuse eussent mérité un cloître ou une principauté; dont l'esprit fin et turbulent était aussi propre à diriger des intrigues qu'incapable d'écrire avec fidelité les scènes d'horreur où elle n'avait pas craint de jouer un rôle.
>
> Mallet du Pin, 1798[1]

So far, one of the major themes of this book has been the construction of human bodies, predominantly male, as arenas of public authority. We have looked in some detail at the very male ethos of Stoicism, dignity and self-containment, the political practices to which it gave rise, and its insertion into political culture as a whole. We have not yet asked, however, whether such an ethos can be examined wholly as a self-sustaining entity: was it self-supporting, or was it sustained by a continuous relocation, within the culture at large, of physical and political attributes antithetical to it? We may ask if the male Stoicism which appears as the dominant political ethos of the Revolutionary period could have been so without the formation of a contrasting ethos of women's public responses. In trying to answer this question we can gain much additional insight into the public embodiment of this period, for clearly, if we look at only one side of the making of public physical representation – the side of the male actors we have so far discussed – we do not go very far towards understanding, for either sex, the problem of public physical embodiment.

It is also, however, important to lead on from the criticisms of Foucault expressed earlier in this volume, and not explore this theme 'from the outside'. We have to ask too how, and to what extent, women in this period constructed their own physical self-image and how that self-image was related by them to experiences in the public realm. In particular, how did women begin to deal with experiences of the body necessarily denied to men, such as childbirth and breast-feeding, or with experiences which weighed more heavily on them, such as life in the family? How, if at all, could they relate such gender-specific experiences in the lived body, to the creation of a body which could carry public weight?

The period of the French Revolution is a key one in the evaluation of this problem. It is not only that then, for the first time, though for a brief period only, a minority of women, especially in Paris, began to be politically visible.[2] It was also that the Revolution defined its difference from the old regime partly in terms of a difference in the impact of women on politics. In the rhetoric, the monarchy was *par excellence* a regime characterized by the corruption of power through the agency of women. Boudoir politics, the exchange of political gifts for sexual favours, were seen both as a cause of the weaknesses of the old regime, and as a justification for the Revolution itself. Perhaps the most visible example of this attitude is constituted by the trial of Queen Marie-Antoinette, in 1793. The 'political' counts against her – instigating the flight of the royal family which ended at Varennes, inciting foreign states to invade France – were inseparable from, and bolstered by, the accusations of sexual perversion and incest which accompanied them. In corrupting the Dauphin, heir to the throne of France, her accusers implied that she had corrupted the body politic at one and the same time as she had corrupted the actual physical body of her son.[3] As Furet remarks, the Revolution could only legitimate its own seizure of power, and distinguish itself from the corrupt power of the old regime, by attacking power itself.[4]

To the degree that power in the old regime was ascribed to women, the Revolution was committed to an anti-feminine rhetoric, which posed great problems for any women seeking public authority. Male politicians, on the other hand, could find in this rhetoric an escape from the guilt arising from the destruction of the French monarchy and its complex religious sanctions: what looked like a sacrilegious act had *in fact* been a crusade for virtue; what looked like an attack on the supreme political symbol, the king's body, had *in fact* been a purging of the female from the body politic. As the woman activist Olympe de Gouges remarked, 'Women are now respected and excluded; under the old regime they were despised and powerful'.[5] Thus, in the rhetoric of the Revolution, the entire struggle for the achievement of legitimacy, for the creation of a new legitimate public embodiment by the Revolutionary governing class, was predicated not on an inclusion of the female, but on its exclusion. The production of male political embodiment cannot be understood as a self-standing development; it has also to be read as a process of exclusion, and differentiation.

Nowhere was this process of exclusion and differentiation more marked than in the case of the most important word of the Revolutionary political vocabulary: 'virtue'. We have already seen how strong was the presupposition that political revolution could only take place if the niche formerly occupied by women's vice was taken over by male virtue. Of that male virtue, Brutus was the supreme personification, Brutus who put the safety of the republic above private emotion, or the protection of his family, in agreeing to the execution of his sons on the discovery of their involvement in a conspiracy to overthrow the Roman republic and restore the monarchy.[6] Brutus could not have been a woman. The embodiment of female virtue, Lucretia, who killed herself after her rape by King Tarquin, was defending virtue in quite a different sense, that of intimate physical reserve. And although the stories of the virtue of both Brutus and Lucretia were ultimately concerned with the defence of the republic against monarchy, their juxtaposition demonstrates, none the less, the immense gulf between men's and women's virtue: the one public, the other private. The word 'virtue', in the Revolutionary context, existed in a perpetual slide between these two meanings, rather than in the rigid 'discourse of the Revolution' of which Furet speaks. The existence of this continuum between virtue as chastity or female fidelity within marriage, and virtue as the upholding of the republic at whatever private cost, carries a whole series of messages: that female chastity is the prerequisite for political innovation undertaken in the name of the general will and against monarchy; that women threaten the revolution, because any deviation from chastity/virtue involves the collapse of republic/virtue; and because through their unrestrained sexuality women can personalize politics and factionalize it with competition for their 'favours' (a significantly two-edged word). Virtue, far from being the linchpin of a monolithic 'discourse of the Revolution', in fact bisected the apparently universalistic discourse of the general will into distinct political destinies, one male and the other female. Both were part of *le souvereign*, but somehow one half of *le souvereign* could function only at the price of the sexual containment of the other.[7]

But somehow, women's desires and passions, and the bodies through which they expressed these passions and desires, refused to abandon the consciousness of the Revolution. The trial of Marie-Antoinette was staged virtually as a morality play on the evil impact of women on the body politic, as well as an epitome of monarchical corruption. Charlotte Corday's assassination of Marat, *'L'Ami du Peuple'*, and Mme Roland's allegedly fatal influence on her husband, twice Minister of the Interior in 1792–3, and on members of the group loosely called Girondins, were test cases of the female potential for danger in the new politics. Contemporaries were quick to link the three women together, whatever their differences in birth and outlook, and to use their common fate of condemnation and execution as a warning to other women who attempted, like the members of women's political clubs in Paris, to gain visibility for themselves in the political process.[8] Women's virtue, it was felt, disappeared when subject to public exposure in the arena of politics: the same arena which created public man, made woman into *fille publique*. Connections with women were also a favourite stick to beat political enemies. Nothing was simpler, for example, than for Marat to trivialize attacks in the Convention on the Jacobin, Pache, in November 1792 by Buzot and Barbaroux, both friends of Mme Roland, by allegations of a sexual reward:

> Ce n'est qu'à cette condition [of making the attack on Pache] qu'on a laissé à Barbaroux l'espoir de continuer ses fonctions de premier frère servant. On dit même que c'est dans l'espoir d'avoir la clef du boudoir que Buzot a donné dans cette affaire un si grand coup de collier.[9]

It is unfortunately true that the historiography of women's experience in the French Revolution for a long time did little else but reproduce the prejudices of the Revolution itself. An image of women, as destructively propelled by physicality, passion and desire, was adopted whole by the nineteenth century. As Louis Devance puts it:

> ...the way in which the 'famous women' of the Revolution have been studied, and the fatal role which historians such as Michelet have ascribed to them, and above all the equation of the three terms 'women', 'madness', and 'revolution', have meant that a mythical or stereotyped approach to women has often predominated in historical writing.

In particular, it was an approach which emphasizes the 'unnatural fury' of the women of the Revolution. It functions to distract attention from the fact that the 'so-called special cruelty' of the 'furies of the guillotine' and others was nothing more than a response by women to 'sadistic spectacles thought up and executed by men'.[10]

Later in the nineteenth century, historians continued this tradition but medicalized its explanation. 'Hysteria' rather than 'fury' became the main description of alleged episodes of feminine destructive ruthlessness, a hysteria arising out of the subjects' physical constitution as women. If Elias's identification of the modern state with the restraint of drives and affects is true, then no wonder women were identified as the enemies of political virtue precisely at the moment of the creation of the first modern state, during the Revolution, precisely by virtue of their lack of control of emotion and their physical violence. It is only in the twentieth century, with the rise of a 'women's history', that an attempt has been made to see women's role in the Revolution as anything more than a 'dark history' of the male revolution. But for all its feminist credentials – or maybe even because of them – even the new history of women poses considerable problems. It has, first of all, very often been tempted to see the actions of militant women during the Revolution, and their political clubs in particular, as forerunners of modern feminist movements, rather than examining them in the context of the history of the Revolution. Because of this, few historians have attempted to isolate the causes of the failure of the clubs in terms of the problems raised by the political culture of the Revolution for *all* its participants, including women – problems such as the mastery of public discourse, and the achievement of public embodiment. The implication often remains that the minority of female activists or 'first feminists' within the Revolution failed because of male hostility to 'feminism'.

Concentration on the activists also means in effect that women's history of the Revolution has stayed well within the canon of 'famous women of the Revolution' first established by nineteenth-century male historians such as Michelet, in his *La Femme et la Révolution*. The only change made is that upper-class or non-activist 'famous women', such as Mme Roland, have been dropped from the canon, as there has also been little interest in searching out hitherto unknown private responses by non-activist, non-canonical 'founding mothers'.[11] Sadly, concentration on a small band of female activists such as Etta Palm, Théroigne de Méricourt or Pauline Leclerc means that women's history in the Revolutionary period has remained isolated from that of the general history of the Revolution, and that mainstream history has accordingly taken little note of the conclusions of the feminist historians, just as they themselves have taken little note of the reactions and responses of the vast numbers of women caught up in the Revolution. Concentration on the small band of female extra-Parliamentary activists has had several other consequences: most importantly, it has led to a neglect of women's self-consciousness. It is precisely the aim of this book to restore that self-consciousness, by examining the interaction, as we will later do in the case of Mme Roland, between private experience of the body and the problems of the achievement of public embodiment. Such an enquiry would, it is clear, tell us much not only about women's difficulties under the Revolution, but also about the stresses within Revolutionary political culture.

In the modern historiography of women during the Revolution, we also find, surprisingly, an almost circular movement towards the revival of some of the basic nineteenth-century approaches to the topic. The concentration of social historians such as Olwen Hufton on the actions of working-class women – often, thanks to their family responsibilities, in the forefront of the food riots and the great *journées* of the Revolution – arose from a laudable desire to end a situation where the attitude of working women and their Revolutionary experience remains an 'enigma, conceded but passing reference even in works concerned exclusively with the attitudes and actions of the working class'. But in spite of these aims, to a disturbing degree Hufton's working women remind one of the passionate 'furies' of the older historians, when she writes that: 'In every outward manifestation in 1793, women were more frenzied, more intense, doubly gullible, doubly credulous, doubly vindictive and the only exception to this is that they were less publicly garrulous than men – but here it may merely be a question of lack of opportunity'.[12]

The modern 'feminist' history of the women of the Revolution has in fact not succeeded either in creating a new and satisfactory history of women, or of laying the ghost of the old. Even more surprising, in view of the importance of the problem of political embodiment in the Revolutionary period, and the efforts of modern feminists to recapture the female body from male appropriation, is the fact that recent women's history of the Revolution has considered its female actors as without embodiment. In the rest of this chapter I am going to consider, through the medium of a case study of an exceptionally well-documented life, that of Mme Roland, what such a reconstruction of female embodiment would involve, and how a specifically female physical consciousness could overlap with, and be transformed into, a series of responses to political situations. I also intend to show how such responses were inextricably linked to the way that the pre-Revolutionary culture of the eighteenth century had given drama and visibility to women's physicality.

The life of Mme Roland has always attracted attention.[13] Partly this has been due to the enormous volume of self-documentation which she produced. She is probably the most extensively intimately documented woman of the French eighteenth century. Her voluminous correspondence, running from early adolescent years to her death in 1793 at the age of thirty-nine, and the lengthy and detailed *Mémoires* written in her imprisonment during the Revolution, have been impeccably edited by Claude Perroud; there also exist from her pen writings on her journeys to England and Switzerland, and about Roman history and its moral lessons – volumes of standard eighteenth-century interest which, together with a harrowing and minutely detailed account of the birth of her only child, Eudore, were issued in a collected edition very shortly after her execution.[14] Mme Roland's was a life in which the art of writing played an almost obsessionally large part; it was also one in which, particularly in the *Mémoires*, writing is used repeatedly to create both the self and its physical embodiment. Editors before Perroud were often perturbed by the mixture of frankness and *risqué* coyness in these writings, to the extent that much material relating to Mme Roland's physical experiences of all kinds, and her celebration of her physicality, was expurgated from early editions of her works.[15] Present-day historians are perturbed by the strength with which her writings demand that we consider the close links between the written word and the growth of a physical identity.

That to consider Mme Roland from this standpoint appears as a new enterprise merely bears out our earlier remarks about certain features of the historiography of women in the Revolutionary period. Apart from a fairly recent and intelligently written biography, and another study of her literary output, both by Gita May, Mme Roland has been conspicuously neglected by the most recent generation of women's historians of the Revolution, being neither working class, nor a radical political activist.[16] For nineteenth-century historians, however, Mme Roland was one of the canonical *femmes célèbres de la Révolution*. Apart from her famous apostrophe on the scaffold, variously rendered as 'Liberty, what crimes are committed in your name' and 'O Liberté, comme l'on t'a jouée', she was seen as having a preponderant influence over her husband, Jean-Marie Roland, as Minister of the Interior, and also over the fall of the Girondin faction, in the purge of the Convention of 31 May and 2 June 1793 which established Jacobin predominance and war government in France. It was she, it was alleged, who was the true author of her husband's famous letter of resignation of 1792 to Louis XVI, which was the first overt challenge to Louis's adherence to the new constitution; and it was also she, as even her husband's biographer claims, in terms which could have been borrowed from the classic historiography of women and the Revolution, who, contributing violence and acrimony, heightened the factional struggles of the Convention by working on the passions of her 'champions', the deputies Buzot and Barbaroux.[17] It took the Girondins' first English chronicler, Martin Sydenham, to begin to dismantle this myth, to point out how difficult it was to isolate 'the Girondins' as a coherent political group, how few of them Mme Roland actually knew, and how little real influence she seemed to have exerted on the passage of events. Sydenham's path-breaking work on the problem of 'the Girondins' also allowed it to become visible for the first time that the myth of Mme Roland's involvement with the Girondins had existed to absolve the Girondins themselves of responsibility for their downfall: it also had had the merit, for the hard-pressed historian, of resolving the problem of defining just who *were* the 'Girondins': by definition, they became that group of politicians known to Mme Roland.[18]

This historiography has been rehearsed at length, not only to be the more effectively discarded for the remainder of this chapter, but also as a measure of the variety of the questions we propose to ask of Mme Roland's life, which will be questions not relating to her alleged historical responsibility for and relations to male political actors, but to and for herself; and by attempting an answer to that question, we may end up with a far truer picture of her real importance in the French Revolution than it has hitherto been possible to draw, and also a far better picture of the way in which male and female political embodiment interacted with each other. Neither makes sense alone.

We approach this project through an area neglected in the historiography at large, and in studies of Mme Roland in particular: her attitudes to her own physicality and to that of men and other women. These are important to understand on many different levels. Firstly, they represent an area of her experience which, in spite of its copious documentation in the correspondence, *mémoires* and other writings produced by her, has received little attention even from twentieth-century biographers, and was the first area to be excised from the early editions of her writings. Where these attitudes have been examined, as in recent work by Marie-France Morel, it is within the straitjacket of the now conventional historiography on women and the family in the Enlightenment, 'medicalizing' the experiences of childbirth and breast-feeding, and relating them to the alleged emergence of the warm, nuclear family in this period.[19]

The production of a new interpretation of the area of physicality in Mme Roland's life, however, does not simply aid us to gain a more accurate idea of an individual experience. It enables us to chart, in the case of a woman, as well as for the men whose experiences have so far concerned us, the interaction of physical self-consciousness, reactions to the physicality of others, and the delineation of the public realm. These interactions emerge far more clearly and directly in the case of Mme Roland than in the case of many of the male actors we have so far considered, not only because she left extensive autobiographical materials and correspondence, and they did not, but also because of her femininity, a condition which required her to be both explicit and circumspect in relation to the area of the physical in a way unnecessary for a man, with his greater freedom. There are two final reasons for our interest in Mme Roland's account of her self. Firstly, Mme Roland constructed her own self-image, in which physicality played a great part, through the medium of words. And the enormous size of her written output, and the immensely important part it played in her life, was matched only by the intensity of her relationship with the experience of reading. Indeed, as we will see, for Mme Roland the experience of reading and the experience of physical arousal were never far apart. Reading also supplied her with roles to play, roles which contributed decisively to the public personifications she would adopt. It is thus an important component in the discussion of public personification which we have identified as one of the major problems of Revolutionary politics. As against the arguments of many feminist historians, we may insist from the example of Mme Roland that women's actions are not determined simply by their biologically given bodies, but also by the repertoire of images which they use to recreate those bodies, and which may be drawn from *both* male and female experience.

One of the major purposes of this chapter is to release one woman's history from a historiography of women which is either overmedicalized or overmaternalized. Mme Roland created her own physical self-consciousness and in doing so, created her own public fate. She ended her life in a considerable blaze of public notoriety owing to the contemporary estimate of her influence on politics; moreover, she ended it in exactly the same way as the majority of the men whose reactions we have been examining: in prison, and under sentence of death. In other words, her search for a self-image and for physical dignity ended by facing exactly the same challenge as theirs. In her reaction to that challenge we may try out the degree of difference, if any, which existed in the male and female response to the challenges of political life in the Revolution.

From the beginning, Mme Roland's relationship with her own body was a focus of contradiction, and irreconcilable demands. The first physical experience she recounts in her *Mémoires* sets the pattern for the future. Having partly encouraged, partly rejected, the fumbling physical contact offered her by one of her father's apprentices, intrigued, yet terrified that the young man would bring their meetings to their logical conclusion, she confessed the episode to her mother, who reacted in horrified panic, lectured the young girl on the sinfulness of sexual acts and thoughts, and hurried her off to make amends in the confessional. She was, as she remarks, treated as the sinner before she had sinned, to such a degree that she became virtually unable to confront sexual topics openly for many years afterwards, and was never able to mention the incident even to

Roland.[20] The problem was that her mother's response had identified the degree to which Manon Phlipon had indeed been 'guilty' in the episode, and on the basis of the ambiguity in the girl's feelings had managed also to instill in her feelings of guilt and shame in the whole sexual area, far more effectively than if Manon had either straightforwardly repulsed the young man with horror, or straightforwardly encouraged his dishonourable intentions. Was she chaste, or was she not? The question lay unresolved in Mme Roland's mind – unresolved even at the time of the writing of the *Mémoires*, so shortly before her death. She admits: 'Je suis un peu embarassée de ce que j'ai à raconter ici, car je veux que mon écrit soit chaste, puisque ma personne n'a pas cessé de l'être, et pourtant ce que je dois dire ne l'est pas trop'.[21]

It is important to link these uncertainties in Mme Roland's own self-portrait with the uncertainties which prevailed in the culture at large in relation to women's public role. Mme Roland's uncertainty as to whether to regard herself as chaste or not, exactly mimicked the way in which, under both the old regime and the Revolution, chaste women were denied public authority and confined, for the preservation of that chastity, to their domestic roles, while women who aspired to public authority or influence were automatically regarded as sexually uncontrolled and thereby threatening to the political order. Unable to define herself as either chaste or unchaste, Mme Roland's attitude to the influence she did wield during her husband's brief tenure of office was equally ambiguous, as we will see when we turn to an examination of her attitudes and actions in this period, and in doing so attempt to resolve the question of the real extent of her political importance – a problem which has eluded each successive generation of commentators.

Mme Roland's ambiguities in relation to her own physicality, it must also be noted, were hardly startlingly personal; they show her efficiently internalizing the presuppositions of her culture at large. What is unusual is the extent to which her *Mémoires* insist upon the relationship between female physicality and the public world. This is a theme to which she returns time and again, and in ways which mirror the conflict between her own fascination with sexuality, and her efficient rejection of it. It is clear that Mme Roland found the use of eroticism by other women at once fascinating and disturbing: fascinating in its attractiveness, disturbing in its ability to corrupt the public sphere. Let us take as an example of this, her detailed description in the *Mémoires* of an acquaintance of her family, the middle-aged novelist Mme Benoît, whom Mme Roland encountered as an adolescent. The passage is worth quoting at length:

> Mme Benoît avait été belle; les soins de la toilette, et le désir de plaire, prolongés au delà de l'âge qui assure d'y réussir, lui valaient

encore quelques succès. Ses yeux les sollicitaient avec tant d'ardeur, son sein toujours découvert jusqu'au delà de la petite rose dont la fleur se réserve ordinairement pour les secrets mystères, palpitait si vivement pour les obtenir, qu'il fallait bien accorder, à la franchise du désir et à la facilité de le satisfaire, ce que les hommes accordent d'ailleurs si aisément dès qu'ils ne sont pas tenus à la constance. L'air ouvertement voluptueux de Mme Benoît était tout nouveau pour moi; j'avais vu dans les promenades ces prêtresses du plaisir dont l'indécence annonce la profession d'une manière choquante; il y avait ici une autre nuance. Je ne fus pas moins frappée de l'encens poëtique qui lui était prodigué et des expressions de sage Benoît, chaste Benoît, plusieurs fois répétées dans ces vers, qui lui faisaient porter de temps en temps devant ses yeux un modeste éventail, tandis que quelques hommes applaudissaient avec transport à des éloges qu'ils trouvaient sans doute bien appliqués. Je me rappelai ce que mes lectures m'avaient mis à portée de juger de la galanterie, ce que les moeurs du siècle et les désordres de la cour devaient y ajouter de corruption du coeur, de fausseté de l'esprit; je voyais les hommes efféminés prodiguer leur admiration à des vers legers, à des talents futiles, à la passion de les séduire tous, sans les aimer sans doute, car quiconque se dévoue au bonheur d'un objet préféré ne se prodigue point aux regards de la foule.[22]

This passage is an important one for what it reveals about the links in Mme Roland's mind between overt eroticism (she has great difficulty in distinguishing between Mme Benoît and genuine prostitutes), emotional falsity, corruption, court 'disorder', male effeminacy, and the undermining of privacy. An absolute polarity is revealed between the Good, meaning female chastity and the veiling of the erotic, the private, and the ordered, on the one hand, and on the other, the exposure of the female body, the undermining of manhood, the weakening of royal authority, and the corruption of public order associated with giving too much away to the eyes of '*la foule*'.

So far, however, we have simply noted Mme Roland reproducing the prejudices of her age. But also at work in the passage about Mme Benoît is a considerable degree of erotic response to the other woman's frank display of her charms, a response which Mme Roland attempts to hide by the use of language of extreme coyness ('cette petite rose...'), but which none the less vibrates through her writing even while it is ostensibly concerned with the rejection of unchastity. This point leads us on to the observation, which at first sight contradicts much of what we have said so far, that in her *Mémoires* Mme Roland displays a considerable concern with establishing for the reader her own physical self-portrait, and does so in a way which reveals a degree of appreciation of her own erotic charms. Rejecting, in highly moral vein, the sensuality of other women, Mme Roland yet seems eager and ready to claim it for herself. Again, a long extract will reveal more than many pages of detailed explication:

> C'est peut-être ici le lieu de faire mon portrait.... À quatorze ans, comme aujourd'hui, j'avais environ cinq pieds, ma taille avait acquis toute sa croissance; la jambe bien faite, le pied bien posé, les hanches très relevées, la poitrine large et superbement meublée, les épaules effacées, l'attitude ferme et gracieuse, la marche rapide et légère, voilà pour le premier coup d'oeil. Ma figure n'avait rien de frappant qu'une grande fraîcheur, beaucoup de douceur et d'expression; à detailer chacun des traits, on peut se demander où donc en est la beauté? aucun n'est régulier, tous plaisent. La bouche est un peu grande, on en voit mille de plus jolies, pas une n'a le sourire plus tendre et plus séducteur. L'oeil, au contraire, n'est pas fort grand, son iris est d'un gris châtain; mais placé à fleur de tête, le regard ouvert, franc, vif et doux, couronné d'un sourcil brun comme les cheveux et bien dessiné, il varie dans son expression comme l'âme affectueuse dont il peint les mouvements; sérieux et fier, il étonne quelque fois, mais il caresse bien davantage et réveille toujours. Le nez me faisait quelque peine, je le trouvais un peu gros par le bout; cependant considéré dans l'ensemble, et surtout du profil, il ne gâtait rien au reste. Le front large, un peu couvert à cet âge, soutenu par l'orbite très élèvé de l'oeil, et sur le milieu duquel des veines en y s'épanouissaient à l'émotion la plus légère, était loin de l'insignificance qu'on lui trouve sur tant de visages. Quant au menton, assez retroussé, il a précisément les caractères que les physiognomistes indiquent pour ceux de la volupté. Lorsque je les rapproche de tout ce qui m'est particulier, je doute que jamais personne fût plus faite pour elle et l'ait moins goûtée. Le teint, vif plutôt que très blanc, des couleurs éclatantes, fréquemment renforcées de la subite rougeur d'un sang bouillant excité par les nerfs les plus sensibles; la peau douce, le bras arrondi, la main agréable, sans être petite, parce que ses doigts allongés et minces annoncent l'adresse et conservent de la grâce, des dents saines et bien rangées, l'embonpoint d'une santé parfaite, tels sont les trésors que la bonne nature m'avait donnés.[23]

Mme Roland can hardly tear herself away from the prolonged and minutely detailed evocation of her own physical charms.

At first sight, this is a puzzling passage to encounter in the work of a woman who was so energetically to condemn such displays by other women. And more is at work here than merely the consistent human foible of condemning in others what one commends in oneself. Mme Roland is in fact trying in this passage, through its length, and its insistent evocation of detail, to overcome precisely the continuing contradiction contained in its closing lines, of being a person made for physical desire and pleasure, and yet never experiencing it. This is still precisely the split between appearance and reality, between chastity and unchastity, contained in the episode of her father's apprentice. We may perhaps be able to resolve many of these problems by treating the self-portrait not merely as a literal, almost narcissistic, description of her physical appearance, but even more as the description which Mme Roland creates, following widely available literary models, of herself as a 'heroine'. In the description, Mme Roland is seeking to overcome the ambiguities in her relationship with her physical self, ambiguities which were not to be lessened by marriage and motherhood, by externalizing her physicality and casting herself in the role of the virginal, and yet voluptuous, besieged and yet always chaste, heroine who abounded in the contemporary novel.[24]

There are several arguments in favour of this view. Gita May has recently emphasized the importance to Mme Roland of writing as a bulwark against painful and confusing discrepancies: '...d'affirmer la consistence de sa personnalité et la constance de ses principes et ceci malgré des événements qui semblent en détruire toute cohérence'. Through the novel, Mme Roland could come to terms with herself. As she wrote of the *Nouvelle Héloïse*: 'Il me rend content de moi, et m'apprend à me tolérer en me donnant toujours l'envie d'être meilleure et l'espérance de le devenir'.[25]

The extent to which Mme Roland in her 'self-portrait' reproduces the commonplaces of the conventional evocation of the body of the heroine is striking. Pierre Fauchéry has described its emphasis upon the erotic potential of the eyes, the hands, and the posture of the body, which form a

> sémantique gestuelle, au jeu de laquelle participent divers phénomènes vasculaires (rougeurs, paleurs), musculaires (action des mains, de la tête, agenouillements, convulsions etc).... L'inventaire et la mobilisation, la 'mise en service' romanesque de cette rhétorique du geste constitue à n'en plus douter une des acquisitions progressives du roman; elle contribue fortement à enrichir le monde de signes, utilisables en des circonstances quotidiennes dont la littérature fait don à la vie.[26]

By the late eighteenth century, there were, too, further advantages in playing oneself into the heroine's role, advantages which related very specifically to the dilemmas over the repression or enjoyment of physicality faced by women in real life; dilemmas which were lifelong, and concerned other events than the loss of virginity. Firstly, from Richardson onwards, the female's struggle to preserve her vir-

XIII Mme Roland: an eager intelligence looking out of a body 'made for pleasure and never experiencing it'.

tue had been placed at centre stage in novels which had both male and female authorship and readership. Secondly, from Rousseau onwards, the heroine did not even have to preserve her virtue throughout the novel in order to remain at centre stage; indeed, her struggle over her sensuality, rather than her chastity, became the central motor of action, for instead of there being only one physical event to justify the heroine's role, that of the conflict over virginity, the whole of her bodily history became the matrix of plot. As Fauchéry has put it: 'C'est Rousseau, qui, le premier, brouille les cartes du roman virginal, en concédant à son héroine une sensualité agissante; il n'est plus question, pour les imitatrices de Julie, de rester à l'écart de l'événement dont leur corps est le théâtre'.[27]

It is in fact impossible to overstress the importance of certain novels in the formation of Mme Roland's self-image. Her very Christian name, as she once commented, was that of a novel's leading character – and not a particularly virtuous one. We know from the correspondence and *Mémoires* that Mme Roland was deeply affected by four novels in particular, Mme de Lafayette's *La Princesse de Clèves*, Samuel Richardson's *Pamela* and *Clarissa*, and above all, by

Rousseau's *Julie, ou la Nouvelle Héloïse*, as well as by the epic poem, Tasso's *Jerusalem Delivered*.[28] There are many points of contact between these works. All of them, with the possible exception of the Tasso epic, centre on women's choices in the disposal of their bodies. All the novels, with the exception of *La Princesse de Clèves*, are written in the form of exchanges of letters. That by Rousseau, as well as that by Mme de Lafayette, places great stress on an episode in which a young wife confesses to her older husband her love for another man. The plots of both foreshadow Mme Roland's own confession to her husband of her unconsummated passion for the *conventionnel* Buzot, which was followed shortly by her death, just as Julie's avowal to her husband, Wolmar, of her love for Saint-Preux, is shortly followed by her fatal boating accident.

Mme Roland's relationship with Buzot was more like an epistolary novel than a real-life, realistic passion. Her refusal to consummate the relationship, her almost sadistic insistence on revealing it to the unsuspecting and politically beleaguered Roland (in the name of marital loyalty), her refusal to leave Roland, while continuing the relationship with Buzot by letter even during her own imprisonment and his flight from Paris after the Jacobin coup of 31 May 1793, all point to the extent to which she succeeded in turning, through the medium of models provided by her favourite reading, what should have been an event of physical commitment into a series of episodes conducted through highly organized words, whether addressed to Roland or to Buzot. In doing so, by substituting the verbal for the physical, she could overcome the contradiction between the unchastity of her desires and the self-portrait she cherished, as chaste wife, and could also keep to herself the heroine's role in her domestic drama.

Nor is this series of parallels between Mme Roland's life and her novel-reading entirely the work of coincidence. It was the result of a willed internalization of these novels, in particular the *Nouvelle Héloïse*, until each became part of the very fabric of her being. As she wrote to Roland, apropos of Rousseau's novel:

> Je viens de dévorer *Julie*, comme si ce n'était pas pour la quatrième ou la cinquième fois. Mon ami, j'aimerai toujours ce livre-là, et si jamais je deviens dévôte, c'est là seulement que l'on en prendrai l'envie; il me semble que nous aurions bien vécu avec tous ces personnages et qu'ils nous auraient trouvés de leur goût, autant qu'ils sont du nôtre.[29]

Such a continuous work of identification had great effects on Mme Roland's self-perception. As she confessed to Roland before they married, it enabled her to see herself as a perpetual heroine: 'Je l'avoue à toi, qu'en lisant un roman ou un drâme, je n'ai jamais été éprise du deuxième rôle; je n'ai pas lu le récit d'un seul acte de courage ou de vertu que je n'aie osé me croire capable d'imiter cet acte dans l'occasion'.[30]

It is not surprising that under these conditions words became important elements in, and indeed substitutes for, physical experience. We need not go as far as to make a total equation between erotic acts and the act of writing or reading, as some modern literary critics have done, to realize the extent to which, for Mme Roland and for others like her, the novel broke down barriers between intellect and sensibility, affect and action, and became imbued with physical messages and responses.[31] Mme Roland herself gives us many indications of the extent to which this happened in her own case. It was not only that through the medium of models provided by her reading she was able to turn a potentially threatening physical outcome, such as that in the relationship with Buzot, into a verbal performance. It was also the way in which, given the continuum between the novel, the heroine-role, and the resolution of real-life conflicts centring on the physical disposal of the body, such reading became charged with the erotic. As Mme Roland recalled of her adolescence:

> Quelques fois je lisais haut, à la demande de ma mère...mais j'aurais plutôt avalé ma langue que de lire ainsi l'épisode de l'île de Calypso et nombre de passages du Tasse. Ma respiration s'élevant, je sentais un feu subit couvrir mon visage, et ma voix altérée eût trahi mes agitations. J'étais Euchris pour Télémaque, et Herminie pour Tancrède; cependant toute transformée en elles, je ne songeais pas encore à être moi-même quelque chose pour personne; je ne faisais point de retour sur moi, je ne cherchais rien autour de moi; j'étais elles et je ne voyais que les objets qui existaient pour elles: c'était une rêve sans réveil.[32]

This was something which remained with Mme Roland till the end: the inventory of the Rolands' flat, taken after their deaths in 1793, included, in a library otherwise entirely composed of non-fiction works, not only an edition of Tasso of 1783, but also the best-selling *risqué* novel by Mme Roland's friend, the *conventionnel* Louvet de Couvray, *Les Aventures du chevalier de Faublas*.[33]

In many ways, Mme Roland's relationship with the printed and written word, which was so strongly influenced by her response to her own physicality, was not unique. It has often been remarked that the eighteenth-century cult of sensibility, and the immense up-swing in the vogue of the novel from the 1740s onward, coinciding with the publication of Richardson's *Pamela*, permitted to readers of both sexes an emotional exaltation which broke down the barriers between affect and response, emotion and reason. It has also often been remarked that the patterns of behaviour which both male and female readers discovered in the novel were deeply internalized, and re-emerged intact in autobiography of the period.[34] Without necessarily taking on board Eagleton's argument that the novel, almost always preoccupied (in Patricia Spacks's words) with 'the trial of a young woman on the grounds of her virginity', produced a 'feminization' of public discourse in the eighteenth century, we can say that this discourse and this set of responses, which were unique to the eighteenth century, co-existed very uneasily with the far older discourse of Stoicism. The novel in fact did not constitute a new public realm; rather it conflicted with it. The eighteenth century saw, for both men and women, a conflict between the Romantic, sentimental response on the one hand, and control and containment on the other, a conflict increasingly carried on through the medium of a literature which itself increasingly insisted on the link between public order and the female body. This rather contradicts Elias's position that this period saw the increasing triumph, especially for the middle classes, of the ethos of physical containment. The Stoic ethos was to win out only precariously during the period of the Revolution itself; then it was swamped under the wave of Romanticism, to surface again in the late nineteenth and twentieth centuries as an ethos of self-control, efficiency and the power of the will which underlay many of the ideologies of the Fascist period. It is, rather, the case, that the eighteenth-century novel, particularly after Rousseau, implied all the Revolution's obsessive connection between the history of the heroines' bodies and the nature of the public order itself.[35]

Thus we should not be surprised to find that Mme Roland, at the same time as proclaiming her devotion to the Rousseau of the *Nouvelle Héloïse*, was also strongly influenced by the Rousseau of *Emile* and by the reading of the classic texts of Stoicism and Roman republican history.[36] But we have still to wonder at the special problems which such Stoic role-modelling might present to a woman. In terms of marriage and family life, as Mme Roland herself made explicitly clear, such an ethos of dignified containment could easily crumble, and crumble through the impact of the different physical histories, expectations, and constitutions, of men and women. On her marriage to Roland, she discovered that what might be conquest for the one was invasion for the other:

> Lorsque je suivis les anciennes sectes de philosophes, je donnai la palme aux stoïciens, je m'essayai comme eux à soutenir que la douleur n'était point un mal, et cette folie ne pouvant durer, je m'obstinai du moins à ne jamais me laisser vaincre par elle; mes petites expériences me persuadèrent que je pourrais endurer les plus grandes souffrances sans crier. Une première nuit de mariage renversa mes prétentions que j'avais gardées jusque-là; il est vrai

que la surprise y fut pour quelque chose et qu'une novice stoïcienne doit être plus forte contre le mal prévu que contre celui qui frappe à l'improviste lorsqu'elle attend tout le contraire.[37]

In entering marriage and the life of the family Mme Roland in fact had abandoned the potential for self-defence and self-command to be found in Stoicism, and instead entered an arena where ideologies and expectations ground against each other with maximum force. This is a point worth stressing, because of the degree to which modern histories of the eighteenth-century family have pictured the rise of the warm, caring, nuclear family, as if that family were itself an effective solvent of all contradiction.[38] The new family of the eighteenth century in fact demanded those involved in it, and especially the mother, to play out roles at maximum variance with each other. The century saw a new definition of childhood as dependent and in need of physical nurturing which women were 'naturally' suited to provide, in practices such as breast-feeding, instead of relying on the wet-nurse, and in the direct involvement of the mother in the rearing of her children while small, rather than leaving the task to servants. This was demanded in virtue of women's 'natural' physical abilities to bear young and to feed them from their own bodies. It was also demanded in virtue of an increasing identification of women with emotional warmth, intimacy, private life and domesticity, and conversely of men with rigour, hardness, and the external public world. However, the simultaneous rise of a new ethos of companionate marriage also demanded of women that they be helpmates to their husbands, sharing in their enterprises in so far as their other domestic duties allowed.

This dual role of wife and mother – of wife defined largely in intellectual terms, and of mother described largely in physical and emotional ones – in fact typified a split between mind and body. Mme Roland lived out this split in precise terms. After the birth of her only child, her daughter Eudore, on 4 October 1781, she carried on working on Roland's great project of an *Encyclopaedia of Manufactures*. She described herself to Roland as writing with one hand, while with the other she supported the perpetually suckling baby on her knee:

Tu trouveras ceci bien griffonnée, je n'ai qu'une main de libre, et je n'y regarde que de côté, ma petite est sur mes genoux, où il faut la garder la moitié du jour. Elle tient le sien deux heures de suite en faisant de petits sommeils qu'elle interrompt pour suçer. Si on l'ôte, elle pleure et mange ses poings.[39]

The conflicts within sexuality for Mme Roland – the desire to remain intact, and the desire to experience sensual pleasure – were doubled by the conflict between the roles of wife and mother, between the head and body. But there were other conflicts as well. The eighteenth-century family, so often presented in recent literature as a haven of emotional warmth, was in fact experienced by its inmates, as much in Mme Roland's *Mémoires* makes clear, as a coercive institution which insisted as much, if not more than, on the attainment of drive-control as on the production of emotional warmth. We may here endorse Elias's argument, produced long before the emergence of 'family history' as a distinct sub-discipline, that the late eighteenth century was a time when the middle-class family finally took over the roles of cultural enforcement, of drive- and affect-control, which had belonged to 'court society' in previous centuries.[40] For mothers and small children, families became institutions where children were not simply nurtured; they were also heavily controlled, through the acquisition of body-management.

Yet, simultaneously, a new, almost utopian rhetoric became available to disguise and obscure these conflicts. Often experienced as coercion and contradiction, the family was described in terms of pastoral. Hence the importance in family life of books, linguistic creations, which emerged with an impact not previously experienced in the eighteenth century. Previous eras had seen the writing of many books of parental advice to children, and guides to manners and morals composed for them. But the family of the late eighteenth century was the first to compile manuals of actual care of the infant and small child which went into minute detail about the direction of its physical existence. And such books not only gave mothers detailed advice; they also offered a view of the family as an innocent idyll which was yet the basis of society, and by combining these two aspects managed to reconcile the contradictions between them. Mme Roland, of course, as an admirer of Rousseau, was a keen student of *Émile*; but in the infancy of her daughter, she also placed great reliance on books which were much closer to modern 'baby books'.[41] Just as, in other words, she had used the written word to create her own self-image, and to take the place of physical events in her own life, so she did also to reconcile the contradictions in her roles as wife and mother.

Mme Roland's relationship with her daughter repays close study, because it shows so well the eighteenth-century family's uneasy swings between pastoral and coercion, between idyll and body-management. In spite of this, very few of Mme Roland's innumerable biographers have paid much attention to the years between 1781 and 1788 when Mme Roland was almost wholly preoccupied with her care of Eudore and her duties to Roland.[42] Many of these biographers have then announced themselves puzzled that the preoccupied wife and mother of those years, whose letters betray few if any 'political' concerns, should suddenly have metamorphosed into the political hostess of 1791–3. But in fact this problem is an unnecessary result of the assumption, itself an eighteenth- and nineteenth-century product, that family life and public life have nothing to do with each other. If we discard the rhetoric of utopian warmth which surrounds the family and look, as Elias recommends us to do, at the functions the family actually performs for its members, we find that the family was the matrix of the new emphasis on control of the affects and physical responses which was the prerequisite for political personification in the Revolutionary era. It is also the case that the conflicts experienced by women in playing out the role which was demanded of them as mothers produced a need for the reconciling devices of the public realm, its rhetoric and its physical manifestation, no less pressing than that experienced by male public figures.

Mme Roland's relationship with her small daughter was minutely chronicled in her letters, in her *Mémoires*, and in her own 'Avis à ma fille'. In them, she provides a detailed description of Eudore's birth, its impact on her own health and physical confidence, and the course she followed during Eudore's early infancy. Mme Roland decided to feed Eudore herself, as a good follower of Rousseau, and it was on this decision that most of her relationship with the child was based. At first easy, the breast-feeding became increasingly difficult when Mme Roland became ill a few weeks after the birth, and she was forced to send Eudore out to a wet-nurse. During her convalescence, she made strenuous efforts to regain her supply of milk, completely altering her diet and daily routine, and hiring women from the village of Clos, near Roland's country residence, to suck at her breasts in order to re-start the flow. Having, against all expectation, succeeded in this, she continued to feed Eudore herself until the child was weaned at around two years.

There are several points to make about this story. Firstly, Mme Roland's decision to breast-feed was by no means a foregone conclusion even by 1781. The practice remained in question even after the publication of *Émile*, and in fact during Eudore's early days of life, in Amiens where Roland's work as inspector of manufactures had taken him, Mme Roland was daily confronted by the carefree existence of her nearest neighbour, Mme d'Eu, who also became a mother at around the time of Eudore's birth, and had immediately handed over her child to a rural wet-nurse. Even in the sentimental novels of the time, as Fauchéry has pointed out, breast-feeding was a rarity; the roles of heroine and breast-feeding mother were, it was realized, difficult to combine.[43] This did not prevent Mme Roland, searching as ever for the heroine's role, from playing out her struggle to breast-feed Eudore as a drama of heroic proportions, with herself, rather than the baby, in the leading role. Rather than dismiss the whole matter, as had her frivolous neighbour Mme D'Eu, as a tiresome problem of early infancy, easily solved by entrusting the child to another woman, Mme Roland preferred to turn it into a drama of control which she presented as a moral epic, and described in minute detail in her letters to Roland. While the feeding was going well, initially, she was easily able to joke about Eudore's unrestrained appetite: 'Elle prend étonnement et elle en rend bien la moitié; j'ai conclu que la fable d'Ève n'était pas si bête, et que la gourmandise était véritablement un péché original'.[44]

But once the feeding had begun to go wrong, yet other aspects of the maternal role, and very coercive ones, began to appear. Forced to give the increasingly suffering Eudore over to a wet-nurse, Mme Roland suffered agonies which focused on the issue not of Eudore's welfare, but on that of her future emotional leverage over the child:

> ...je me suis chargée de l'enfant; a peine à-t-il été dans mes bras, qu'il s'est mis à crier en me fixant; il m'a semblé qu'il me cherchait après sa bonne; j'en ai conclu qu'il se déplaisait avec moi, et ce soupçon m'a désesperée.... Il ne faut pas se le dissimuler, elle aura l'enfant plus que moi dans ces premiers temps; surtout durant cette malheureuse convalescence où je suis privée de mes forces; elle aura aussi ses souris; et moi, qui aurai plus de douleurs, je ne serai pas dédommagée par ses premières caresses qui m'auraient fait tout oublier.... mon enfant ne connaîtra pas mon sein; il ne s'y jettera plus avec cet empressement si touchant tous les mères. Pourquoi n'ai-je plus de lait? Voilà ce que tant de gens ne sentent pas, quand ils convient me consoler entièrement en m'assurant que mon enfant vivra.[45]

The last sentence makes it clear how secondary, in Mme Roland's drama of heroic motherhood, was Eudore's welfare, compared to her obtaining power over the infant through the 'bonding' which breast-feeding was assumed to produce, an exercise of power which also extends to Mme Roland's social inferiors, such as the wet-nurse herself. If the breast-feeding were going well, Mme Roland would not be dependent on the services of servants. Mme Roland's attitude to breast-feeding, as an instrument of emotional domination, rather than a *means to* her baby's welfare, in fact comes very close to what Freud was later to describe in his theory of anal eroticism as the manipulation of body products for the control of others. Through the tissue of the body, products may emerge to dominate or cajole, gifts which are also weapons, artfully wrought communications than which nothing, after all, could be more 'natural': this was how breast-feeding had been vaunted by Rousseau, and countless other contemporary apologists for the practice.[46] Mme Roland's use of it in her relationship with her daughter might well lead us to ask, was this not the point in time at which, over a far wider span of conflict, the 'natural' became the coercive? So much was this so, that the definitely *non*-natural ethos of Stoicism, which constrains only the individual who practices it, begins to look positively libertarian by contrast.

We can see very fully how this could be worked out in Mme Roland's 'Avis à ma fille en âge et dans le cas de devenir mère', first published in 1799 but written shortly after Eudore's birth. Ostensibly a paean to the joy and glory of motherhood, it is in fact a minute description of the physical horrors of childbirth and its aftermath, with a full account of the whole breast-feeding epic. The 'enfant chéri qui m'a coûté tant de douleurs', reading such a message from its parent, would not have seen it as a proclamation that motherhood is worth such sufferings, but rather, felt guilt at the pain which its entry into the world had produced. Mme Roland details her post-partum experiences of mastitis, dysentery, dysuria, broken sleep, severe constipation, before even beginning on the struggle to regain her lost flow of milk.[47] Her comments on this make it even clearer that the struggle to breast-feed was a struggle not for Eudore's benefit, but for her own self-validation, and self-justification. The repeated personal pronoun in the following passage from the 'Avis' emphasizes the point:

> Quand même enfin *mes* efforts eussent dû être sans succès, un besoin de *me* rendre dans tous les temps le témoignage d'avoir tenté pour *mon* enfant tout se qui était dans les possibles, *m'*en faisait un devoir; et si la nature devait *me* refuser de nourrir, il fallait que le tort fut entièrement de son côté [*italics mine*].[48]

As the last phrase implies, the breast-feeding saga did function thereafter in her relations with Eudore as moral alibi. Having battled to feed the infant, it must remain forever attached to her, whatever her subsequent actions in relation to it. By suffering as a mother, in the body, Mme Roland purchased moral immunity and emotional power. Motherhood became an arena of control where 'l'oeil des mères doit surveiller tout ce qui les entoure'.[49]

Nothing, therefore, could have been more surprising, or more reprehensible on the part of the child – or so the mother felt – than the increasing difficulty of their relationship once early infancy had passed. After leaving her child for three months (March–May 1784) to lobby for a brevet of nobility for her husband, Mme Roland was amazed to find that her daughter rejected her on her return. Efforts to teach the child to read, or to enjoy classic authors, by the age of six were uphill work, enforced by an increasingly grim and distant Mme Roland as her moral due. By 1789, mentions of Eudore virtually cease in the correspondence, and when, in March 1789, Mme Roland

XIV The silhouettes by Mme Roland's friend, the Swiss physiognomist Lavater, clearly show the basic structures of her family: Eudore marginalized, husband and wife communicating around the printed word.

accompanied her husband to Paris when he led a municipal delegation from Lyons to the National Assembly, Eudore was not even allowed to share her parents' Paris flat, but was put out to board with the Froissard family, friends of the Protestant pastor and Assembly member, Rabaut Saint-Etienne. Mme Roland's attempts to act out the maternal role had clearly been acknowledged as a failure – but, of course, through Eudore's fault rather than her own.[50]

Her actions thereafter, however, during her husband Roland's two periods as Minister of the Interior in 1792–3, were hardly less ridden with frustration and conflict. We have now returned to our point of departure: the problems faced by Revolutionary political culture in its attitude to female participation. Mme Roland certainly did not escape the 'Catch-22' situation of women; respect could be bought only at the price of inaction, non-participation. To try to bridge this gap, Mme Roland offered her husband's associates a forum in which others, men, could speak, whilst herself remaining silent, and hence respected. Few more frustrating ways of becoming one of the best-known figures of the Revolution can be imagined:

> Je savais quel role convenait à mon sexe et je ne le quittai jamais. Les conférences se tenaient en ma présence sans que j'y prisse

aucun part; placée hors du cercle et près d'une table, je travaillais des mains, ou faisais les lettres, tandis qu'on déliberait...je ne perdit pas un mot de ce qui se débitait et il m'arrivait de me mordre les lèvres pour ne pas dire le mien....

Se taire quand on est seule n'est pas chose merveilleuse; mais garder constamment le silence au milieu des gens qui parlent des objets auxquels on s'intéresse, réprimer les saillies du sentiment qui vous opprime lors d'une contradiction, arrêter les idées intermédiaires qui échappent aux raisonneurs, et faute desquelles ils confluent mal ou ne sont pas entendus, mesurer ainsi la logique de chacun en se commandant toujours soi-même, est un grand moyen d'acquérir de la pénétration, de la rectitude, de perfectionner son intelligence et d'augmenter la force de son âme.

Mme Roland's continual emphasis in her *Mémoires* on her private, domestic, solitary life, even during Roland's two ministries, comes straight out of her efficient internalization of the idea that women can only have a public existence in as much as they wield corrupt power: '...on n'avait cherché à me voir que dans l'idée qu'il pouvait en être dans l'ancien régime, où l'on engageait les femmes à solliciter leurs maris'. When she was finally arrested and imprisoned in Sainte-Pélagie, she found with a degree of shock explicable only on these lines, that the authorities had taken little care to segregate her from the ladies of easy virtue (revealing phrase) also held within its walls: 'Voilà donc le séjour qui était réservé à la digne épouse d'un homme de bien. Si c'est la prix de la vertu sur la terre, qu'on ne s'étonne donc plus de mon mépris pour la vie'.[51]

In entering prison, however, Mme Roland was able for the first time, apart from these brief encounters with other prisoners, to escape the world of contradiction and confusion. For the first time her physical being and her sanctioned role-playing could come together in ways which formed an uncontroverted whole. Thus, it is not surprising that her immediate reaction on entry into her cell was not the abject lethargy or glazed shock of many male prisoners, such as Riouffe, but was devoted to an easy, almost cheerful adaptation of physical regime to her present circumstances:

Je n'aime point à en faire une grande [dépense] pour ma personne, et j'ai quelque plaisir à exercer mes forces dans les privations. L'envie m'a pris de faire une expérience et de voir jusqu' où la volonté humaine peut réduire les besoins; mais il faut procéder par gradations, c'est la seule manière d'aller loin. J'ai commencé, au bout de quatre jours, par retrancher les déjeuners, et substituer au café, au chocolat, du pain et de l'eau.... Si je reste ici six mois, je veux en sortir grasse et fraîche, n'ayant plus besoin que de soupe et de pain, et ayant mérité quelques bénédictions incognito.[52]

In fact, what she was doing was putting away the difficult female body for the Stoic body which she had had to abandon at marriage, a body deliberately chosen, invaded by no extraneous desires or appetites, and not subject to the uses of others. Later on in the *Mémoires*, she was to make this point explicitly, again in relation to the physical regime she chose to adopt in prison, and makes an equivalence between her moral and physical regimes:

> La fermeté ne consiste pas seulement à s'élever au-dessus des circonstances par l'effort de sa volonté, mais à s'y maintenir par un régime et des soins convenables. La sagesse se compose de tous les actes utiles à sa conservation et à son exercice. Lorsque des événements fâcheux ou irritants viennent me surprendre, je ne me borne pas à me rappeler les maximes de la philosophie pour soutenir mon courage; je ménage à mon esprit des distractions agréables, et je néglige point les précepts de l'hygiène pour me conserver dans un juste équilibre.[53]

But if Mme Roland's first reaction to prison was to begin the Stoic role-playing, through body-management, already so familiar to us, she was also more explicitly aware than many of those we have so far encountered, of the function of the whole prison experience as a retreat, almost as escapist as the powerlessness induced by illness. Comparing imprisonment with illness, she remarks:

> Du moment où je me mets au lit, il me semble que tout devoir cesse, et qu'aucune sollicitude n'a de prise sur moi; je ne suis plus tenue qu'à être là et à y demeurer avec résignation, ce que je fais de fort bonne grâce. Je donne carrière à mon imagination; j'appelle les impressions douces, les souvenirs agréables, les sentiments heureux: plus d'efforts, plus de calculs, plus de raison; toute à la nature, et paisible comme elle, je souffre sans impatience, ou me repose ou m'égaye. Je trouve que la prison produit sur moi à peu près le même effet que la maladie: je ne suis tenue aussi qu'à être là, et qu'est ce que cela me coûte?[54]

It is also important to remember that a very large part of Mme Roland's time in prison was devoted to the production of verbal images of her physical history and reactions, such as the one immediately above, and indeed, the majority of the passages cited in this chapter. The entire two volumes of her *Mémoires*, over 500 printed pages, were written between June and November 1793. Prison in fact became a central ground for the reconstitution, through the written word, of a physical history divorced from the role of motherhood which dominates to the virtual exclusion of all else in the two other major works written before her imprisonment: the correspondence, and of course in the 'Avis'. Prison was the place where Mme Roland felt able for the first time to write for herself and to reconstitute her physical history, not as it concerned other living beings, Eudore and Roland, but as it had concerned herself. In the *Mémoires* she could write of episodes which she had never revealed to Roland, such as that with her father's apprentice. As she wrote from prison to her friend the geographer Edmé Mentelle, 'Je dirai tout, absolument tout'.[55] Imprisonment also enabled her to write not only the autobiography she could never otherwise have produced, but also to write the letters she could not otherwise have countenanced in her role as the chaste 'digne épouse d'un homme de bien'. It enabled her, with complete self-approbation, to continue the passionate relations with Buzot which she had renounced in their physical reality. Through imprisonment, the ultimate reconciliation could be performed, as 'virtue' was preserved, yet passion satisfied. Both the *Mémoires* and the letters such as those to Buzot, written in prison, are fine examples of Lacan's famous 'mirror-stage', in which literary creations reflect back to their author an image of idealized self-unity.[56]

We have already seen in a previous chapter that the pinnacle of the self-unity which was Stoicism was the act of heroic suicide. It thus seems quite logical that Mme Roland should seriously, during October 1793, have contemplated committing such an act during her imprisonment.[57] Deciding to starve herself to death, by 14 October her condition was serious enough for her to be moved to the infirmary at Sainte-Pélagie. She was, however, dissuaded by another friend, the naturalist Louis-Guillaume Bosc, from persisting in her plan. Viewing her death as inevitable, he persuaded her that it was her duty to go through with the actual execution as an example to the rest of the nation of political rectitude. In any case, death was certain whichever option was chosen. And in either case, a role, and an uncontroverted one at that, could be made out of it.

Our focus here should not be on the fact that Mme Roland chose execution rather than suicide, but that she proceeded along the path to suicide, and then was persuaded to reject it. The rejection of suicide itself was nothing unusual for a woman, as we have seen in a previous chapter; but it was Mme Roland's approach to suicide, and her achievement of execution instead, which points up her capacity to use more than one register of a heroic role, and to amalgamate in herself the totality of those potential roles, just as she could amalgamate within herself both chastity and unchastity. In reconciling the disparate elements of her physical self-consciousness, Mme Roland succeeded in becoming a heroine at last. It is this capacity which gave her, precisely through her confusions and conflicts, her capacity in the nineteenth century and since, to attact a mythology and historical attention out of all proportion to her actual influence on events.

Such figures must either emerge from an extreme of simplicity, as in the case of Charlotte Corday, or an extreme of confusion between warring elements of self-image, as in the case of Mme Roland.

It is valuable to study Mme Roland's career for what it tells us about the use of fictions and role-playing in the Revolution. We make the point, that it seems useless to proceed on the assumption of two separate repertoires of roles for men and for women. The arguments recently put forward by some literary critics that the eighteenth-century novel, with its concentration on feminine fates, and its avid readership of both sexes, somehow 'feminized' the public cultural zone, is obviously too extreme. But it is true that after Rousseau and Richardson, as never before, for both sexes fiction offered a way into the adoption of a political role. Many were those men, such as the Comte de Vaublanc with his *Télémaque* tucked into his coat pocket, who read themselves into their roles, as surely as Mme Roland read herself into hers, with a mixture of classical Stoic texts, *Clarissa*, *La Princesse de Clèves* and the *Nouvelle Héloïse*. Nor do the similarities stop there. Just as death, firmness under physical trial, and the preservation of physical intactness, validated the Stoic role-player, so did they the female heroine. As Nancy K. Miller has remarked, 'Clarissa must, like Julie, die to be restored to the self of her exemplarity'.[58] And, unlike the heroes of the classical world or medieval romance, whose heroic status is not solely constituted by their deaths, but by their deeds while living, death was practically the only guarantee for the men and women of the French Revolution of heroic status. Death, by 1789, had become part of the cultural 'plot', in Margaret Mead's sense,[59] of French culture, and one of extreme importance because it was one of the few elements which could reconcile all the confused and worrying aspects which that culture presented.

It is, however, perfectly possible to argue that it was made much more difficult for women to *achieve* personification than it was for men, in so far as that personification was based on the successful display of physicality. It was certainly the case that physicality operated as a reservoir of authority for men, but of potential humiliation and certain restriction for women. The roles allotted to women in virtue of their physical attributes were, moreover, different from male roles and incompatible with many aspects of the Stoic persona. As mothers and wives, women played roles which involved them in orienting both the shape of their lives and the use of their bodies outwards, on to the needs and demands of others, rather than inwards, on to the self. Marriage and motherhood also involved them in roles which were defined by physical processes, rather than the resolutely fixed heroic image of Stoic calm. Women thus faced great difficulties in becoming the heroines of their own real, lived, lives.

The way out of these problems was through identification with the heroines of fiction, heroines of novels which had greater currency, and more power and vigour, than in any preceding century. Certain novels enabled both women and men, but especially women, to verbalize their own desired identity. These novels became virtually part of their physical being, in the same way as food eaten. Mme Roland, for example, repeatedly speaks of 'devouring' the *Nouvelle Héloïse*.[60] The cultural practice of such an intense identification with heroines of novels must surely be seen as an important contributory factor in the central feature of Revolutionary political discourse, which is the personification of representative virtue. The breakdown of distinctions between the self and the characters of the novel rapidly turns into the converse process of turning the real self into a heroic fiction. There was not much distance between 'devouring' Julie and dying as Cato.

Mme Roland's enduring appeal for the historians and myth-makers comes not from her importance as a political actor, which was virtually nil, but precisely from her ability, throughout her life, to maximize the number of roles she played, demonstrating the fluidity of the boundary between men's and women's cultures which feminist historians try so hard to separate. In order to create that identity Mme Roland produced a body which existed as much as a verbal creation as a lived physical experience. If cultural expectations in the late eighteenth century pressed heavily on the physical self-perceptions of individuals, those individuals could still re-shape their physical self-consciousness by verbal means. Physicality was always mediated, for individuals, by words. Accordingly, such descriptions could take place on many levels, with many restraining conventions.

When Mme Roland declared that she wished to 'say everything' in her *Mémoires*, she was not simply stating a desire to achieve a frankness comparable to that of the Rousseau of the *Confessions*. She was also opening up her account of herself to invasion by many different and conflicting conventions of what a woman's physicality might symbolize in the public and private worlds. Such were the conflicts between those conventions, and hence between her images of herself, that they may well have rendered her, as the royalist journalist Mallet du Pin was so devastatingly to charge, 'incapable d'écrire avec fidelité'. She could not write in a trustworthy way because there was no means by which she could have achieved an undivided vision of herself, and hence of her surroundings. The self-confidence necessary to such a task was lost in her perpetual conflicts between chastity and desire, intellect and body, conflicts which were just as strong in her domestic life as they were in her relations with the political world which she briefly entered in 1792.

Above all, Mme Roland was undermined by the Revolution's strong wish to remove, with women, 'l'intrusion du désir dans la vie intellectuelle ou politique', as Aline Rousselle has termed it.[61] The Revolution found both its energy and its fragility in this urge to create polarity, to define by exclusion. In the struggle between Cato and Circe, the former won, with results that affect our politics, and our domestic lives, today.

# 9

# THE FRENCH REVOLUTION, MODERNITY AND THE BODY POLITIC

Non, nous ne pouvons pas renier notre guerre.

Pierre Drieu la Rochelle[1]

Throughout this book, we have been tracing three closely interwoven themes: the history of the body, the history of the modern state, and the history of the political culture of the middle class. In order to focus this complex enquiry, we have examined the point in European history, the French Revolution, where these three stories are the most closely mingled. The Revolution has also been identified by many historians as a decisive time for the seizure of power in state and civil society by the middle class. In this book, I have been explicitly arguing for a rejection of the Marxist identification of the Revolution as a time when the mode of production represented by feudalism was replaced by capitalism, the mode of production represented by the bourgeoisie. This does not mean, however, that we can deny that the French Revolution saw the first emergence, in a major Western European state, of the middle class as firmly dominant in a new republic.

But what do we mean by this 'middle class'? Not only have we rejected any economic definition of it, but historians have become fond of reminding us of the complexity of the definition of social-status labels in the eighteenth century. On this problem, I have implicitly relied throughout this book upon the definition of class produced by the French sociologist Pierre Bourdieu, in his book *Distinction*, where he uses the word 'class' not as a *group* label, but as a *location* label.[2] Class for Bourdieu is located by the multiplicity of its practices, in their interrelationship rather than their specificity. Class, for Bourdieu, is not definable in terms of any single variable, whether it be economic or juridical. It is, rather, an approach which treats the attempt to 'define' 'the middle class' as an essentially ahistorical question and focuses instead on the question of 'how is the middle class *being constituted* at any particular time?'. That process of constitution necessarily includes an account of the subjectivity and self-definition of those involved. This is the approach to the history of the political culture of the social strata that were neither aristocratic nor engaged in manual labour, agriculture or petty trade which has been adopted in these pages.

I also, in these pages, link up the constitution of the political culture of the French middle class in the years following 1789, with more generalized crises in the nature of the modern state, of modern subjectivity, and the history of the body in western political culture as a whole. This linking is possible because the constitution of the French middle class and its political culture rapidly took on a representative status for other European middle classes in their struggles for power. If by the end of the nineteenth century, in both state and civil society, the position of the middle class was immeasurably stronger than it had been in 1789, this was in large part due to the effect and generalization of the French example. Marx perceived that this was the case, that the French middle-class experience of the forging of a political culture had become a universal middle-class experience, when he made his famous comment on the bourgeois revolutions of the nineteenth century, each of them, he said, re-enacting as farce the original tragedy of 1789.

However, although the French Revolution may have been the point in time at which the middle class began to be constituted, it is as well to remember how profoundly conservative an event that Revolution actually was. While changing the form of government, challenging the political culture of the old regime and destroying many of its actual representatives, it thrust the bourgeoisie into power in a way which did not entail the inclusion in the political nation, except very briefly, of elements in society – the workers, peasants and women – which had been excluded under the old regime. As we have seen, while using a universalistic political discourse, it excluded workers and peasants from formal political participation on the basis of criteria (poverty, illiteracy) which made a mockery of a 'natural right' of all 'citizens' to *act* politically. Even more interestingly, the middle-class revolution in France developed an ideology whereby women were excluded by virtue of characteristics ascribed to them which defined them as different from men and *hence* defined their political unacceptability.

The political culture of the middle class in the French Revolution was constituted by the construction of images of masculinity and femininity which served to exclude all women and validate some men. As the nineteenth century progressed, scientific 'facts' would increasingly be pressed into the service of maintaining the perceived differences between masculinity and femininity, until, and to such an extent that, the historically specific origins of such stereotyping were forgotten and feminists had to struggle to convince an unwilling public, just as they do in the twentieth century, that such differences were not somehow 'natural'. Nor are these exclusionary ideas of femininity simply a gendered way of reading off what the middle class thought of the working class. Both middle- and working-class culture had, and have, difficulty in accepting women as equal public actors. And while the emergence of a predominantly middle-class state and society had not prevented the emergence in much of Europe by 1914 of specifically working-class political movements, the story was quite other, until very recently, in the case of women. In other words, the conflict between 'labour' and 'capital', 'masters' and 'men', may, *pace* Marxist theory, have been superficial by comparison with the determination of *all* political groups to leave unchallenged the basically patriarchal character of society.

We are thus led back to the essential paradox that the French Revolutionary middle class probably actually produced an intensification of the pre-existing patriarchal political culture which they alleged they were attempting to replace. As the French Revolution *did* become the universal representative experience of rising and revolutionary middle classes, it is not surprising that successive revolutions followed the French pattern in this as in much else. The Russian Revolution of October 1917, for example, rapidly drew back from its initial support for women's rights, in spite of the contribution of women activists to its success. The same process has been observed in colonial revolutions, such as that in Algeria, where the contribution of women to the revolution has been denigrated and women's position in society actually worsened relative to the pre-revolutionary situation. Nor is this surprising: in a situation of patriarchy, the oppressive regime is seen by those who challenge it as a threat to their authentic wholeness, their masculinity, in the same way that parents threaten children; hence the importance of constructing perceptions of the old ruling power as 'bad parents'. In these 'family stories', the weakness of the king (who should be, but is not, a strong father) and the wickedness of the queen (who should be, but is not, a virtuous, submissive spouse) are often alleged as justification for the overthrow of their authority. As Ronald Paulson has remarked, it was in this way that Louis XVI and Marie-Antoinette were portrayed by both pre- and post-Revolutionary propagandists, as were the contemporary king and queen of Spain, and the contemporary king and queen of Naples, all of whom suffered middle-class revolutions against their power in this period.[3] Such regimes were characterized by dominance which women, through their sexuality, enjoyed over the kings, and hence over the conduct of government. It was by reference to this illegitimate use of femininity that the revolutionaries justified their sacrilegious uprising against God's Anointed; and it was in virtue of this too that the nineteenth century proceeded to construct a political culture, justifying the exclusion of women, and the feminine principle, from public life.

The Revolution in France can thus be seen as a contestation between male and female, in which the result of the middle-class revolutionary creation of political culture was to validate the political participation of men and culpabilize that of women, in both cases by the creation of images of heroic masculinity, often drawn, as we have seen, from the Stoic movement in classical antiquity. This was insisted upon at all levels of Revolutionary political culture, from the struggles over the implementation of sovereignty to the creation of images of heroic revolutionary dignity for men, to the very dress fashions of the Revolutionary period. Such fashions radically simplified the clothes and styles worn under the old regime, replacing its high-built artificial hair-styles with simply swept-back or closely cropped heads; replacing the wide paniers by narrow skirts and close-fitting jackets. Eighteenth-century clothes were designed for artifice, display and disguise; Revolutionary styles for authenticity, simplicity, and transparency to the gaze of others. No longer seducing the eye of the beholder with artifice, they emphasized the actual gender of the wearer. Dress practices, like the use of make-up, jewellery, artificial hair and facial patches, which had been common to both sexes before 1789, began to be rigidly differentiated by gender and their use confined to women. The new 'minimalist' clothes of the Revolution, and the forbidding to men of disguise, display and artifice in dress and body adornment, meant that Revolutionary fashions echoed the new political culture's emphasis on sharpening differentiation between the sexes and insisting that members of each sex appear for what they 'really' were. At the same time, it is interesting to note, *class* lines in dress were often deliberately blurred, as ardent male middle-class revolutionaries donned the trousers identified with the working man and escaped the knee-breeches associated with the aristocracy. The clothes expressed the profound truth that while the line between middle-class men and working-class men might, on strategic occasions, be blurred, that between men and women had at all costs to be made visible.

How is it, then, that this political culture, so vital for the formation of the middle class, and so preoccupied with the body as the location for the construction of the ground-plan of that culture, should have produced in the still-bourgeois twentieth century, the trivialized body described in the opening pages of this book? Part of the answer to this question is to be found in the inherent weaknesses of Revolutionary political culture itself. Partly it is that the public importance of the body became lost to visibility because it was lost to history itself. During the early nineteenth century, histories of the French Revolution, while not formulating an explicit 'history of the body', at least kept before their massive readership the possibility of a link between the history of the Revolution and the history of the body, by retelling in a compulsive and detailed way the episodes of physical trauma with which that history was interspersed. As professionalized historical scholarship came to the fore by the close of the century, the body was no longer a legitimate object of historical writing. Trying to legitimize itself by reference to alleged scientific norms of 'objectivity', the new history rejected the older 'traumatic' version of the Revolution, and along with it the compulsive retelling of violent episodes involving the bodies of Revolutionary participants, episodes where emotionality and subjectivity were clearly seen to cluster. A whole genre of historical writing emerged, concerned with the 'deconstruction' or expulsion from the range of 'real history' of these stories which were identified as 'counter-revolutionary' or Thermidorean; so successful in their project were the founders of the 'professional' history that it is only very recently that historians such as Linda Orr have been able to call for a 're-traumatization' of the Revolution.[4] Major revisionist versions of the Revolution, such as that by François Furet, have still been able to produce an account where the body is absent, where therefore the interpretation is gender-blind, and where the record of discourse is separated from that of behaviour, embodiment and subjectivity. Furet's attack on Marxism as an overdetermining force in Revolutionary historiography was not accompanied by any equally fierce critique of the other implicit agendas for historical enquiry into the Revolution introduced by the Marxist 'professionalized' historians.

Evacuated from the history of the great paradigmatic experience in the formation of bourgeois culture, it is not surprising that the history of the body has until very recently only been applied to those groups also excluded from the 'universal' bourgeois experience. Histories of the body are very largely connected with 'women's history', or 'histories of sexuality'. In spite of the widespread respect accorded to the works of Elias and Foucault, writers who do try to address the crucial problem of the relationship between state formation and individual bodies, their work has not become an integral part of the history of political culture. All this only shows, paradoxically, what Foucault himself has confirmed in the opening volume of his history of sexuality, about the 'compulsive' yet hidden, and till recently marginalized discourse on the body-as-sexuality, which was created in the nineteenth century.[5] Such a discourse has operated very effectively to contribute to the marginalization and de-legitimization of body history, and has been highly effective in blotting out very ancient ideas of the intimate link between private physical bodies and public politics. In accepting this agenda, historians have colluded with the impoverishment of our public world, and of our private consciousness of ourselves.

Why did this happen? Why has the middle class been so concerned to obscure its links with its origins, which lie in an intense debate on the public body? The answer to this is partly to be found in the idea that the public body on which the middle class founded its political legitimation during the Revolution was that of *homo clausus*, the male type validated by his separation of affect from instinct, by body-control leading to an increasingly painful yet necessary sense of separation from other individual human beings. *Homo clausus* legitimated himself by his superiority to the somatic relationships enjoyed by other classes – aristocracy, peasants and workers – and by the other gender. In other words, what he possessed was a body which was also a *non*-body, which, rather than projecting itself, *retained* itself. In doing so, it became the location of abstract value-systems, such as rationality and objectivity. As Pierre Bourdieu has remarked, such a move is integral to the production of middle-class systems of cultural hegemony, which privilege over-arching *languages*, such as the language of objectivity and rationality, rather than privileging energy or displays of integration between body and personality: display is characterized as aristocratic, emotionality and subjectivity as feminine, physical energy as plebeian. The new world of the middle class in the nineteenth and twentieth centuries gained authority from distance, refusal to engage, or to be self-revelatory, and it is no coincidence that areas of knowledge whose value-systems collude with these norms, as do those of the sciences, should have emerged as privileged at exactly the same time as the middle class emerged as culturally hegemonic; or that by the mid-century the state bureaucracy itself should be the carrier of these same values.

In the French Revolution, the newly dominant middle class acted out and made publicly visible the bodily behaviours and projected the images on which these claims to hegemony were based. *Homo clausus* embodied the new world of distance, division and restraint which were the prerequisites for the legitimization of rationality and objectivity. But there was a price to pay here and it is one which we are still paying. In basing their claims to hegemony on a non-body, the body of *homo clausus*, the middle class admittedly found it easy to remove the body itself completely from public consciousness by the time, the late nineteenth century, that the *values* carried by that body had achieved domination of public space. But in doing so they also deprived the physical body of many other significances as well. It is this process which led to the ultimate trivialization of the body and its separation from public space in our own time, earlier remarked on: and so it is as well to examine this process in some detail.

Firstly, the Revolution destroyed the historical French monarchy and substituted for the power of the monarch the power of the 'sovereign' people, as expressed in the general will. Each individual made manifest in his body the sovereignty which had been reserved before for the body of the king alone. The Revolution invested with public significance pre-existing ideologies produced in the eighteenth century, which validated ideals of personal autonomy, and re-emphasized their values in specifically revolutionary forms of public political behaviour, such as heroic suicide. These new public bodies provided the only images which could effectively bring together individual and general will, since the general will cannot be represented and Rousseau's social contract is an unusable concept without its representation in a public body. So, even before 1789, the 'body politic', far from becoming an increasingly depersonalized image, in fact stood at the heart of the problem and presentation of theory connected with the representation of political society to itself. In doing so, it also produced, not a stable state, but rather a highly sensitized public realm in which different 'practices' could lock across each other, forming as they did so both the identity of the middle class and the range of alternative political expressions.

None the less, this was a curious public space. It included women only as a source of imagery for male political debate. And even as it established the male body as a site of resistance, and the site of the creation of new public spaces and audiences, it also relieved that body of half its power. It denied an acceptable, forceful public body to women. It also evacuated religious meaning from the body. This desacralization occurred at a time when the new Revolutionary order was intent on dispossessing the Catholic Church of its pre-eminent position in the state, confiscating its property, abolishing its teaching and welfare functions, and turning it into an organ of state, by the Civil Constitution of the Clergy of 1790. Wings of the Revolutionary middle class also promoted a strong campaign to discourage Christian allegiance as such in 1794, and throughout the Revolution, middle-class groups in power tried to create and enforce substitute religions of humanity, like that of the Supreme Being envisaged by Robespierre.

By 1792, the Revolution had succeeded in uprooting the monarchy and with it the whole validation of political power through a sacral body. The public body produced by the Revolution had little to do with the sacralized bodies on which the Church had insisted for so many centuries, on the model of the eternal, suffering and redemptive body of Christ. Throughout the nineteenth century and into our own day, the desacralized bodies of the modern public world and the sacralized body still insisted upon by the Catholic Church, have remained in conflict; what is different in the twentieth century, however, is a gradual victory for the desacralized body, as the Church itself more and more focuses its pronouncements on the body purely on sexual and reproductive issues. Public dignity, physical suffering and bodily death receive relatively little attention, and in this the Church has in fact adopted the implicit agenda of the secularized society of the twentieth century, which also defines bodies largely in terms of their sexuality and ignores the question of their capacity to fill and create public space.

What the public bodies constructed by the Revolution did, in other words, was to hurl individuals, in the sense of their public bodies, out of the world of 'being', in Heideggerian terms, out of the world of the eternal public bodies of monarch and Christ, into the world of time, where public bodies had to be continually remade as they are today. In this sense, Tocqueville was wrong to say that the French Revolution was a revolution against the state, not a revolution against religion. The two cannot be separated, in the sense that the public images and public space created by the Revolution cannot be understood except in terms of a change-over from a public world constituted as conterminous with sacral bodies, and one conceived as a scene of conflicts over the achievement of heroic bodies which had to be recreated anew by each individual. The regicide – and regicide was a sacrilegious act – of King Louis XVI, and the abolition of the aristocracy by a middle class that had never been awarded the status of possessing bodies which were truly public, was of enormous significance. The members of the new political class after the Revolution do not have sacralized bodies and do not seriously try to create them – in fact, in many instances, as we have seen, go out of their way to *desacralize* their public/physical persona. The figure of heroic dignity, who is an intensification of Elias's *homo clauses*, is the nearest they come to producing a sacralized body, and that is not very close. That is the basic reason for the fragility of the poses of heroic dignity: unlike fully sacralized bodies which exist *above* time, desacralized ones exist *in* time. They can only really find validation through death – not through re-creation.

It is thus not surprising that those who belonged to the Revolutionary middle class should have struggled hard to maintain control over the manner of their death. They committed suicide to avoid public execution, in large numbers, while, conversely, the forces of state power struggled to show, by guillotining even the bodies of the already dead or dying, such as Robespierre and his follower Lebrun in 1794, that the final arbitration of death was still its own. Such a struggle only makes sense when both the state and the condemned believe that death brings existence to an absolute end. To control the actual act of execution is to control the total significance of death, which both in the prison suicides and the public guillotinings was wholly devoid of the religious trappings which had played a large part in public execution in previous centuries. Death truly was the end, and this also makes the public executions of the French Revolution very different from those of earlier 'repressive' organizations of terror, such as the Inquisition. There, the victim's death was seen as a liberation into spiritual truth beyond death. The Revolution, on the other hand, executed for acts or thoughts manifesting a disloyalty perceived as ineradicable. Death simply ended the physical existence of one more carrier of disloyalty, nothing more.

In fact, the Revolution's public manifestation of a desacralized death has far more in common with the attitudes of our own day. The apathy which accompanies the mass mechanization of death is visible for the first time in the demeanour of the guillotine victims, and with it, the terrible ambiguities involved in the adoption of models of Stoic calm in keeping with the image of *homo clausus*. The apathetic demeanour of the guillotine victims tells us first that such poses were conspiring to maintain the pretence, in spite of the overwhelming presence of death, that death was not somehow real or imminent. This demeanour hid death, rather than reacted to it, or challenged it. In the same way, in modern societies, we pretend to have overcome the fear of death when in fact we have only made it invisible. In doing so, we use 'management' of such a life-event to mediate between our knowledge of what must be so, and what it is to make visible. In doing so, we deprive the dying of authority, just as all other 'managed' life-events, such as birth and sex, are also deprived. As Walter Benjamin pointed out:

> ...in the course of the nineteenth century bourgeois society has, by means of hygienic and social, private and public institutions, realized a secondary effect which may have been its subconscious main purpose: to make it possible for people to avoid the sight of the dying. Dying was once a public process in the life of the individual and a most exemplary one: think of the medieval pictures in which the death-bed has turned into a throne toward which the people press through the wide-open doors of the death-house.... Today, people live in rooms that have never been touched by death, dry dwellers of eternity, and when their end approaches they are stowed away in sanatoria or hospitals by their heirs. It is however characteristic that not only man's knowledge or wisdom, but above all his real life – and this is the stuff that stories are made of – first assumes transmissable form at the moment of his death....suddenly, in his expressions and looks

the unforgettable emerges and imparts to everything that concerned him that authority which even the poorest wretch in dying possesses for the living around him.[6]

All this may appear to dwell at too great length on the darker side of Revolutionary body-culture. Was it not, many will object, also the era of the creation of images of active heroism, of military dynamism and popular energies? For a short time, this was indeed true. But it must also be pointed out how quickly the images, and indeed the reality, of popular energies, the 'people's revolution' which had manifested itself in the storming of the Bastille in July 1789, or the overthrow of the monarchy on 10 August 1792, were to be quashed in the futile risings of Germinal and Prairial 1795. The major image of the people's strength, the 'Hercules' statues and prints, became weakened very early on in the Revolution, and was rapidly replaced by representations of the Republic as the classical female figure usually known as 'Marianne'. As to the figures of heroic military glory which the Revolution produced, they too were ultimately ambiguous. While seeming to validate the energies of the Revolution, and the conquests of the Revolutionary state, their appeal was also short-lived. Stendhal's novel *Le Rouge et le noir* is in some sections a prolonged lament for the disappearance of such images which the collapse of the French Empire in 1814 had brought with it. Nor were such images radically different in kind from those which surrounded the more melancholy themes of death and imprisonment. Like them, they presupposed that validation occurred through death; like them, they were reserved exclusively for males, and their very existence, if canonizing the heroic energies of the (male) political nation, could be viewed only as a symbol of their exclusion by the female element of the population. The positive and active features of the Revolution's body-culture tend to be so only from a male perspective.

In many ways, in fact, the Revolution gave promises to the future which it was unable to fulfill. While appealing to universalistic freedoms, the Revolution in fact set up a state which excluded the majority of the population from political creativity. Liberty, equality and fraternity, while brandished around throughout the nineteenth century, in fact translated out very badly as an actual political culture. The Revolution also established the body as the site of struggle and the site of political creativity. At the same time, the way that the new political class in France created that body culture partook of trends which deprived the body of much of its significance, and privileged a notion of political authority which only gave models for dignified or heroic death, not for resistance or political innovation.

Thus, although the French Revolution was different from twentieth-century revolutions in that it did not use state, routine, torture on any wide scale, nor intern its enemies on a permanent basis in any institutions which can be seen as forerunners of concentration camps, neither did it place obstacles in the way of their appearance. The whole tendency of its political culture was to collude with state terror rather than to resist it. This was important because of the very success of the Revolution in constructing the body as a site of political creativity and visibility. The body was crucial to the redefinition of sovereignty in the state, and the definition of middle-class political culture itself. But that very same body, because it was based on *homo clausus*, rather than the carnivalesque body described by Bakhtin, also weakened models for change. It thus opened the way for the emergence of modern totalitarian states led by charismatic figures who were able to focus the unspoken desires of individuals, inexpressible because of the culture's validation of *homo clausus*, upon their own public performances. This was a pre-condition for the establishment of the totalitarian regimes of the 1930s, based as they were on the mass mobilization of bodies who submerged their autonomy in the will of the leader.

In the later twentieth century, the Revolution has started to matter in a different, although connected way. The Revolution and the Enlightenment which preceded it had, as we have seen, produced a cacophony of competing prescriptions through which individuals might attain real selfhood. Many of these prescriptions linked the attainment of selfhood to the erection of prescriptive models of society or state. After the Revolution, selfhood and political structures progressively cut loose from one another. This has led to a deep slippage between morality and legality, where the absence of an idea of community renders many issues of public policy irresolvable except through force. In the twentieth century, the nature of the relations between individuals and the state is emerging as probably the dominant and certainly the most morally crucial area of politics, especially in the increasing number of states which use physical coercion of individual bodies deprived of public resonance to delegitimize dissent and stabilize their regimes. For all the emphasis in the West on models of radical personal autonomy, very little is provided for individuals to *do* with that autonomy. As the body is the only irreducibly personal space solely 'owned' and completely experienced by any individual, what happens to it is a measure of the nature of public society. In the twentieth-century West, seen solely as a collection of desires or a production of outputs, the body either becomes frivolous or is reduced to an economic definition.

The Revolution constructed a political culture which seemed, though through different forms of expression, to be as profoundly concerned as had been the eighteenth century with radical personal autonomy. Yet that culture was also constructed on the basis of the exclusion, except as rhetorical resource, of social elements rigidly designated as 'other', most notably women, and lower social classes. The ultimate symbol of its political culture, the body, could not operate as a unifying device, as had the sacral bodies which it replaced. Not only did it have to be re-created anew, perpetually, by every public individual: it had also been constructed on the basis of the exclusion of other parts of the potential body politic. Such a situation led directly to the extreme paranoia of nineteenth- and twentieth-century politics, in which individuals seek to lose their consciousness of the frailty of their own public personification either in the charismatic self-presentation of political leaders, or in the compulsive representation of social groups such as women, Jews, homosexuals or the poor, as that which is so alien that it must be either mastered or exterminated before 'normal' individuals can exercise what remains of their autonomy in security. It is in this sense that Max Horkheimer's and Theodor Adorno's idea that Enlightenment is peculiarly prone to turn into its opposite, is correct.[7]

The history of Revolutionary bodies is the history of a self-image of rationality, reflexivity, universalism, autonomy, individuation and emancipation always containing the potential for transposition into its direct opposite: in other words, it is the history of the mounting sense of paradox and impasse with which the post-modern twentieth century confronts its problems. This is the real reason why we need to 're-traumatize' the history of the Revolution: in the history of its bodies, desacralized, public, dignified, suicidal, the object of massacre and dismemberment, was inscribed the future histories of the nineteenth and twentieth centuries. Rethinking that history and revitalizing that body, into an instrument of personal authority, may be one of the few options left open to us to produce a creative public world. Above all, the history of the body in the creation of Revolutionary political culture supports the conclusion for the future, that only when the link between physical constitution and public authority is broken will we have real political change, for it is only then that a non-masculinist public world can be established. Any other way of absorbing the legacy of the Revolution simply runs the risk of repeating, as tragedy, its more tragic themes.

# NOTES

Sources are cited in full in the first instance, and thereafter by author's surname and short title only; when a source previously cited recurs in a subsequent chapter, a cross-reference (e.g., [ch. 2, n. 5]) is given to the first full citation. For works in English where more than one place of publication is given, references are to the London or U.K. edition unless otherwise indicated.

## CHAPTER 1

[1] Tom Paine, *The Rights of Man* (New York, 1973), 320; first published 1791.

## CHAPTER 2

[1] Jean de La Salle, *Traité de la civilité* (Paris, 1774), 23.

[2] Roland Barthes, *Mythologies* (Paris, 1957), sel. and tr. Annette Lavers as *Mythologies* (London, 1972), 129.

[3] Esp. Michel Foucault: *Surveiller et punir* (Paris, 1975), tr. Alan Sheridan as *Discipline and Punish* (New York and London, 1977); *La Volonté de savoir* (Paris, 1976), vol. I of a projected 6-vol. *Histoire de la sexualité*, tr. Robert Hurley as *The History of Sexuality* (New York, 1978; London, 1979). See also Jean Blot, 'Michel Foucault: *Surveiller et punir*', *Nouvelle Revue Française* 276 (1975), 89–92; François Ewald, 'Anatomie et corps politiques', *Critique* 343 (1975), 1228–65.

[4] Norbert Elias: *State Formation and Civility* [U.S. title *Power and Civility*]: *The Civilizing Process*, tr. Edmund Jephcott (Oxford, 1982; New York, 1986) from *Über den Prozess der Zivilisation*, 2 vols. (Basle, 1939), vol. II; *The Court Society*, tr. E. Jephcott (Oxford, 1983) from *Die Höfische Gesellschaft* (Darmstadt and Neuwied, 1969, 1975); The Civilizing Process: *The History of Manners*, tr. E. Jephcott (New York, 1978; Oxford, 1983) from *Über den Prozess der Zivilisation*, vol. I.

[5] E.g., Edward Shorter, *A History of Women's Bodies* (London and New York, 1982); Linda Gordon, *Women's Body, Women's Rights: Birth Control in America* (New York, 1976); C. Smith-Rosenberg, 'Puberty to Menopause: the Cycle of Femininity in Nineteenth-Century America', in M.S. Hartman and Lois Banner, eds., *Clio's Consciousness Raised* (New York, 1974), 25–7; Jean-Pierre Peter, 'Entre femmes et médicins: violence et singularités dans le discours du corps et sur le corps d'après les manuscrits médicaux de la fin du XVIII$^e$ siècle', *Ethnologie française* 6 (1976), 341–8; Natalie Zemon Davis, 'La storia delle donne in trasizione: il caso europeo', *Donna-woman-femme* 3 (1977), 7–33.

[6] E.g., Aline Rousselle, *Porneia: De la maîtrise du corps à la privation sensorielle: II$^e$–IV$^e$ siècles de l'ère chrétienne* (Paris, 1983); M. Foucault, *L'Usage des plai-*

sirs (*Histoire de la sexualité*, II), (Paris, 1984).

[7] Max Weber had already linked bodily restraint with early capital accumulation and hence with the formation of capitalist bourgeois society in the Renaissance period. The anthropologist Marcel Mauss was also pursuing similar connections in his 'Body Techniques', first pub. 1935, repr. in M. Mauss, *Sociology and Psychology: Essays*, tr. Ben Brewster (London, 1979). It was undoubtedly the sociologists rather than the professional historians who first found ways of linking the history of bodily consciousness to the history of state society and capital formation.

[8] Gregory Bateson and Margaret Mead, *Balinese Character: A Photographic Analysis* (Special Publications of the New York Academy of Sciences, II) (New York, 1942); P. Eisenberg, 'Expressive Movements Related to Feelings of Dominance', *Archives of Psychology* 30 (1937), 5–72; H. Sperber, 'Expressive Aspects of Political Language', in H. Werner, ed., *On Expressive Language* (Worcester, Mass., 1955); D. Efron, *Gesture and Environment* (New York, 1941); W.H. Blake, *A Preliminary Study of the Interpretation of Bodily Expression* (New York, 1933); sigmund Freud, *Civilization and Its Discontents*, tr. Joan Rivière (London and New York, 1930), from *Das Unbehagen in der kultur* (Vienna, 1930).

[9] B.S.T. Turner, *The Body and Society: Explorations in Social Theory* (Oxford, 1984), 36; Max Beloff, *Wars and Welfare, 1914–1945* (London, 1984).

[10] Mikhail Bakhtin, *Rabelais and His World*, tr. Helena Iswolsky (Cambridge, Mass., 1968). Erving Goffman, *The Presentation of the Self in Everyday Life* (London, 1969), was another work to achieve classic status from this period in its description of 'body-work' as constitutive of individual strategies of survival and control.

[11] Keith Walden, 'The Road to Fat City: An Interpretation of the Revolution of Weight Consciousness in Western Society', *Historical Reflexions* 12 (1985), 331–73; Leslie M. Thompson, 'People as Machines and the Body as Property', *Midwest Quarterly* 27 (1986), 163–80; Ted Polhemus, ed., *The Body Reader: Social Aspects of the Human Body* (New York, 1978); Leonard Barkan, *Nature's Work of Art: the Human Body as Image of the World* (New Haven, Conn., and London, 1975); Turner, *Body and Society*; M. Featherstone, 'The Body in Consumer Culture', *Theory, Culture and Society* 1 (1982), 18–33; T. Hanna, *Bodies in Revolt: a Primer in Somatic Thinking* (New York, 1970); M. Mead, 'Biosocial Components of Political Processes', *Journal of International Affairs* 24 (1970), 18–28.

[12] Elias, *Civilizing Process: The History of Manners*, 258.

[13] Ibid., 258–9. For Bakhtin, however, the 'public body' is the unrestricted body; Elias argues that it is the closed, formal body which is given public validation.

[14] Ibid., 261.

[15] Theda Skocpol, *States and Social Revolutions: A Comparative Analysis of France, Russia and China* (Cambridge, London and New York, 1979); François Furet, *Marx et la Révolution française* (Paris, 1986). More extended discussion of this point follows in ch. 3.

[16] Freud's work on anal eroticism also complements Elias's assumption by documenting subjects possessing a body-image with a 'real', 'central' body, also provided with a detachable part such as limbs, or excrement. These subjects appear trapped by the very distinction between inner and outer world, centre and periphery, expressed through the body, which Elias is describing.

[17] Carl Schmitt: *The Crisis of Parliamentary Democracy* (Cambridge, Mass., 1985), tr. from *Die Geistesgeschichtliche lage des heutigen Parlamentarismus* (Munich, 1923, 1926); *Leviathan: Significance and Failure of a Political Symbol* (Cambridge, Mass., 1985), from *Der Leviathan in der staatslehre des Thomas Hobbes* (Hamburg, 1938);

[18] See the argument in Richard Sennett, *The Fall of Public Man* (Cambridge, London and New York, 1977), 195–268.

[19] Foucault's *Histoire de la sexualité* (see n. 3), left incomplete at the philosopher's death, is not so directly concerned with the constitution of the body for the exercise of state power, more with the constitution of 'sexuality' as an object of discourse. It is thus less relevant to the theme of this work, in the form conceived by Foucault. The themes of the relations between sexuality, reproduction and power are, however, treated here in ch. 8.

[20] For a more prolonged exploration of the history of the concept of the mystical 'body politic', see ch. 5.

[21] Foucault, *Discipline and Punish*, 25, 7. Other writers following this approach include Francis Barker, *The Tremulous Private Body: Essays in Subjection* (London and New York, 1984); François Guéry and Didier Deleule, *Le Corps productif* (Paris, 1972).

[22] M. Foucault, *Les Mots et les choses* (Paris, 1969), tr. Alan Sheridan as *The Order of Things* (London and New York, 1970).

[23] M. Corvez, 'Le Structuralisme de Michel Foucault', *Revue Thomiste* 68 (1968), 101–24.

[24] M. Foucault, *Power/Knowledge: Selected Interviews and Other Writings 1972–1977*, ed. and tr. Colin Gordon (Brighton and New York, 1980).

[25] Foucault, *Discipline and Punish*, 28.

[26] A wider survey of the philosophical problems raised here is offered in R.M. Zaner, *The Problem of Embodiment: Some Contributions to a Phenomenology of the Body* (The Hague, 1964).

[27] François Furet, *Penser la Révolution* (Paris, 1978), tr. Elborg Forster as *Interpreting the French Revolution* (Cambridge and Paris, 1981). Other works along this line include L.A. Hunt, *Politics, Culture and Class in the French Revolution* (Berkeley, Los Angeles and London, 1984); Brian C.J. Singer, *Society, Theory and the French Revolution: Studies in the Revolutionary Imaginary* (New York, 1986); Ronald Paulson, *Representations of Revolution 1789–1820* (New Haven, Conn., and London, 1983).

[28] Ray L. Birdwhistell, *Kinesics and Context: Essays on Body-Motion Communication* (Philadelphia, 1970; London, 1971), 75.

[29] Furet, *Interpreting the French Revolution*; Richard Cobb, *Paris and Its Provinces 1792–1802* (Oxford, London and New York, 1972); Albert Soboul, *Les Sans-culottes parisiens en l'an II: Mouvement populaire et gouvernement révolutionnaire, 2 juin 1792–9 thermidor an II* (Paris, 1965); Colin Lucas, *The Structure of the Terror: The Example of Javogues and the Loire* (Oxford, 1973); J. Goulemot, ed., *Gilbert Romme et son temps* (Paris, 1966).

[30] This willingness to see the body as a creator of public space has been carried forward into Elias's most recent work: N. Elias and Eric Dunning, *The Quest for Excitement: Sport and Leisure in the Civilizing Process* (Oxford, 1986).

[31] See the argument in Edward Peters, *Torture* (Oxford, 1985).

[32] Jacobo Timerman, *Prisoner Without a Name, Cell Without a Number*, tr. Toby Talbot (New York, 1981); Michael Walzer, 'Timerman and His Enemies', *New York Review of Books*, 24 Sept 1981.

[33] Turner, *Body and Society*, 110, 174. It is interesting that Elias should have identified the typical 'modern man' of the 1930s as *homo clausus*; now sociologists' worries focus on the 'collapse of the unitary personality' as the hallmark of man in the 1980s.

[34] Turner, *Body and Society*, 174; see similar arguments in Sennett, *Fall of Public Man*, 195–268.

[35] Bateson and Mead, *Balinese Character*; Birdwhistell, *Kinesics and Context*.

[36] M. Mead, 'On the Concept of Plot in Culture', *Transactions of the New York Academy of Sciences* (2nd ser.) 2, no. 1 (1939), 24–31; A.L. Kroeber and C. Kluckhohn, 'Culture: A Critical Review of Concepts and Definitions', *Papers of the Peabody Museum of American Archaeology and Ethnology* 47, no. 1 (1952), 1–223; Kirsten Hastrup, 'Anthropology and the Exaggeration of Culture', *Ethnos* 50 (1985), 313–24; Clifford Geertz, *The Interpretation of Cultures: Selected Essays* (London, 1975).

## CHAPTER 3

[1] Paul Valéry, 'Mauvaises pensées et autres', in *Oeuvres* (Paris, 1957), II: 715.
[2] For a comprehensive review see Alice Gérard, *La Révolution française: mythes et interpretations* (Paris, 1970), and Linda Orr, 'The Romantic Historiography of the Revolution and French Society', *Consortium on Revolutionary Europe, Proceedings* 14 (1984) (Athens, Ga., 1986), 242–8; F. Furet: *Marx et la Révolution française* [ch. 2, n. 15] and *La Gauche et la Révolution française au milieu du XIX<sup>e</sup> siècle* (Paris, 1986). Novels based on the Revolution include Balzac's *Les Chouans*, Victor Hugo's *Quatre-vingt treize*, Anatole France's *Les Dieux ont soif*, Dickens's *A Tale of Two Cities*; films might include such masterpieces as Abel Gance's epic *Napoléon* (1926) and the more recent and hotly debated film by Andrzej Wajda, *Danton*.
[3] E.g., Bernardine Melchior-Bonnet, *Charlotte Corday* (Paris, 1972); Françoise Kermina, *Mme Roland ou la passion révolutionnaire* (Paris, 1976); journals such as *Histoire* and *Histoire Magazine*.
[4] Gerald J. Cavanaugh, 'The Present State of French Revolutionary Historiography: Alfred Cobban and Beyond', *French Historical Studies* 7 (1972), 587–606; Alfred Cobban: *The Myth of the French Revolution* (London, 1975) and *Aspects of the French Revolution* (Cambridge, 1964).
[5] F. Furet and Denis Richet, *La Révolution française*, 2 vols. (Paris, 1965–6), tr. Stephen Hardman as *The French Revolution* (London, 1970); Furet, *Interpreting the French Revolution* [ch. 2, n. 27].
[6] Soboul's counter-blast to Furet is the significantly titled collection *Comprendre la Révolution: problèmes politiques de la Révolution française, 1789-1797* (Paris, 1981), esp. no. 16, pp. 323–45. Recent accounts dependent on Furet include Carol Blum, *Rousseau and the Republic of Virtue: The Language of Politics in the French Revolution* (Ithaca, N.Y., and London, 1986), and Hunt, *Politics, Culture and Class* [ch. 2, n. 27].
[7] Furet, *Interpreting the French Revolution*, 48–50.
[8] Ibid., 50.
[9] Roger Barny: 'Les Mots et les choses chez les hommes de la Révolution française', *La Pensée*, no. 202 (1978), 96–115: 109–10.
[10] Skocpol, *States and Social Revolutions* [ch. 2. n. 15], 174–205; similarly, Jean Baechler, 'Le Problème de rupture révolutionnaire: à propos des origines de la Révolution française', *Archives Européennes de sociologie* 15 (1974), 3–32.
[11] With the exception of J.L. Talmon, *The Origins of Totalitarian Democracy: Political Theory and Practice during the French Revolution and Beyond* (London, 1952, 1986).
[12] Hunt, *Politics, Culture and Class*; a more sophisticated examination of the philosophical bases of the notion of political-culture-as-discourse is contained in K.M. Baker, 'On the Problem of the Ideological Origins of the French Revolution', in D. LaCapra and S.L. Kaplan, eds., *Modern European Intellectual History: Reappraisals and Perspectives* (Ithaca, N.Y., and London, 1982), 197–219, and in J. Guilhaumou, 'Idéologies, discours et conjoncture en 1793: quelques réflexions sur le jacobinisme', *Dialectiques*, nos. 10–11 (1975), 33–55.
[13] John Searle, *The Expression of Meaning* (Cambridge, 1968). On 'thick des-

cription', see Geertz, *Interpretation of Cultures* [ch. 2, n. 36].

14 Furet's Marxist predecessors were of course even less likely to do so; in fact those writers explicitly dismiss such factors as part of historical explanation; e.g., George Rudé, *Robespierre* (London, 1975), 10: Robespierre's personal characteristics, he says, 'have not seemed to me to be of more than marginal relevance to the study of a political leader and practitioner of revolution and of the impact he made on the history of his times'.

15 For an exception see Guéry and Deleule, *Le Corps productif* [ch. 2, n. 21].

16 See ch. 8 on Mme Roland, for a case-study in this process.

17 Baker, 'Ideological Origins', 210; similar comments in Baechler, 'Problème de rupture', 31.

18 E.g., Serge Bianchi, *La Révolution culturelle de l'an II: Elites et peuple, 1789–1799* (Paris, 1982); Daniel Hermant, 'De la contestation à l'orthodoxie, la révolution culturelle en France après 1789', *Contrepoint*, no. 17 (1975), 167–77; Bronislaw Bazcko, *Lumières de l'Utopie* (Paris, 1978); P. Goujard and Claude Mazauric, 'Dans quel sens peut-on dire que la Révolution française fut une révolution culturelle?', *Europa* 2 (1971), 14–27.

19 Basil Bernstein, 'Elaborated and Restricted Codes', in *Class, Codes and Control: Theoretical Studies Towards a Sociology of Language* (London, 1971).

20 John F. Laffey, 'Cacophonic Rites: Modernism and Post-Modernism', *Réflexions historiques/Historical Reflections* 14 (1987), 1–33.

21 F. Furet, 'Beyond the *Annales*', *Journal of Modern History* 55, no. 3 (1983), 389–410.

22 Talmon, *Origins of Totalitarian Democracy*.

23 As Linda Orr has remarked ('Romantic Historiography', 242): 'Nineteenth-century histories of the French Revolution are exasperating: the authors hiss, boo and cheer; they seem to relish the cup of blood and body parts hiked up on pikes [but these anecdotes have] a purpose and force we might do well to interrogate rather than dismiss...'.

24 Furet, 'Beyond the *Annales*', 409.

## CHAPTER 4

1 Italo Calvino, *Italian Folktales*, tr. George Martin (London, 1986), xviii.

2 Françoise Piponnier and Richard Bucaille, 'La Bille ou la belle? Remarques sur l'apparence corporelle de la paysannerie médiévale', *Ethnologie française* 6, nos. 3–4 (1976), 227–32.

3 R. Grew, 'Picturing the People', *Journal of Interdisciplinary History* 17 (1986), 201–31.

4 Arlette Farge, 'Les Artisans malades de leur travail', *Annales E.S.C.* 32 (1977), 993–1006.

5 K.M. Figlio, 'Theories of Perception and the Physiology of Mind in the Late Eighteenth Century', *History of Science* 13 (1975), 177–212.

6 Jean-Pierre Goubert, ed., *La Médicalisation de la société française, 1770–1830* (Waterloo, Ont., 1982), and *Maladies et médicins en Bretagne, 1770–1790* (Rennes and Paris, 1974); M. Foucault: *Naissance de la clinique* (Paris, 1972), and *Les Machines à guérir: aux origines de l'hôpital moderne* (Paris, 1976); Toby Gelfand: *Professionalizing Modern Medicine: Paris Surgeons, Medical Science and Institutions in the Eighteenth Century* (Westport, Conn., 1980), and 'The Decline of the Ordinary Practitioner and the Rise of the Modern Medical Profession' in M.S. Staum and D.E. Larsen, eds., *Doctors, Patients and Society: Power and Authority in Medical Care* (Waterloo, Ont., 1981), 106–29.

7 N.D. Jewson, 'The Disappearance of the Sick Man from Medical Cosmology, 1770–1870', *Sociology* 10 (1976), 225–44; Georges Canguilhem, *Le Normal et le pathologique* (Paris, 1972), 50–1: '[Modern clinicians are led] ...à tenir l'expérience pathologique directe du patient comme négligeable, voir même comme systématiquement falsificatrice du fait pathologique objectif'.

8 Gelfand, 'Decline of the Ordinary

Practitioner', 122.
9 Foucault, *Naissance de la clinique*. See also, for the twentieth-century hold of hospital medicine, David Armstrong, *Political Anatomy of the Body: Medical Knowledge in Britain in the Twentieth Century* (Cambridge, 1983).
10 Foucault, *Discipline and Punish* [ch. 2, n. 3], 193.
11 J.P. Goubert: 'L'Art de guérir: médicine savante et médicine populaire dans la France de 1790', *Annales E.S.C.* 32, no. 5 (1977), 908–26, and 'The Extent of Medical Practice in France around 1780', *Journal of Social History* 10, no. 4 (1977), 410–27; Toby Gelfand, 'Deux cultures, une profession: les chirurgiens français au dix-huitième siècle', *Revue d'histoire moderne et contemporaine* 27 (1980), 468–84.
12 Gelfand, 'Decline of the Ordinary Practitioner', 122.
13 E.g., Goubert, 'L'Art de guérir'; Foucault, *Naissance*.
14 Foucault, *Naissance*; Harvey Mitchell: 'Rationality and Control in French Eighteenth-Century Medical Views of the Peasantry', *Comparative Studies in Society and History* 21 (1979), 81–112, and 'The Political Economy of Health in France, 1770–1830: The Debate over Hospital and Home Care and Images of the Working-Class Family' in Staum and Larson, *Doctors, Patients and Society*, 71–104.
15 W.C. Coleman, 'Health and Hygiene in the *Encyclopédie*: A Medical Doctrine for the Bourgeoisie', *Journal of the History of Medicine* 29 (1974), 339–421.
16 Ibid.
17 Dora B. Weiner, 'Le Droit de l'homme à la santé: une belle idée devant l'Assemblée Constituante, 1790–1791', *Clio médicale* 5 (1970), 209–23.
18 See below, chs. 6 and 7.
19 Quoted in Coleman, 'Health and Hygiene', 411.
20 Robert Mandrou, 'Histoire sociale et histoire des mentalités', *La Nouvelle Critique* 49 (1972), 44.
21 G. Bollème: (ed.) *La Bibliothèque bleue: littérature populaire en France du XVII$^e$ au XIX$^e$ siècle* (Paris, 1971), and 'Littérature et littérature de colportage au XVIII$^e$ siècle' in F. Furet, ed., *Livre et société dans la France du XVIII$^e$ siècle* (Paris, 1965).
22 L.J. Jordanova, 'Guarding the Body Politic: Volney's *Catéchisme* of 1793', in Francis Barker, ed., *1789: Reading, Writing and Revolution* (Colchester, 1982), 12–22; J.V. Pickstone, 'Bureaucracy, Liberalism and the Body in Post-Revolutionary France: Bichat's Physiology and the Paris School of Medicine', *History of Science* 19 (1981), 115–42.
23 For developments of this idea after 1800 by Saint-Simon and others, see B. Haines, 'The Inter-Relations between Social, Biological and Medical Thought, 1750–1850: Saint-Simon and Comte', *British Journal for the History of Science* 11 (1978), 19–35.
24 Sergio Moravia, 'From *homme machine* to *homme sensible*: Changing Eighteenth-Century Models of Man's Image', *Journal of the History of Ideas* 39 (1978), 45–60.
25 Albrecht von Haller, *De partibus corporis humani sensibilibus et irritabilibus* (Göttingen, 1752–3), tr. Simon-André Tissot as *Dissertation sur les parties irritables et sensibles des animaux* (Lausanne, 1755).
26 E. Haigh, 'Vitalism, the Soul and Sensibility: the Physiology of Théophile Bordeu', *Journal of the History of Medicine* 31 (1976), 30–41; E.T. Carlson and Meribeth Simpson, 'Models of the Nervous System in Eighteenth-Century Neurophysiology and Medical Psychology', *Bulletin of the History of Medicine* 44 (1969), 101–15.
27 Quoted in Moravia, 'From *homme machine*...', 56, from Bordeu, *Recherches anatomiques sur la position des glandes* in *Oeuvres complètes*, 2 vols. (Paris, 1828), I: 187.
28 Geoffrey Sutton: 'The Physical and Chemical Path to Vitalism: Xavier Bichat's *Physiological Researches on Life and Death*', *Bulletin of the History of Medicine* 58 (1984), 53–71; W.R. Albury, 'Heart of Darkness: J.N. Corvisart and the Medicalization of

Life' in Goubert, *Médicalisation*, 17–31.
[29] Mitchell, 'Rationality and Control'.
[30] Goubert, 'L'Art de guérir'.
[31] Marie-France Morel, 'Ville et campagne dans le discours médical sur la petite enfance au XVIII$^e$ siècle', *Annales E.S.C.* 32 (1977), 1007–24; M. Duchet, *Anthropologie et histoire au siècle des lumières* (Paris, 1971), 11.
[32] Jacques Revel and Jean-Pierre Peter, 'Le Corps: l'homme malade et son histoire', in Jacques Le Goff and Pierre Nora, eds., *Faire de l'histoire: nouveaux objets* (Paris, 1974), 169–91: 173–4.
[33] Mitchell, 'Rationality and Control', 105.
[34] Goubert, 'L'Art de guérir'.
[35] R. Chartier, 'Les élites et les gueux: quelques représentations', *Revue d'histoire moderne et contemporaine* 21 (1974), 376–88; Jean-Paul Desaive, 'Le Nu hurluberlu', *Ethnologie française* 6, nos. 3–4 (1976), 219–26.
[36] Morel, 'Ville et campagne', 1013.
[37] Alain Corbin, 'L'Hygiène publique et les "excreta" de la ville pré-haussmannienne', *Ethnologie française* 12 (1982), 127–30; Richard Allan Etlin, *The Cemetery and the City: Paris 1744–1804* (Princeton Univ. Ph.D. thesis, 1978).
[38] Quoted in Morel, 'Ville et campagne', 1019, from J. Ballexserd, *Dissertation sur l'éducation physique des enfants, depuis leur naissance jusqu'à l'âge de puberté* (Paris, 1767), 125.
[39] F. Loux and Marie-France Morel, 'L'Enfance et les savoirs sur les corps: pratiques médicales et pratiques populaires dans la France traditionelle', *Ethnologie française* 6 (1976), 309–24; F. Loux and Philippe Richard, *Sagesses du corps: la santé et la maladie dans les proverbes français* (Paris, 1978); F. Loux, *Le Corps dans la société traditionelle* (Paris, 1979); Jacques Gélis, 'Refaire le corps: les déformations volontaires du corps de l'enfant à la naissance', *Ethnologie français* 14 (1984), 7–28.
[40] J. Devlin, *The Superstitious Mind: French Peasants and the Supernatural in the Nineteenth Century* (New Haven, Conn., and London, 1987), 72–99; G. Bollème, 'L'Enjeu du corps et la Bibliothèque bleue', *Ethnologie française* 6 (1976), 285–92.
[41] R. Muchembled, *Culture populaire et culture des élites, dans la France moderne* (Paris, 1977).
[42] P. Caron, *Les Massacres de septembre* (Paris, 1935); M. Mortimer-Ternaux, *Histoire de la Terreur*, 8 vols. (Paris, 1862), IV: 493–8.
[43] Paulson, *Representations of Revolution* [ch. 2, n. 27], 71–9.
[44] For a full discussion of the legend of Charlotte Corday's head and its diffusion, see Mortimer-Ternaux, *Histoire de la Terreur*, VIII: 147–67; 519–25. See also ch. 7 of the present work.
[45] S. Thompson, *Motif-Index of Folk-Literature*, 6 vols. (Bloomington, Ind., 1932–6), s.v. 'head'.
[46] Paulson, *Representations*, 363; see also ch. 7. M.S. Staum, *Cabanis: Enlightenment and Medical Philosophy in the French Revolution* (Princeton, N.J., 1980), 201; 69–77, 89–90.
[47] For this mythology, see the comprehensive discussion in Paulson, *Representations*, 75, 363–73. Mortimer-Ternaux, *Histoire de la Terreur*, III: 286–8.
[48] Ibid.

CHAPTER 5

[1] 'Une autobiographie du Baron Ramond', ed. H. Dehérain, *Journal des savants*, Mar 1905, 121–9: 128; F.V.A. Aulard, *L'Éloquence parlementaire pendant la Révolution française: les orateurs de la Législative et de la Convention*, 2 vols. (Paris, 1886), II: 475.
[2] 'O courageux Caton, ce ne sera plus de toi seul qu'on apprendra de quelle manière les hommes libres savent se soustraire à la tyrannie', quoted in Alessandro Galante Garrone, *Gilbert Romme; Storia di un rivoluzionario* (Turin, 1959), 492. See also the comment, from another point on the political spectrum, of the Committee of Public Safety member Bertrand Barère, on his proscription in 1795:

'J'avais souvent dans la pensée ces mots si rassurants de Caton: que la lutte d'un homme vertueux aux prises avec l'infortune est un spectacle digne de fixer les regards de la Divinité. Cette confiance de Caton était passée dans mon âme oppressée par l'adversité et la consolait', in *Mémoires de Barère...précédés d'une notice historique*, ed. Hippolyte Carnot and R. David d'Angers, 4 vols. (Paris, 1842), II: 169–70.

3 Alberto Grilli, *Il problema della vita contemplativa nel mondo Greco-Romano* (Milan and Rome, 1953); for the Renaissance and Baroque reworking of this theme see Michael O'Loughlin, *The Garlands of Repose* (Chicago and London, 1978); N.Z. Davis, 'Boundaries and the Sense of Self in Sixteenth-Century France', in T.C. Heller et al., eds., *Reconstructing Individualism: Autonomy, Individuality and the Self in Western Thought* (Stanford, Calif., 1986).

4 Pierre Thévenaz, 'L'intériorité chez Sénèque', in Thévenaz et al., eds., *Mélanges offerts à M. Max Niedermann à l'occasion de son soixante-dixième anniversaire* (Université de Neuchâtel: Receuil de travaux publiés par la Faculté de Lettres, fasc. 22) (Neuchâtel, 1944), 189–94; Miriam Griffin, *Seneca: A Philosopher in Politics* (Oxford, 1976), 360–6.

5 H.T. Parker, *The Cult of Antiquity and the French Revolutionaries: A Study in the Development of the Revolutionary Spirit* (Chicago, 1937).

6 Griffin, *Seneca*.

7 Gerhard Oestreich, *Neostoicism and the Early Modern State*, tr. David McLintock (Cambridge, London and New York, 1982).

8 See F. van der Haeghen, *Bibliographie Lipsienne*, 3 vols. (Ghent, 1886–8); Justus Lipsius: *Politicorum libri sex* (1589), and *De constantia libri duo qui alloquium praecipue continent in publicis malis* (1584). A new edition of the *Constantia* was produced in 1802 (Leipzig), influenced military reform in Prussia in the early nineteenth century, and was current in European military circles in the late eighteenth, through the excerpts contained in the influential J.E. von Beust, *Observationes militaires* (Gotha, 1743–57). Its ideals of disciplined military leadership cast a long shadow into the Revolutionary period; see R. Vanpel, ed., *Das Preussiche Heer von Tilsiter Frieden bis zur Befreiung: 1807 bis 1814* (Publikation en aus den Preussischen Staatsarchiv, bd. 94) (Leipzig, 1938), 463–84; Oestreich, *Neostoicism*, 57.

9 Griffin, *Seneca*, 360–6; P. Pecchiura, *La figura di Catone Uticense nella letteratura latina* (Turin, 1965); R.L. Herbert, *David, Voltaire, 'Brutus' and the French Revolution: An Essay in Art and Politics* (London, 1972).

10 Oestreich, *Neostoicism*, 1 passim.

11 Ibid., 53.

12 Ibid., 71.

13 Nannerl O. Keohane, *Philosophy and the State in France: the Renaissance to the Enlightenment* (Princeton, N.J., 1980), 431; Edouard Guitton, *Jacques Delille et la poème de la nature en France de 1750 à 1820* (Paris, 1974). These were ideals which were not confined to poetry, but influenced the lifestyles of many individuals, including those later politically prominent: see Maurice Prouteaux, 'La Maison des champs de Creuzé-Latouche', *Bulletins de la Société des Antiquaires de l'Ouest* (3rd ser.) 13 (1939–41), 369–92. Creuzé (1759–1800) was one of the few men who pursued a continuous political career in this period, as, successively, member of the Estates-General, the Legislative Assembly, the National Convention, the Conseil des Anciens, and the Conseil des Cinq-cents under Napoleon. See also his 'Reflexions sur la vie champêtre: mémoire lu à la séance publique de l'Institut National de France, 20 messidor an VIII'. In similar vein, Mme Roland complimented herself on the *aurea mediocritas* of her retired country life (*Lettres de Mme Roland*, ed. Claude Perroud, 2 vols. [Paris, 1900–1], I: 21–2, letter to Lavater of 7 July 1788). For the growth of the related ideal of privacy, see David H. Flaherty, *Privacy in Colonial New England*

(Charlottesville, Va., 1972). Solitude, an intensification of the 'rural retreat', was also vaunted by such widely sold and much translated works as George Zimmerman, *La Solitude considérée relativement à l'esprit et au coeur* (Paris, 1788). The attainment of individual apartness and autonomy was also stressed in the writings on 'cosmopolitanism' produced in great numbers in the late eighteenth century; D. Outram, *Georges Cuvier: Vocation, Science and Authority in Post-Revolutionary France* (Manchester and Dover, N.H., 1984), 69-86; I.D. McKillop, 'Local Attachment and Cosmopolitanism: The Eighteenth-Century Pattern', in *From Sensibility to Romanticism: Essays presented to F.A. Pottle* (London, 1965), 191-218.

[14] Robert Darnton, 'Readers Respond to Rousseau: The Fabrication of Romantic Sensitivity', in id., *The Great Cat Massacre and other Episodes in French Cultural History* (London, 1984), 215-25; Terry Eagleton, *The Rape of Clarissa: Writing, Sexuality and Class Struggle in Samuel Richardson* (Oxford, 1982). See also ch. 8, below, for a much more detailed account of this theme.

[15] J.-J. Tatin, 'Relation de l'actualité, reflexion politique et culte des grandes hommes dans les almanachs de 1760 à 1793', *Annales historiques de la Révolution française* 57 (1985), 307-16; Jean-Claude Bonnet, 'Naissance du Panthéon', *Poétique* 33 (1978), 46-55; M. Ozouf, 'Le Panthéon: l'Ecole Normale des morts', in P. Nora, ed., *Les Lieux de mémoire*, vol. I: *La République* (Paris, 1984). For the incorporation of this pantheon into domestic settings with house decoration and furnishing, see Prouteaux, 'La Maison des champs'.

[16] C.A. Lopez, *Mon cher papa: Benjamin Franklin and the Ladies of Paris* (New Haven, Conn., 1966); for the construction of another such reference-figure, see B. Schwartz, 'The Character of Washington: A Study in Republican Culture', *American Quarterly* 38 (1986), 202-22.

[17] Oestreich, *Neostoicism*, 259-60.

[18] Daniel Roche, *Le Siècle des lumières en province: académies et académiciens provinciaux, 1680-1789*, 2 vols. (Paris, 1978), I: 391; Fritz Hartung, 'L'Etat c'est moi', *Historische Zeitschrift* 169 (1949), 1-16.

[19] Heinz H.F. Eulau, 'The Depersonalization of the Concept of Sovereignty', *Journal of Politics* 4 (1942), 3-19; Paul Archambault, 'The Analogy of the "Body", in Renaissance Political Literature', *Bibliothèque d'humanisme et Renaissance* 29 (1967), 21-53. For the medieval elaboration of these ideas, see the classic study by Ernst H. Kantorowicz, *The King's Two Bodies: A Study in Medieval Political Theology* (Princeton, N.J., 1957), 207-32, 496-506. The implications of these ideas for our period are discussed in Michael Walzer, *Regicide and Revolution: Speeches at the Trial of Louis XVI* (Cambridge, 1974), 1-89.

[20] Keohane, *Philosophy and the State*, 399, 459.

[21] Ibid., 459.

[22] Baker, 'Ideological Origins of the French Revolution' [ch. 3, n. 12].

[23] Cp. J.-J. Rousseau: 'as nature gives every man absolute control over all his members, so the social contract gives to the body politic an absolute power over all its members', quoted in Charles E. Merriam, *History of the Theory of Sovereignty since Rousseau* (New York, 1900), 34, from Rousseau, *Le Contrat social*, Bk. 2, § 4; see also the definition of sovereignty offered by Merriam, of 'owing obedience to none' (p. 67).

[24] The Revolution also saw an explosion of writing, from many different points of view, on the whole problem of sovereignty: Merriam, ibid.; Joseph de Maistre, *Étude sur la souveraineté* (Paris, 1794-6).

[25] Roger Barny, 'Les Aventures de la théorie de la souveraineté en 1789', in 'La Révision des valeurs sociales dans la littérature européenne à la lumière des idées de la Révolution française', *Annales Littéraires de l'Université de Besançon* 109 (1970), 65-93: 70, 84.

[26] Ibid., 79.
[27] Keohane, *Philosophy and the State*, 408; Oestreich, *Neostoicism*, 36.
[28] Merriam, *Theory of Sovereignty*, 37.
[29] C. Matson and Peter Onuf, 'Toward a Republican Empire: Interest and Ideology in Revolutionary America', *American Quarterly* 37 (1985), 496–531.
[30] Furet, *Interpreting the French Revolution* [ch. 2, n. 27], 56. By placing the emphasis on personification, Furet begins to move away from the purely verbal emphasis of Parker's earlier account (n. 5); but he does not produce a full account of the behaviour which accompanied personification.
[31] E.g., Anon., 'Instruction pour les hommes publics: traduction de Plutarque', *Décade philosophique*, an IV (1795), 8, trimestre II, 420–3: 420. This article is a very free paraphrase, with significant alterations of passages, from Plutarch's *Moralia*; in the Loeb edn., tr. H.N. Fowler (Cambridge, Mass., 1936), 169–271: 229, 253–5.
[32] Oestreich, *Neostoicism*, 44; Richard Brilliant, *Gesture and Rank in Roman Art: The Use of Gestures to Denote Status in Roman Sculpture and Coinage* (Memoirs of the Connecticut Academy of Arts and Sciences, 14) (New Haven, Conn., 1963); Averil Cameron, 'Images of Authority: Elites and Icons in Late Sixth-Century Byzantium', *Past and Present* 84 (1979), 3–35; M.P. Charlesworth, 'Roman Imperial Deportment', *Journal of Roman Studies* 37 (1947), 34–8.
[33] Honoré Riouffe, *Mémoires d'un détenu pour servir à l'histoire de la tyrannie de Robespierre*, 2 vols. (Paris, 1823; first pub. 1795), I: 50.
[34] J. Dulaure, *Supplément aux crimes des anciens comités de gouvernement* (Paris, an III), 71: quoted in Aulard, *Eloquence*, I: 187 n. 2. The image of a 'Socratic' death was also in widespread use: see Raymond Trousson, *Socrate devant Voltaire, Diderot et Rousseau: la conscience en face du mythe* (Paris, 1967). It is noticeable that those public figures, such as Marat, who were identified with an extravagant political style far removed from Stoic reserve, were also usually identified as populist in their appeal. The existence of these differing political styles is examined more closely in ch. 6.
[35] *Oeuvres complètes de Saint-Just*, ed. Charles Vellay, 2 vols. (Paris, 1908), I: 349, letter of 20 July 1792.
[36] Quoted in Aulard, *Éloquence*, II: 26, speech by Louvet of 16 Dec 1792.
[37] *Mémoires de M. le Comte de Vaublanc*, ed. M.F. Barrière (Paris, 1857), 270.
[38] A. Gooden, *Action and Persuasion: Dramatic Performance in Eighteenth-Century France* (Oxford, 1986); Marian Hobson, *The Object of Art: The Theory of Illusion in Eighteenth-Century France* (Cambridge, 1982), 194–208. The famous actress Mlle Clairon was, however, in no doubt that, particularly for a public man, 'La principale attention de l'orateur doit donc être de ne laisser voir que son personnage': Hérault de Séchelles, 'Reflexions sur la déclamation', *Magasin encyclopédique* 1 (1795), 396–416: 397.
[39] Anon., 'Instruction', 420. The passage quoted significantly intensifies a passing reference in the original (see n. 31) to the 'open stage' of public life, into an all-embracing metaphor.
[40] Ibid., 421.
[41] Riouffe, *Mémoires*, I: 70; André Fribourg, *Discours de Danton: édition critique* (Paris, 1910), 701, quoting from the *Bulletin du Tribunal criminal révolutionnaire*, 13–16 germinal an II (2–5 Apr 1794).
[42] Bailly (1733–94) had been at the centre of the controversy surrounding the 'massacre' of the Champ de Mars on 17 July 1791, during which a crowd, gathered to sign a public petition for the establishment of a republic in France, was fired on by troops under the orders of the municipality of Paris: Edwin Burrows Smith, 'Jean-Sylvain Bailly: Astronomer, Mystic and Revolutionary', *Transactions of the American Philosophical Society*, n. ser. 44 (1954), 427–538; L. Audiat, 'Le Mot de Bailly

allant à l'échafaud', *Revue des questions historiques* 20 (1876), 544–53. This anecdote is also retailed in Riouffe, *Mémoires*, I: 50–1, and in J.-B. Delambre, *Histoire de l'astronomie au dix-huitième siècle* (Paris, 1827), 563, 748.

[43] Louis-Philippe de Ségur, *Mémoires*, 2 vols. (Paris, 1825), I: 3. The only general discussion of the problem of rapid role-change in this period is Marguerite Vergnaud's study of the chemist Lavoisier, 'Un savant pendant la Révolution', *Cahiers internationaux de sociologie* 17–18 (1954–5), 123–39.

[44] Vaublanc, *Mémoires*, 264; *Mémoires de La Révellière-Lépaux...publiés par son fils* [Ossian de La Révellière-Lépaux], ed. Robert David d'Angers, 3 vols. (Paris, 1895), 1: 162–3; *Mémoires de Mme Roland; nouvelle édition critique: contenant les fragments inédits et les lettres de prison*, ed. Claude Perroud, 2 vols. (Paris, 1905), II: 455–6, reprinting MS 872 of the Central Library of the Musée national d'histoire naturelle, Paris, by Bosc.

[45] When Saint-Just arraigned Danton before the Convention, he cried, 'In our stormy debates, we were outraged by your absence and your silence: you, you were talking of the countryside, of the delights of solitude and leisure'; quoted in P. Trahard, *La Sensibilité révolutionnaire* (Paris, 1936), 134–5.

[46] Some would argue that such an autonomy, emphasizing the separation between self and other, internal and external worlds, is a necessary precondition for *any* revolutionary activity. Pocock asserts that revolutionaries are 'those whose identities can only be created by transforming the world *seen as other*': J.G.A Pocock, *Politics, Language and Time: Essays on Political Thought and History* (London, 1972), 284. Furet, *Interpreting the French Revolution*, 45–9; 69.

[47] Quoted in Aulard, *Éloquence*, I: 71, speech to the National Convention of 15 Mar 1793.

[48] E.g., M. Sydenham, *The Girondins* (London, 1961); Alison Patrick: *The Men of the First French Republic; Political Alignments in the National Convention of 1792* (Baltimore and London, 1972), and 'Political Divisions in the French National Convention, 1792–1793', *Journal of Modern History* 41 (1969), 473–89; Michel Pertué: 'Remarques sur les listes de Conventionnels', *Annales historiques de la Révolution française* 53 (1981), 366–89, and review of A. Patrick, *Men of the First French Republic*, ibid., 661–5.

[49] Sophie Grandchamp's comment on her reaction to Roland is revealing: 'Ses principes d'une austère vertu, dont tout en lui portait l'empreinte, me donnait le désir d'obtenir son suffrage': Mme Roland, *Mémoires*, II: 461–97: 464. For Robespierre, see the reactions catalogued in Louis Jacob, *Robespierre vu par ses contemporains: témoignages* (Paris, 1938), and D. Blottière, 'Robespierre apprécié par une contemporaine: Mme Julien de la Drôme', *Annales révolutionnaires* 4 (1911), 93–6.

[50] E.g., Gabriel-Marie-Jean-Baptiste Legouvé, *Le Mérite des femmes: Poëme* (Paris, 1801); this was still in print in 1881. See also Joseph-Alexandre de Ségur, *Les Femmes, leur condition et leur influence, dans l'ordre social chez différents peuples anciens et modernes*, 3 vols. (Paris, 1803), III *passim*. Both Legouvé and Ségur found their major quarry for material in H. Riouffe, *Mémoires*. The 'canon' which these three authors established also found its way into other widely disseminated works such as Mme Fortuné Briquet, *Dictionnaire historique, littéraire et bibliographique des françaises et des étrangères naturalisées en France...*(Paris, 1804), and later works in the same vein such as E. Lairtullier, *Les Femmes célébrées de 1789 à 1795 et leur influence dans le Révolution*, 2 vols. (Paris, 1840).

[51] See J.-J. Süe, *Essai sur la physiognomie des corps vivans considéré depuis l'homme jusqu'à la plante: ouvrage où l'on traîte principalement de la nécessité de cette étude dans les arts d'imitation, des véritables règles de la beauté et les grâces, des proportions du corps humain, de l'expression, des passions, etc.* (Paris, 1797), iii–iv. Similar statements in Ségur, *Les*

*Femmes*, 27. It may be no accident that Süe, father of the nineteenth-century novelist, and Legouvé were the first and second husbands respectively of the same woman, Adelaide Rosalie Souvan (1776–1810): J.-L. Bory, *Eugène Süe* (Paris, 1962), 27.

[52] Legouvé, *Le Mérite*; Ségur, *Les Femmes*. Another significant example is provided by the case of Charlotte Corday, whose own claims to have murdered Marat to serve the royalist cause were countered, at her trial, by attempts to prove that her act was motivated entirely by a love affair with one or more of the Girondin deputies who had taken refuge in her home town of Caen.

[53] It is no accident that an influential myth-maker such as Honoré Riouffe should devote much attention to physical descriptions of his political heroes, descriptions which were an integral part of their heroic status. To take only one example, here is his description of the arrested Girondin deputy Gaspard Severin Duchâtel, who was to be guillotined at Paris on 31 Oct 1793: 'ce jeune homme retenait des larmes d'indignation qui roulaient dans ses yeux; la tête haute et le regard *courageux et terrible, son caractère de représentant se traçait sur son front*, en traits d'autant plus *augustes* qu'il était méconnu: sa taille était avantageuse, l'intrépidité respirait tellement dans tout son visage, *d'une beauté mâle et vigoureuse*, sa jeunesse paraissait tellement indépendante et libre, que, tant qu'a duré la route, je ne me souviens pas d'avoir vu un seul moment de sécurité aux gendarmes, quoiqu'il eût des fers aux pieds et aux mains... il traversa *avec majesté* tout le long corridor et une partie de la place. Les hommes que le conduisaient avaient les yeux baissés comme honteux de descendre du rang de citoyen français au rôle de sbire de la tyrannie' (Riouffe, *Mémoires*, I: 29–30 [italics mine]). This passage shows clearly how Riouffe combined images of imperial majesty with those of male physical beauty to validate the politics of 'Girondins' like Duchâtel, and assert their intrinsic political primacy in spite of their temporary defeat by the Jacobin faction. Such a concentration on the physical appearance of the Girondins is still seen in historical work today, e.g., Jacqueline Chaumié, 'Les Girondins', in *Actes du Colloque Girondins et Montagnards*, ed. Albert Soboul (Paris, 1980). Riouffe also drew heavily on available classical models of the physical description of great men and emperors; see, for example, the passages cited in P. Jal, 'Images d'Auguste chez Sénèque', *Revue des études latines* 35 (1957), 242–63. In tactics such as these employed by Riouffe, we see a literal redistribution of the physical attributes of classical majesty to the heroic person of a republican representative. Others sought to create such heroic images by the use of costume: Anon., 'Les Costumes de Thibaudeau', *Bulletins de la Société des Antiquaires de l'Ouest* 13 (1939–41), 444–51.

[54] This conflict is dramatically represented in J.-L. David's picture, *Brutus* (Louvre), in which the canvas is sharply divided between the dark, rigid, angular, self-contained figure of Brutus, on the one side, and the brightly lit, swirling, demonstrative and passionate figures of his wife and daughters lamenting the executed sons. See also ch. 8 for more extended treatment of male/female conflict in the Revolution.

[55] The struggle for 'objectivity' is treated in more detail in D. Outram: 'Before Objectivity: Women and Cultural Reproduction in Nineteenth-Century French Science', in D. Outram and P. Abir-Am, eds., *Uneasy Careers and Intimate Lives: Women in Science, 1789–1979* (New Brunswick, N.J., 1987), 19–31, and *Georges Cuvier*, 118–41. For the accompanying 'abstraction' of feeling, see A. Heller, *A Theory of Feelings* (Assen, 1979).

[56] They surface in the twentieth century in that section of society which has effectively remained locked on to the image of *homo clausus*: the military.

Here, such attitudes were still powerful enough to lead, as late as 1956, to the 'heroic suicides' of disgraced French officers at Dien Bien Phu.
[57] Élites in general utilized heroic images in this way even after the end of the Revolution: D. Outram, 'The Language of Natural Power: The Funeral *éloges* of Georges Cuvier', *History of Science* 16 (1978), 153-78.
[58] E.g., Robespierre: 'J'en suis venu au point de soupçonner que les véritables héros ne sont pas ceux qui triomphent, mais ceux qui souffrent': letter to Pétion of 1792, quoted in Trahard, *La Sensibilité révolutionnaire*, 122. This is also the tenor of the anecdote on the death of Bailly recounted above.

## CHAPTER 6

[1] Karl Marx, *Early Writings*, ed. R. Livingstone (New York, 1975), 276.
[2] Figures based on A. Kuscinski, *Dictionnaire des Conventionnels* (Paris, 1916).
[3] For Soubrany, see Galante Garrone, *Gilbert Romme* [ch. 5. n. 2], 479; for Ducos, see Riouffe, *Mémoires* [ch. 5, n. 33], I: 51; for Lavoisier, Edouard Grimaux, *Lavoisier, 1743–1794* (Paris, 1899), 269–70.
[4] Henri Wallon, *Histoire du Tribunal Révolutionnaire de Paris, avec le journal de ses actes*, 6 vols. (Paris, 1880-2), II: 433; III: 242, 336, 386-7; IV: 59, 191, 254, 293; V: 8, 157, 163; VI: 69. We are not attempting here to compile a statistical portrait of such acts; merely to show that they occurred.
[5] Albert Bayet, *Le Suicide et la morale* (Paris, 1922), 709–20, argues that suicide was a rare act, confined only to political leaders, but his own documentation points in the opposite direction.
[6] E.g., John McManners, *Death and the Enlightenment: Changing Attitudes to Death among Christians and Unbelievers in Eighteenth-Century France* (Oxford, 1981), 410–33; Lester G. Crocker, 'The Discussion of Suicide in the Eighteenth Century', *Journal of the History of Ideas* 13 (1952), 47-72; J.M. Goulemot, 'Montesquieu: du suicide légitime à l'apologie du suicide héroïque', in Goulemot *et al.*, *Gilbert Romme et son temps* [ch. 2, n. 29], 163–74; Michel Launay, 'Contribution à l'étude du suicide vertueux selon Rousseau', in ibid., 175–82; for Socrates see Trousson, *Socrate devant Voltaire, Diderot, et Rousseau* [ch. 5, n. 34].
[7] E.g., McManners, *Death and the Enlightenment*, 427, quotes Lefebvre de Beauvry, *Dictionnaire sociale et patriotique* (Paris, 1770), 510: '[Heroic suicides were] plutot martyrs de leur amour-propre, que de leur patrie'. See also Jean Dumas, *Traité du suicide ou du meutre volontaire de soi-même* (Amsterdam, 1773).
[8] Bayet, *Le Suicide et la morale*, 666–77; 695 gives the repeal date of these measures as 13 floréal an III.
[9] For the prevalence and predictability of suicide in imprisonment, Alexandre Tuetey, *Répertoire général des sources manuscrits de l'histoire de Paris pendant la Révolution française*, 11 vols. (Paris, 1890-1914), VIII: col. 2867, where the Commission de Police de la Section Henri IV points out the danger for the Revolutionary Tribunal of confiding '...à la surveillance d'un concierge, vingt-quatre condamnés à mort qui cherchent à chaque instant à attenter leurs jours'; VII: col. 1892, the Minister of the Interior writes of the '...état déplorable des prisons de la Conciergerie où vingt-sept condamnés à mort cherchent à s'échapper ou à se détruire'. After the Senecan suicide of Clavière, prisoners were regularly searched for weapons – not, significantly, because they were expected to turn them on their gaolers, but to forestall their own suicides: ibid., VIII: col. 1774. For the rarity of suicide after 1795, Kuscinski, *Dictionnaire*, cites among the *conventionnels* only the isolated instance of the suicide of the republican Frécine, in June 1804, as a protest against the proclamation of the Empire.
[10] Eighteenth-century suicide, for ob-

vious reasons, was grossly underreported, and it would be impossible to reconstruct an accurate estimate of its incidence from which to draw a comparison with the Revolutionary experience. Even after 1814, there were still serious problems involved in the compilation of statistical data: see Bayet, *Le Suicide et la morale*, 680; Armand des Étangs, *Du suicide politique en France depuis 1789 jusqu'à nos jours* (Paris, 1860), Introduction and p. 215. For the prison population of the Revolution itself, loss of the documents registering prisoners' entry, or the manner of their exit, again make calculations doubtful. Group biographies such as Kuscinski's are thus all the more vital in enabling us to assess the incidence of suicide in any given group.

[11] Riouffe, *Mémoires*. Sources dependent on Riouffe include Ségur, *Les femmes* [ch. 5. n. 50], III: *passim*, and Legouvé, *Le Mérite des femmes* [ch. 5, n. 50], which went through six editions by 1802.

[12] Riouffe, *Mémoires*, I: 23.

[13] E.g., J.A. Roucher, *Consolations de ma captivité ou correspondance de Roucher, mort victime de la tyrannie décemvirale, le 7 thermidor an II de la république française* (Paris, 1797).

[14] Much of what follows is based on Parker, *Cult of Antiquity* [ch. 5, n. 5].

[15] I am also indebted to J.M. Rist, *Stoic Philosophy* (Oxford, 1969), 233–41.

[16] Ibid.

[17] Charlesworth, 'Roman Imperial Deportment' [ch. 5, n. 32].

[18] Rist, *Stoic Philosophy*, 241.

[19] Ibid., 246–8.

[20] An attitude taken over fully by the revolutionaries: Mme Roland urges Buzot to suicide with the words 'Meurs libre, comme tu sus vivre'; *Mémoires* [ch. 5, n. 44], II: 270; cp. S.R.N. Chamfort, *Oeuvres complètes*, 12 vols. (Paris, 1812), I: 'Notice' (unpaginated), '...déclare avoir voulu mourir en homme libre', in relation to his suicide attempt at the time of his arrest in 1794.

[21] Riouffe, *Mémoires*, I: 50.

[22] Rist, *Stoic Philosophy*, 250–3.

[23] Ibid., 252. This point appeared obvious to late contemporary commentators, e.g. J.P. Falret, *De l'hypochondrie et du suicide: considérations sur les causes, sur le siège et le traitement de ces maladies, sur les moyens d'en arrêter les progrès et d'en prévenir le développement* (Paris, 1822), 36–7: 'L'orgueil humilié est sans contredit une des choses les plus propres à entraîner au suicide. N'est-ce point à cette passion violente qu'il faut rapporter la fréquence du suicide chez les stoïciens...[each of whom would]...fait attention au théâtre, aux spectateurs, et au temps qu'il choisit pour son suicide'.

[24] An exception was the suicide of the *représentant en mission* Brunel, which although it took place in a crowded house, was carried out while Brunel was alone: Anon., 'Procès-verbal de constat du suicide d'Ignace Brunel député de l'Hérault à la Convention', *La Révolution française* 43 (1902), 363–71.

[25] Thévenaz, 'L'Intériorité chez Sénèque' [ch. 5, n. 4], 193.

[26] Riouffe, *Mémoires*, I: 52.

[27] See also the examination of this point in Bayet, *Le Suicide et la morale*, 687–93.

[28] Even after Thermidor, the cultural imperative remained. Men such as the royalist Vaublanc, who had saved their lives by rejecting Stoic dignity for life on the run, found they had to justify their actions in face of a predominant hostility: 'Des députés, anciens membres du la Convention, en avaient conservés des idées bien singulières; l'un d'eux m'interrompit au moment où je prononcais quelques phrases sur le courage qu'on devait opposer aux factieux; il s'écria, d'un ton de reproche, que je m'étais soustrait par la fuite. "Oui, lui repondis-je, comme un certain poltron romain qui se cacha pendant quatre ans pour éviter les fureurs de Sylla. Ce poltron était César".' Vaublanc, *Mémoires* [ch. 5, n. 37], 309. We shall see in ch. 7 how role-playing continued right up to the foot of the guillotine.

29 La Révellière-Lépaux, *Mémoires* [ch. 5, n. 44], I: 152. Similar remarks to the imprisoned Girondins, significantly enough by a woman, Mme Roland, are reported even by Riouffe, *Mémoires*, I: 56.

30 Vaublanc, *Mémoires*, 262. Such ideas of 'awaiting fate' were an intrinsic part of Stoicism's response to political misfortune. Cp. K.F. Roche, *Rousseau, Stoic and Romantic* (London, 1974), 9: '(Fate was)...a law of necessity... something extra-human in origin, over which the individual has no control, and submission to which is freedom. To struggle against it is the mark of the slave'.

31 Falret, *De l'hypochondrie et du suicide*, 82.

32 Riouffe, *Mémoires*, I: 33, 47.

33 Ibid., I: 44.

34 It was only in January 1794 that the Conciergerie prison was emptied of its ordinary criminal population, and reserved specifically for prisoners charged with offences within the purview of the Revolutionary Tribunal. For statistics of imprisonment, see Donald Greer, *The Incidence of the Terror during the French Revolution: A Statistical Interpretation* (Cambridge, Mass., 1935), 166, and Table VI: estimates of 500,000 cases of imprisonment against 35,000–40,000 deaths in prison or by execution, or 'sans jugement', with a disproportionately high incidence among the middle class. This figure is unaffected by Richard Louie, 'The Incidence of the Terror: A Critique of a Statistical Interpretation', *French Historical Studies* 3 (1964), 379–89.

35 Riouffe, *Mémoires*, I: 45; it is interesting to note that Riouffe locates energy and emotionalism with the people, and control with the élite, remarking, 'J'ai vu au contraire des hommes de la dernière classe du peuple qui, en allant au supplice, prenaient à témoin le ciel et la terre, et faisaient tout retentir de leurs lamentations' (I: 85n). One of the main concerns of Riouffe's whole account is to drive home this difference in comportment, or 'body-management', between upper and lower classes.

36 Ibid., I: 77.

37 For Malesherbes see, most recently, G.A. Kelly, *Victims, Authority and Terror: The Parallel Deaths of d'Orleans, Custine, Bailly and Malesherbes* (Chapel Hill, N. Car., 1982), 234 ff.; like Riouffe, Malesherbes's hagiography comes out of conversations recorded at the time, by fellow prisoners (ibid., 274). For accounts using the Cartouche story: J.B. Delisle des Sales, *Malesherbes* (Paris, 1803); J.-D. Dubois, *Notice historique sur...Malesherbes* (Paris, 1804); M. Gaillard, *Vie et éloge historique de M. de Malesherbes* (Paris, 1805); A.A. Martainville, *Vie de...Malesherbes* (Paris, 1802); Comte Boissy d'Anglas, *Essai sur la vie, les écrits, et les opinions de M. de Malesherbes*, 3 vols. (Paris, 1819–21); the story also appears in the *Biographie universelle (Michaud)* account of Malesherbes. Riouffe, *Mémoires*, I: 72, comments: 'Ce serait une étrange méprise cependant chez une grande nation, et digne en tout de cette désastreuse époque, que de mettre sous les mêmes verroux ses Brutus avec ses galériens, et de confondre ses Scévola avec ses Cartouche: la postérité jugera'.

38 Galante Garrone, *Gilbert Romme*, 479.

39 Furet, *Interpreting the French Revolution* [ch. 2, n. 27], 53.

40 Hobson, *The Object of Art* [ch. 5, n. 38], 32, 43.

41 Similar tendencies in Revolutionary political culture have been identified in M. Ozouf, 'De thermidor à brumaire: le discours de la Révolution sur elle-même', *Revue historique* 243 (1970), 31–66.

42 See the works cited above in n. 11. There are no heroic sucides by independent women. The two most famous examples, of Mme Clavière and Mme Rabaut Saint-Etienne, are treated entirely as reflex actions to those of their husbands. See Riouffe, *Mémoires*, I: 237; des Étangs, *Du suicide politique*, 119.

43 Roche, *Le siècle des lumières en province*

[ch. 5, n. 18], II: Conclusion.

[44] Soboul, *Les sans-culottes parisiens en l'an II* [ch. 2, n. 29], 407–33.

[45] Riouffe, *Mémoires*, I: 58.

[46] For another account of one who chose flight and disguise rather than wait for arrest, see Claude Perroud, 'Le Roman d'un Girondin: le naturaliste Bosc', *Revue du dix-huitième siècle* 1 (1916), 57–77; 232–57; 348–67. Bosc relates how he wore sans-culotte clothes, and did his own domestic labour in his retreat at Sainte-Radegonde. La Révellière-Lépaux, *Mémoires*, I: 162–3, recounts how the *conventionnels* Leclerc and Pilastre owed their safety to a convincing disguise which involved 'playing the part' of skilled craftsmen: 'Dès les premiers moments de la Convention, Pilastre et Leclerc, forts et adroits, s'étaient, par une sage prévoyance, exercés au métier de menuisier.... Pilastre se fit, sur son passeport, garçon menuisier; il se sauva à la faveur de cet heureux déguisement, en travaillant jusqu'au 9 thermidor, en qualité de simple ouvrier....'.

[47] Cf. Barker, *Tremulous Private Body* [ch. 2. n. 21], and Elias, *Civilizing Process: The History of Manners* [ch. 2. n. 4]; both represent the history of the body as its increasing 'management' or even editing out.

[48] E.g., Sydenham, *Girondins* [ch. 5, n. 48]; Pertué, 'Remarques sur les listes de conventionnels' [ch. 5, n. 48]; Galante Garrone, *Gilbert Romme*, 489.

[49] Riouffe, *Mémoires*, I: 51.

[50] Ibid., I: 58.

## CHAPTER 7

[1] Jean-Paul Marat, *Oeuvres* (Paris, 1790), 90.

[2] Pierre Jean Georges Cabanis, 'Note addressée aux auteurs du *Magasin encyclopédique* sur l'opinion de MM Oelsner et Soemmering, et du Citoyen Süe, touchant le supplice de la guillotine', *Magasin encyclopédique* 5 (an IV/1795), 155–74: 172. The article is reprinted in *Oeuvres philosophiques de Cabanis*, ed. Claude Lehec and Jean Cazeneuve, 2 vols. (Paris, 1956), II: 492–504, and in P.J. Cabanis: *Du degré de certitude de la médecine* (Paris, an XI/1803), 311–45, and *Oeuvres complètes* (Paris, 1823), II: 161–83. All citations of Cabanis's article on the guillotine are here taken from the *Magasin encyclopédique* version. On Cabanis in general, see Staum, *Cabanis* [ch. 4, n. 46].

[3] An exception is the research project of Prof. Alain Ruiz, Université Aix-Marseille, on the symbol of the guillotine in Germany during the Revolutionary period.

[4] Stanley Y. Edgerton, '*Maniera* and *Mannaia*: Decorum and Decapitation in the Sixteenth Century', in F.W. Robinson, ed., *The Meaning of Mannerism* (Hanover, N.H., 1972), 67–103: 93–5. See also the same author's *Pictures and Punishment: Art and Criminal Prosecution during the Florentine Renaissance* (Ithaca, N.Y., 1985).

[5] Trahard, *La Sensibilité révolutionnaire* [ch. 5, n. 45], passim.

[6] We do not concern ourselves here with the controversy over Dr Ignace-Joseph Guillotin's responsibility for the machine which bears his name. The machine and its design modifications are described in Antoine Louis, 'Avis motivé sur le mode de la décolation', *Réimpression de l'ancien Moniteur depuis la réunion des Etats-Généraux jusqu'au Consulat, mai 1789–novembre 1799* (Paris, 1842), XI: 689, 22 mars 1792. The 'Avis' itself is dated 7 March, and was presented to the Legislative Assembly on 21 March. See also G.D.F. [Guyot de Fère], *Notice historique et physiologique sur le supplice de la guillotine* (Paris, 1830); Alister Kershaw, *A History of the Guillotine* (London, 1958).

[7] Jean Goulet, 'Robespierre, la peine de mort et la Terreur', *Annales historiques de la Révolution française* 43 (1981), 219–38; Jean Imbert, 'La Peine de mort et l'opinion au dix-huitième siècle', *Revue de science criminelle et de droit comparée* (sér 4) 52 (1964), 724–46; Gordon Wright, *Between the Guillotine and Liberty: Two Centuries of the*

8. Pierre-Louis Lacretelle (l'aîné), 'Discours sur les peines infamantes, couronné à l'Académie de Metz, en 1784, et ensuite à l'Académie française, en 1785, comme l'ouvrage le plus utile de l'année', in *Oeuvres diverses de Pierre-Louis Lacretelle: philosophie et littérature*, 3 vols. (Paris, an X/1802), I: 171–329: 231, 233, 229. Robespierre was the second-prize winner in this competition, with similar arguments: Goulet, 'Robespierre'.
9. Lacretelle, 'Peines infamantes', 284–5.
10. Emile Littré, *Dictionnaire de la langue française* (Paris, 1958), VII: 1174–5, defines *tragédie* as: 'Pièce de théâtre en vers, dans laquelle figurent des personnages illustres, dont le but est d'exciter la terreur et la pitié et qui se termine ordinairement par un événement funeste'. The application of this definition to public events was well-established by the mid-century.
11. J.B. Duvergier, *Collection complète des lois, décrets, ordonnances, règlemens, avis du Conseil d'Etat depuis 1788* (Paris, 1836), III: 352–66.
12. Quoted in Georges Lenôtre, *La Guillotine et les exécuteurs des arrêts criminels pendant la Révolution, d'après les documents inédits tirés des Archives de l'Etat* (Paris, 1914), 221. There had been few beheadings by axe in the last century of the old regime. The last in Paris had been that of Lally-Tollendal in 1766, for the loss of India to the British; see Marc Chassaigne, *Le Comte de Lally* (Paris, 1938). This was a bungled execution which aroused widespread horror at the time, and to which Antoine Louis specifically refers in making the case for the guillotine: see Louis, 'Avis'; it may well have been in Samson's mind also. In spite of their rarity, however, such executions of the great stayed long in the popular memory, even though, owing to their short life-expectancy, the majority of those of the *petit peuple* who witnessed the Lally execution would not have been alive in 1792. For similar points see Pieter Spierenburg, *The Spectacle of Suffering: Executions and the Evolution of Repression: From a Pre-industrial Metropolis to the European Experience* (London, 1984), 81–9.
13. The pre-1789 figure is from Jeffrey Kaplow, *The Names of Kings: the Parisian Labouring Poor in the Eighteenth Century* (New York, 1974), 138, the 1793–4 total from Greer, *Incidence of the Terror* [ch. 6, n. 34], 166. This last, a simple total, is unaffected by the conclusions of Louie, 'Incidence of the Terror' [ch. 6, n. 34].
14. Ibid., 386.
15. In this the bourgeoisie were echoing a generalized fear amongst the French élite of the humiliation of exposure to the crowd, which existed well before 1789; see, for example, the frantic efforts made by the family of Lally-Tollendal to secure his execution in private: Chassaigne, *Le Comte de Lally*, 305. Soboul, *Les Sans-culottes parisiens* [ch. 2, n. 29], 408–11, shows how sharply the sans-culottes were aware of dress as an indicator of social status and political opinions.
16. For Cabanis, see Staum, *Cabanis*. Charles-Ernest Oelsner (1764–1828), native of Silesia, writer, diplomat and political analyst, was from 1789 Paris correspondent of many German newspapers; he accompanied Siéyès on his mission to Prussia, and during the Restoration was a member of the Prussian legation in Paris. His hostile appreciations of Robespierre have been printed in Jacob, *Robespierre vu par ses contemporains* [ch. 5, n. 49], 78–81. The German physician Samuel-Thomas Soemmering (1755–1830) was already well known for his researches on cranial nerves. The debate related here may be regarded as preparatory to his 1796 publication, *On the Organ of the Soul*. The Parisian physician Jean-Baptiste Süe (1760–1829), father of the novelist and stepfather of the *littérateur* Ernest Legouvé, was well known as a practising physician and popularizer of medical mat-

ters: *Dictionary of Scientific Biography*, ed. C.C. Gillispie, 14 vols. (New York, 1975), XII: 509–11; *Biographie universelle (Michaud) ancienne et moderne, nouv. édn.* (Paris, 1848–65), XXXI: 194; *Biographisches Lexikon der Hervorragenden Äerzte alle Zeiten und Völker*, ed. E. Gurlt and A. Hirsch, 6 vols. (Vienna and Leipzig, 1887), V: 578–9.

17 'Sur le supplice de la guillotine, par le professeur Soemmering: Oelsner aux rédacteurs du *Magasin encyclopédique*', *Magasin encyclopédique* 3 (an III/1795), 463–77: 469, 471.

18 'Opinion du citoyen Süe, professeur de médecine et de botanique, sur le supplice de la guillotine', *Magasin encyclopédique* 4 (an IV/1795), 170–89: 171; reprinted in J.B. Süe, *Recherches physiologiques et expériences sur la vitalité* (Paris, an VI/1797), 51–76. Süe's 'Opinion' was also printed in pamphlet form, and sold out after it had formed the spark-point for another controversy, within the Institut national, on 11 messidor an V: Süe, *Recherches*, v. The *Recherches* themselves contain a very detailed account of Süe's experimentation to establish post-mortem sensation in the decapitated head.

19 Cabanis, 'Note', 170.

20 Oelsner, 'Sur le supplice', 465–6; Soemmering, in ibid., 476. Such fears may well have been enhanced by the practice still current in the French provinces, of stripping the executed corpses; their clothes were a traditional source of income for the executioner and his assistants: Lenôtre, *La Guillotine*, 88.

21 Louis Audiat, 'Le mot de Bailly allant à l'échafaud' [ch. 5, n. 42]; and see ch. 5.

22 Amaury Duval, 'De Beccarie et de son livre', *Décade philosophique* 5 (no. 3) (an III/1794), 137–42: 141. This aspect is undiscussed in Kelly, *Victims, Authority and Terror* [ch. 6, n. 37]: 198–211, for Bailly. An example of literal role-playing on the way to the guillotine is provided by a legend attached to the execution of André Chénier (7 thermidor/2 July 1794), which portrays him declaiming with a fellow victim, the poet Roucher, the first scene of *Andromaque*; a scene in which two separated friends are reunited on a strange and foreign shore, *Biographie universelle* XVIII: 81, article by André Fouquier.

23 Cabanis, 'Note', 171–2.

24 *Chronique de Paris*, 22 Apr 1792. This dating of the first execution by guillotine in France should be substituted for that suggested in 'F', 'Rapport sur les premières exécutions', *Annales révolutionnaires* 5 (1910), 244–5, of 21 Aug 1792, the date followed by later historians, e.g., Furet and Richet, *La Révolution française* [ch. 3, n. 5], I: 240. The April execution was of a common-law criminal, the one in August that of the first 'political', Louis-David d'Aigremont. This confusion of dates attests the extent to which historians have exclusively identified the guillotine with political repression, and have failed to measure the effect on the middle class of execution by a method already in use for the repression of ordinary criminals.

25 Quoted in Lenôtre, *La Guillotine*, 310–11. the deputy referred to here could be either Marc-Antoine-Alexis Giraud (1748–1821), deputy for the Charente, or Pierre-François-Félix Giraud (1745–1821), deputy for the Allier, and regicide.

26 'F', 'Rapport'; George Rudé, *The Crowd in the French Revolution* (Oxford, 1959); Soboul, *Les Sans-culottes*.

27 Spierenburg, *Spectacle of Suffering*, 91–4; Edgerton, '*Maniera and Mannaia*', *passim*; Kaplow, *Names of Kings*, 138–55.

28 E.g., the account of the execution of the Marquise de Noailles by the Abbé Carrichon, quoted in Lenôtre, *La Guillotine*, 176–8.

29 Spierenburg, *Spectacle*, 91–4, describes how such crowds were always perceived by middle-class commentators as composed entirely of the *petit peuple*, even though indirect evidence often in fact shows a considerable middle-class attendance. This is,

again, an indication of the middle-class need to distance its own self-image from the execution crowds.
[30] Soboul, *Les Sans-culottes*, 578–80, 425.
[31] 'F', 'Rapport'; Lenôtre, *La Guillotine*, 260–75. Criminal executions remained at the Place de Grève. For the 'politicals', another guillotine was erected in the Place de la Carrousel on 22 Aug 1792, moved to the Place de la Révolution on 21 Jan 1793 – spectators here would have had to accommodate themselves to the terraces of the Tuileries gardens; on 25 Prairial 1795 it was moved to the other end of Paris, to the Barrière du Trône. The second guillotine was also moved to the Place de Grève, and the two execution spots briefly fused, earlier in 1795.
[32] Cabanis, 'Note', 172. A similar point is made by Riouffe, *Mémoires* [ch. 5, n. 33], I: 84–5, 85n: 'leur jugement semblait avoir fait sur eux l'effect d'un enchantement qui les rendait immobiles'. Riouffe also gives us one of our few glimpses of the behaviour of the *petit peuple* sentenced to the guillotine; contrasting their shrieks and cries for mercy with the somnambulistic self-control of the upper-class victims, he yet commends the superior warmth of heart from which these reactions stem.
[33] Spierenburg, *Spectacle*, 185–95.
[34] Troy Duster, 'Conditions for Guilt-Free Massacre', in Nevitt Sanford and Craig Comstock, eds., *Sanctions for Evil* (San Francisco, 1971), 25–36.
[35] See, however, Riouffe, *Mémoires*, I: 88.
[36] E.g., ibid., I: 50 (account of the last days of the condemned Girondins).
[37] See Walzer, *Regicide and Revolution* [ch. 5, n. 19], Introduction, *passim*; Furet, *Interpreting the French Revolution* [ch. 2, n. 27], 49, 56–7.
[38] Quoted in Melchior-Bonnet, *Charlotte Corday* [ch. 3, n. 3], 302–5, I, from the *Révolutions de Paris*, no. 209 (13–19 July 1793), 302–5.
[39] Ibid., from *Chronique de Paris*, 20 July 1793.
[40] Cabanis, 'Note'; similar argumentation in *Réflexions historiques et physiologiques sur le supplice de la guillotine, par Sédillot, le jeune, docteur en médecine de la ci-devant Académie de Chirurgie de Paris, membre du Lycée des Arts* (Paris, an IV/1795). The author may be identified as Dr Jean Sédillot.
[41] See Steven Shapin and Simon Schaffer, *Leviathan and the Air-Pump: Hobbes, Boyle and the Experimental Life* (Princeton, N.J., 1985), ch. 2, *passim*; S. Shapin, 'Pump and Circumstance: Robert Boyle's Literary Technology', *Science Studies* 14 (1984), 481–520.
[42] Süe, 'Opinion', 179; Soemmering, 'Sur le supplice', 464.
[43] Littré, *Dictionnaire*, VII: 28, defines *sensibilité* as: (1) 'Qualité de sentir, c'est-à-dire propriété dévolue à certaines parties du système nerveux par laquelle l'homme et les animaux perçoivent les impressions...(3) Il se dit de la susceptibilité à l'impression des choses morales...', definitions which make clear the double physiological and moral burden borne by the word.
[44] See, e.g., Mallet du Pin, *Considérations sur la nature de la révolution de France et sur les causes qui en prolongent la durée* (London, 1793), 8; 'les passions brutales et énergiques de la multitude'.
[45] This story is repeated throughout the martyrology of the Revolution, particularly in collections concerned with heroic women; e.g. Ségur, *Les femmes* [ch. 5, n. 50], III: 83: 'Dans la voiture qui la menait au supplice, son fichu tomba. Exposée en cet état aux regards de la multitude, elle addressa au bourreau ce mot memorable, "Au nom de la pudeur, couvrez-moi le sein"'.
[46] Melchior-Bonnet, *Charlotte Corday*, 299–300. For similar concerns in the case of an earlier female heroine also condemned to public execution, see Marina Warner, *Joan of Arc: the Image of Female Heroism* (London, 1981), 15–24, 234–5, 103–8.
[47] Mona Ozouf, *La fête révolutionnaire, 1789–1799* (Paris, 1976), 16–17.
[48] Soboul, *Les sans-culottes*, 677.
[49] Spierenburg, *Spectacle*, 185.

[50] Süe, 'Opinion', 177: 'Je crois entendre ceux pour qui la douleur des autres n'est qu'un songe...'.
[51] Soboul, *Les Sans-culottes*, 550–7.
[52] Spierenburg, *Spectacle*, 109–50.
[53] Michel Vovelle, *Mourir autrefois: attitudes collectives devant la mort au XVII$^e$ et XVIII$^e$ siècles* (Paris, 1974), 161–77.

## CHAPTER 8

[1] Hébert, quoted in Baron Marc de Villiers, *Histoire des clubs des femmes et des légions d'Amazones, 1793–1848–1871* (Paris, 1910), 256; Mallet du Pin from his *Mercure britannique*, in C.A. Sainte-Beuve, *Nouveaux Lundis* VIII (Paris, 1867), 222.
[2] The literature on this topic concentrates on working-class women, and on the women organized into political clubs. Older literature also emphasizes the efforts of organized women to back the war effort of 1792–4. There is little enquiry into the reactions of middle-class women such as Mme Roland, or non-activists. See de Villiers, *Histoire des Clubs*; Camille Bloch, 'Les femmes d'Orléans pendant la Révolution', *La Révolution française* 43 (1902), 49–67; Marie Cerati, *Le Club des citoyennes républicaines révolutionnaires* (Paris, 1966); Mary Durham, 'Citizenesses of the Year II of the French Revolution', *Proceedings of the Consortium on Revolutionary Europe* 1 (1972–4), 87–109; Léon Hennet, 'Une femme-soldat: Anne-Françoise-Pélagie Dulierre', *Annales révolutionnaires* 1 (1908), 610–21; Olwen Hufton, 'Women in Revolution, 1789–1796', in Douglas Johnson, ed., *French Society and the Revolution* (Cambridge, 1976), 148–64; D.G. Levy, H.B. Applewhite and M. Durham Johnson, eds., *Women in Revolutionary Paris, 1789–1795: Selected Documents Translated with Notes and Commentary* (Chicago, Urbana, Ill., and London, 1979); Albert Mathiez, 'Les femmes et la Révolution', *Annales révolutionnaires* 1 (1908), 303–5; Albert Soboul, 'Sur l'activité militante des femmes dans les sections parisiennes en l'an II', *Bulletin de l'histoire économique et sociale de la Révolution française* 2 (1979), 15–26. Some of the historiographical roots of this literature are explored in L. Devance, 'Le Féminisme pendant la Révolution française', *Annales historiques de la Révolution française* 49 (1977), 341–76. D. Outram, 'Le Langage mâle de la vertu: Women, Politics and Public Language in the French Revolution', in R.S. Porter and P. Burke, eds., *The Social History of Language* (Cambridge, 1987), 120–35, critically examines attempts made to link organized female groups in the Revolution with modern feminist movements.
[3] See Wallon, *Histoire du tribunal révolutionnaire* [ch. 6, n. 4], I: 296–350, for the trial record of Marie-Antoinette.
[4] Furet, *Interpreting the French Revolution* [ch. 2, n. 27], 66.
[5] Quoted in Levy, Applewhite and Johnson, *Women in Revolutionary Paris*, 93, from Olympe de Gouges, *Les Droits de la femme* (Paris, 1791).
[6] For the contemporary image of Brutus, publicized in, for example, the painting by Jacques-Louis David (cf. ch. 5, n. 54), see Herbert, *David, Voltaire, 'Brutus', and the French Revolution* [ch. 5, n. 9].
[7] See Outram, '*Le Langage mâle*', for further development of this theme.
[8] E.g., speech by the public prosecutor Chaumette to the Paris Commune, 27 brumaire an II, quoted in Levy, Applewhite and Johnson, *Women in Revolutionary Paris*, 219.
[9] *Journal de la république française*, no. 92 (3 Jan 1793), quoted in Alfred Chuquet, 'Buzot et Mme Roland', *Annales révolutionnaires* 1 (1908), 93.
[10] Devance, 'Le Féminisme pendant la Révolution', 347.
[11] This is the approach of Levy, Applewhite and Johnson, *Women in Revolutionary Paris*. An attempt at rectification is contained in Outram, '*Le Langage mâle*'.
[12] Hufton, 'Women in Revolution', 148, 159.
[13] Mme Roland was born Marie-Jeanne

(Manon) Phlipon in Paris in 1754. Her father was a master engraver and dealer in gem-stones. After being educated in a convent in Normandy, she met Jean-Marie Roland de la Platière, an inspector of manufactures, in 1776, and married him in 1780. Their only child, Eudore, was born on 4 Oct 1781, in Amiens. Between 1784 and 1789, they lived either at Lyons or on Roland's family property at Clos, near Villefranche. In 1791 Mme Roland accompanied her husband to Paris as part of a municipal delegation from Lyons to the National Assembly. They returned to Paris in December 1791 and Roland became Minister of the Interior from 23 Mar 1792 to 13 June 1792, and again from 10 Aug 1792 to 23 Jan 1793. In January 1793 Mme Roland confessed to Roland her love for the deputy Buzot. On 31 May, Roland was proscribed by the Convention, and on 10 Nov 1793 killed himself while in hiding in Normandy. Meanwhile Mme Roland was arrested and spent 1–24 June 1793 in the Abbaye prison; she was re-arrested on 24 June and imprisoned in Sainte-Pélagie prison until 31 Oct, when she was transferred to the Conciergerie. She was guillotined on 8 Nov 1793.

14 Mme Roland: *Lettres* [ch. 5, n. 13] and *Mémoires* [ch. 5, n. 44], both ed. Perroud; *Oeuvres de J.M. Ph. Roland, femme de l'ex-ministre de l'Intérieur*, ed. L.-A. Champagneux, 3 vols. (Paris, an VIII/1799–1800); 'Avis à ma fille en âge et dans le cas de devenir mère', in ibid., I: 301–44, written during Eudore's infancy.

15 The capacity of Mme Roland to act as one of the major reference-figures in the nineteenth-century image of the Revolution is attested by the number of editions of her writings prior to Perroud's:

LETTERS: *Lettres autographes, adressées à Bancal des Issarts* (Paris, 1835); *Lettres inédites de Mlle Phlipon adressées aux Demoiselles Cannet, de 1772 à 1780*, 2 vols. (Paris, 1841); Charles-Aimé Dauban, *Étude sur Mme Roland et son temps, suivie des lettres de Mme Roland à Buzot et d'autres documents inédits* (Paris, 1864); *Lettres en partie inédites de Mme Roland aux Demoiselles Cannet suivies de lettres de Mme Roland à Bosc, Servan, Lanthenas, Robespierre, etc.*, 2 vols. (Paris, 1867); *Lettres choisies de Mme Roland* (Paris, 1867); A. Join-Lambert, *Le Mariage de Mme Roland, trois années de correspondance amoureuse, 1777–1780* (Paris, 1896); C. Perroud, *Roland et Marie Phlipon, lettres d'amour, 1777 à 1780* (Paris, 1909).

MEMOIRS AND OTHER WRITINGS: *Appel à l'impartiale postérité, par la citoyenne Roland, femme du ministre de l'Intérieur, ou Recueil des écrits qu'elle a rédigés pendant sa détention aux prisons de l' Abbaye et de Sainte-Pélagie, imprimé au profit de sa fille unique, privée de la fortune de ses père et mère, dont les biens sont toujours séquestrés*, ed. L.-A.-G. Bosc (Paris, 1795), tr. as *An Appeal to Impartial Posterity*, etc. 12 vols. (London, 1796); *Oeuvres de J.M. Phlipon Roland*, introd. L.A. Champagneux, 3 vols. (Paris, an VIII/1800), tr. as *Works of J.M. Phlipon Roland*, 3 vols. (London, 1803); *Mémoires de Mme Roland avec une notice sur sa vie*, 2 vols. (Paris, 1820), in MM Berville and Barrière, *Mémoires relatifs à la Révolution française* (2nd edn., 1826; 3rd edn., 1827); *Mémoires de Mme Roland*, preceded by a short biography [signed M. Roger], 2 vols. (Paris, 1823); *Mémoires de Mme Roland*, ed. J. Ravenel, 2 vols. (Paris, 1840); *Mémoires particuliers de Mme Roland*, ed. M. Fs. Barrière (Paris, 1855), vol. VIII in *Bibliothèque des Mémoires relatifs à l'histoire de France pendant le dix-huitième siècle; Mémoires de Mme Roland*, ed. C.-A. Dauban (Paris, 1864); *Mémoires de Mme Roland écrits durant sa captivité*, ed. M.P. Faugère, 2 vols. (Paris, 1864); *Mémoires de Mme Roland*, with a preface by Jules Claretie, 2 vols. (Paris, 1884), in *Bibliothèque des Dames*; *Mme Roland, sa détention à l'Abbaye et à Sainte-Pélagie, 1793, racontée par elle-même dans ses Mémoires* (Paris, 1886). For a study of the MS of the *Mémoires*, and a critical estimate of the earlier editions, see Perroud's introduction to his own edition [ch. 5, n. 44], I: liv-xc, xc-cxxvii.

[16] Gita May: *De Jean-Jacques Rousseau à Mme Roland: Essai sur la sensibilité pré-romantique et révolutionnaire* (Geneva, 1964), and *Mme Roland and the Age of Revolution* (New York and London, 1970). Mme Roland does not appear, for example, in Levy, Applewhite and Johnson, *Women in Revolutionary Paris*.

[17] Edith Bernardin, *Jean-Marie Roland et le ministère de l'Intérieur, 1792–1793* (Paris, 1964), 19. This was a view canonized by the influential nineteenth-century critic, Charles Augustin Sainte-Beuve, in *Portraits des femmes*, nouv. édn. (Paris, 1852), 160–86, 187–206. The essay in question was originally published in 1835. Mme Roland makes a number of different statements about her involvement in the letter of resignation, which veer from womanly denials of authorship to proud claims to have been its originator; see *Mémoires*, I: 240–4: '...j'avais *esquissé* la lettre... je *fis* la fameuse lettre...nous *arrêtames entre nous deux* la fameuse lettre' [*italics mine*].

[18] Sydenham, *Girondins* [ch. 5, n. 48]. The image of Mme Roland as a Girondin 'leader', however, lives on in Chaumié, 'Les Girondins' [ch. 5, n. 53], 49–55.

[19] Marie-France Morel, 'Mme Roland, sa fille, et les médecins: prime éducation et médicalisation à l'époque des lumières', *Annales de Bretagne* 86 (1979), 211–19. This article also sees Mme Roland as a Girondin 'leader'.

[20] Mme Roland, *Mémoires*, II: 36, 101–2.

[21] Ibid., 29.

[22] Ibid., 148–9. Parts of this passage were expurgated by editors up to and including Dauban (see n. 15).

[23] Ibid., 97–9. Mme Roland's interest in perpetuating descriptions of her own appearance also found expression in her commissioning numerous portraits, especially during her imprisonment: Claude Perroud, 'Le portrait de Mme Roland aux Archives Nationales', *La Révolution française* 40 (1901), 153–67. Persistent themes in her verbal self-portrait, such as her image of herself as 'legère comme un oiseau', are discussed in Françoise Kermina's intelligent popular account, *Mme Roland ou la passion révolutionnaire* (Paris, 1976).

[24] Other women who adopted roles of high public visibility also tried the same tactic. One example is the famous portrait painter Elisabeth Vigée-Lebrun, whose *Souvenirs* are examined from this point of view in Jean Owens Schaefer, 'The *Souvenirs* of Mme Elisabeth Vigée-Lebrun: The Self-Imagining of the Artist and the Woman', *International Journal of Women's Studies* 4 (1980), 35–49. Nor was this a phenomenon confined to France; see Patricia Meyer Spacks, *Imagining a Self: Autobiography and Novel in Eighteenth-Century England* (Cambridge, Mass., 1976).

[25] May, *De Rousseau à Mme Roland*, 146, 235; Mme Roland, *Lettres*, II: 48. May, however, fails to turn aside from her analysis of Mme Roland's style to enquire into the significance of the sheer *quantity* of writing which Mme Roland produced.

[26] Pierre Fauchéry, *La Destinée féminine dans le roman européen du dix-huitième siècle, 1713–1807: Essai de gynécomythie romanesque* (Paris, 1972), 179–86, 196–7.

[27] Ibid., 320–1. For Richardson, see Eagleton, *Rape of Clarissa* [ch. 5, n. 14].

[28] May, *De Rousseau à Mme Roland*, 146 and *passim*; Mme Roland, *Lettres*, II: 8: 'Oui, Manon, c'est ainsi qu'on m'appelait; j'en suis fâchée pour les amateurs du roman, ce nom n'est pas noble, il ne sied point à une héroïne du grand genre; mais enfin c'était le mien et c'est une histoire que j'écris'.

[29] Ibid., I: 662; cp. *Mémoires*, II: 185.

[30] Mme Roland, *Lettres*, I: 159 (to Roland, 20 Jan 1782).

[31] E.g., Eagleton, *Rape of Clarissa*, 13ff; Rita Goldberg, *Sex and Enlightenment: Women in Richardson and Diderot* (Cam-

bridge, 1984).
32 Mme Roland, *Mémoires*, II: 22.
33 Kermina, *Mme Roland ou la passion révolutionnaire*, 403. In the same way, Mme Roland records how she fell in love with Roland, not through personal contact with him, but by reading his written works: *Mémoires*, II: 423; the mingling of the erotic and the written could hardly have produced a longer-lasting historical effect.
34 Darnton, 'Readers Respond to Rousseau' [ch. 5. n. 14]; Trahard, *La Sensibilité révolutionnaire* [ch. 5, n. 45], 31.
35 This connection is examined in Tony Tanner, 'Julie and "La Maison Paternelle"', in J.B. Elshtain, ed., *The Family in Political Thought* (Amherst, Mass., 1982), 96–124. Fauchéry, *La Destinée feminine*, 414–16, notes the novel's portrayal of marital bliss for the heroine as magically entailing the creation of an entire pastoral social order.
36 Most recently examined in K.A. Kadane, 'The Real Difference Between Manon Phlipon and Mme Roland', *French Historical Studies* 3, no. 4 (1963–4), 542–9.
37 Mme Roland, *Mémoires*, II: 101–2. More than once, Mme Roland describes her sexual experiences inside marriage as 'aussi surprenantes que désagréables': ibid., 36, 101–2.
38 See B.H.E. Niestroj: 'Die Mutterkind Beziehung im Kontinuum von Neuzeit und Moderne, Zwischen Vernunft und Zürtlichkeit', in J.H. Campe, *Über die früheste Bildung Junger Kinderseelen* (1785), ed. Niestroj (Berlin and Frankfurt-on-Main, 1985), 7–73, and 'Affective Individualism: zwischen Nähe und Dist anz: eine bürgerliche-humanistische Revolution? Zür genealogie der Intimität', *Asthetik und Kommunikation* 15 (1985), 14–37; Karl-Heinz Osterloh, 'The Making of Western Industrial Society and the Revolution of Forms of Interaction', *Archiv für Kulturgeschichte* 58 (1976), 87–131; Adrian Wilson, 'The Infancy of the History of Childhood: An Appraisal of Philippe Ariès', *History and Theory* 19 (1980), 137–53; Philippe Ariès, *Centuries of Childhood* (New York, 1965).
39 Mme Roland, *Lettres*, I: 57 (18 Nov 1781).
40 Elias, *Court Society* [ch. 2, n. 4], 137. Historians such as Edward Shorter who link the rise of the modern 'affectionate' family in the middle class with the lessening in risks to women's health through pregnancy and childbirth, fail to realize that such a utopian vision could only apply from a male viewpoint.
41 See Morel, 'Mme Roland, sa fille, et les médecins', for a discussion of these works.
42 This preoccupation is almost or completely passed over in most biographies of Mme Roland: May, *Mme Roland and the Age of Revolution*; Kadane, 'The Real Difference...'; Kermina, *Mme Roland ou la passion révolutionnaire*; Una Birch, *Mme Roland, A Study in Revolution* (London, 1917); Ida Ashworth Taylor, *Life of Mme Roland* (London, 1911); Ida M. Tarbell, *Mme Roland: A Biographical Study* (London, 1896); Catherine Young, *A Lady Who Loved Herself: Mme Roland* (New York, 1930); Madeleine Clémenceau-Jacquemaire, *The Life of Mme Roland* (London, New York and Toronto, 1930).
43 Fauchéry, *La Destinée féminine*, 403.
44 Mme Roland, *Lettres*, I: 57 (18 Nov 1781).
45 Ibid., I: 85 (26 Dec 1781).
46 The growing enforcement of breastfeeding by the biological mother rather than by a wet-nurse, almost always drawn from a lower social class, can of course be interpreted in many other ways: (1) as a drawing of higher boundary lines around the middle class, by the abolition of a practice which linked mother, and particularly child, to the lower-class wet-nurse's own children; (2) as a drawing of increasingly severe boundaries around the physical outline of the middle-class woman, as was also happening to middle-class men, in a different way; mothers no longer

shared the products of their bodies (babies and milk) with other women.
47 Mme Roland, 'Avis', in *Oeuvres*, I: 301, 306–20.
48 Ibid., 328–9.
49 Ibid., 320.
50 Perroud, 'Le Roman d'un Girondin' [ch. 6, n. 46], 57–77, 232–57, 348–67.
51 Mme Roland, *Mémoires*, I: 63–4, 201, 185, 295–6. I have placed these passages against a more general discussion of Revolutionary public discourse in Outram, '*Le Langage mâle*'.
52 Mme Roland, *Mémoires*, I: 46–7. It is tempting to speculate on the links between Mme Roland's cheerful asceticism in prison, and in particular the reduction in her intake of food, and the efforts made by many female saints to achieve religious sanction by fasting. See, recently, Caroline Walker Bynum, *Holy Feast and Holy Fast: The Religious Significance of Food to Medieval Women* (Berkeley, Los Angeles and London, 1987); R.M. Bell, *Holy Anorexia* (Chicago and London, 1985).
53 Mme Roland, *Mémoires*, I: 292–3.
54 Ibid., I: 39.
55 Mme Roland, *Lettres*, II: 396 (October 1793).
56 J. Lacan, 'The Mirror-Stage', *Ecrits: a selection*, tr,. Alan Sheridan (London, 1977). This is probably the significance of the persistent myth, ably analysed in Kermina, *Mme Roland ou la passion révolutionnaire*, 389, that Mme Roland continued to write her impressions even at the foot of the scaffold itself.
57 Discussed in greater detail by Perroud in Mme Roland, *Mémoires*, I: lxxvii–lxxx. Literary models for suicide by women are discussed by Gita May, *De Rousseau à Mme Roland*, 213 (n. 16), and by Ruth P. Thomas, 'The Death of an Ideal: Female Suicides in the Eighteenth-Century French Novel', in S.I. Spencer, ed., *French Women and the Age of Enlightenment* (Bloomington, Ind., 1984), 203–28.
58 Nancy K. Miller, *The Heroine's Text: Readings in the French and English Novel, 1722–1782* (New York, 1980), 95.
59 Mead, 'On the Concept of Plot in Culture' [ch. 2, n. 36].
60 E.g., Mme Roland, *Lettres*, I: 662. She goes so far as to put aside her child, Eudore, the product of physical acts of generation and birth, as her hold on the future, and ascribe instead solely to her writings her hope of posterity. With these, she wrote, 'j' aurai quelque existence dans la génération future': *Mémoires*, II: 141. She speaks explicitly of writing *as* a physical function like digestion, from early on in her marriage: see ibid., 189.
61 Roussell, *Porneia* [ch. 2, n. 6], 10.

# CHAPTER 9

1 Pierre Drieu la Rochelle, *Interrogations* (Paris, 1917), 88.
2 Pierre Bourdieu, *Distinction: A Social Critique of the Judgement of Taste*, tr. Richard Nice (Cambridge, Mass., 1984).
3 Paulson, *Representations of Revolution* [ch. 2, n. 27], 301.
4 Orr, 'Romantic Historiography of the Revolution' [ch. 3, n. 2], 242–6.
5 Foucault, *La Volonté de savoir* [ch. 2, n. 3].
6 Walter Benjamin, *Illuminations*, ed. Hannah Arendt (London, 1982), 93–4.
7 Theodor W. Adorno and Max Horkheimer, *Dialektik der Aufklärung* (Amsterdam, 1947), 35.

# INDEX

ADORNO, Theodor, 164, 188
ALBURY, W.R., 170
Algeria, revolution in, 155
American Republic, 77
ARCHAMBOULT, Paul, 173
ARMSTRONG, David, 170
*Andromaque* (Racine), 182
ARIÈS, Philippe, 187
aristocracy, 42, 74
AUDIAT, L., 174
AULARD, F.V.A., 88, 171
autonomy, 14, 79, 81, 82, 83, 85, 86, 87, 88, 101, 159, 163, 164, 172; and revolution, 175; *see also* cosmopolitanism; Stoicism; virtue

BABEUF, François-Noël, 90
BAECHLER, Jean, 168, 169
BAILLY, Jean-Sylvain, 80, 81, 112–13, 121, 174–5, 177, 182
BAKER, Keith, 35, 160, 169, 173
BAKHTIN, Mikhail, 9, 15–16, 163, 166
BALLEXSERD, J., 171
BALZAC, Honoré de, 168
BARBAROUX, Charles-Jean-Marie, 127, 130
BARÈRE, Bertrand, 171–2
BARKAN, Leonard, 166
BARKER, Francis, 167, 170
BARNY, Roger, 30, 168, 173
BARRÉ, Judge, 99
BARTHES, Roland, 6, 26, 165
BARTHEZ, Paul Joseph, 54

Bastille, 162
BATESON, Gregory, 7, 166, 167
BAYET, Albert, 177
BAZCKO, B., 169
BECCARIA, Carlo, 107
behaviour, 22, 32, 34, 157–9
BELL, R.M., 188
BELOFF, Max, 166
BENDERSKY, V.W., 167
BENJAMIN, Walter, 89, 161, 188
BENOIT, Mme, 133–4
BERNARDIN, Edith, 186
BERNSTEIN, Basil, 36, 169
BESANÇON, Alain, 39
BIANCHI, Serge, 169
BICHAT, Xavier, 67, 170
BIRCH, Una (Mrs Pope-Hennessy), 187
BIRDWHISTELL, Ray L., 167
BLAKE, W.H., 166
BLOCH, Camille, 184
BLOOMFIELD, Leonard, 22
BLOT, Jean, 165
BLOTTIÈRE, D., 175
BLUM, Carol, 168
body, in political culture, 1; French revolution and, 2, 3; privatized, 2; sacralized, 1; totalitarian states and, 2; *see also* desacralization; French Revolution; women
BOISSIER DE SAUVAGES, 54
BOLLÈME, Geneviève, 170, 171
BONNET, Jean-Claude, 173
BORDEU, Théophile, 54, 55, 66, 170
BORY, J.L., 176

# INDEX

BOSC, Louis-Guillaume, 81, 149, 175, 180
BOURDIEU, Pierre, 153, 158, 188
BOYER-FONFRÈDE, Jean-Baptiste, 83, 85, 90, 96
breast-feeding, 142-4, 187
BRILLIANT, Richard, 174
BRIQUET, Mme Fortuné, 175
BRISSOT, Jacques-Pierre, 78
BRUNEL, Ignace, 178
Brutus the elder, 7, 12, 77, 79, 85, 126, 176, 179
BUZOT, François Nicolas Léonard, 79, 103, 127, 130, 138, 139, 149, 178
BYNUM, Caroline W., 188

CABANIS, Pierre-Jean-Georges, 64, 106, 111-15, 116-17, 118-19, 122, 171, 180
CALVINO, Italo, 41, 169
CAMERON, Averil, 174
Campaign for Nuclear Disarmament, 23
CANGUILHEM, Georges, 169
cannibalism, 63, 64
capital punishment, debates on, 107-9, 123; law on, 107, 109; and middle class, 110-11, 120-3; experimentation and, 111-12; mythology and, 118-20, 121
CARLSON, E.T., 170
carnival, 16
CARNOT, Hippolyte, 172
CARON, P., 171
CARTOUCHE, 99, 179
Catholic Church, 159-61
Cato (of Utica), 68, 71, 72, 77, 85, 93, 94, 101, 124, 151, 172
CAVANAUGH, G.J., 168
CERATI, Marie, 184
CHAMFORT, S.R.N., 178
CHARLES IV, King of Spain, 155
CHARLESWORTH, M.P., 174
CHARTIER, R., 171
CHASSAIGNE, Marc, 181
CHAUMIÉ, Jacqueline, 176
CHÉNIER, André, 182
Cicero, 93-4, 95
civilization, 10, 11-13
CLAIRON, Mlle, 174

*Clarissa* (Samuel Richardson), 150
CLAVIÈRE, 90, 96, 102, 103, 104, 105, 177; Mme, 179
CLÉMENCEAU-JACQUEMAIRE, Madeleine, 187
COBB, Richard, 22, 115, 167
COBBAN, Alfred, 28, 29, 168
COLEMAN, William, 47, 170
*Confessions* (Rousseau), 151
consciousness, 112, 119
conspiracy, 30
CORBIN, A., 171
CORDAY, Charlotte, 28, 63, 64, 65, 85, 118-20, 121, 127, 150, 171, 176, 183
CORVEZ, M., 167
cosmopolitanism, 173
COUGHLIN, Patricia, ix
CREUZÉ-LATOUCHE, 172
CROCKER, Lester G., 177
crowds, revolutionary, 113, 114-15, 134, 181, 182, 189; and guillotine, 113-16, 122-3
cynicism, 95

D'AIGREMONT, Louis-David, 182
DANTON, Georges, 80, 90, 100, 110, 175
DARNTON, R., 173
DARTHÉ, 90
D'AUMONT, Arnulf, 51
DAVID, J.-L., 176, 184
DAVIS, Natalie Zemon, 165, 172
death, 88, 101, 118, 123, 150, 160-2; and Stoicism, 96-7, 98, 101, 150; *see also* desacralization; secularization; Stoicism; suicide; women
*Décade philosophique*, 80
DE FÈRE, Guyot, 180
DE GOUGES, O, 126, 184
DEHERAIN, H., 171
DE LAMBALLE, Marie Thérèse de Savoie-Carignan, Princesse, 16, 63
DELAMBRE, J.B., 175
DE LA SALLE, J., 6, 165
DE MAISTRE, Joseph, 173
DERRIDA, Jacques, 32
desacralization, 1, 2, 49, 51, 89, 117-18, 123, 159-61; *see also*

death; suicide
DESAIVE, Jean-Paul, 171
DE SAUSSURE, Ferdinand, 22, 33
DES ETANGS, Armand, 178
DE SOMBREUIL, Mlle de, 64, 66
DE TOCQUEVILLE, Alexis, 11, 31, 38, 160
DEVANCE, Louis, 127, 184
DE VAUBLANC, Vincent-Marie, 79, 81, 97, 100, 150, 174, 178
DE VILLIERS, Baron Marc, 184
DEVLIN, J., 171
DEVOISINS, 91
DICKENS, Charles, 115, 168
DIDEROT, Denis, 55, 79
Dien Bien Phu, battle of, 177
discourse, political, 29–30, 36, 126, 108
disguise, 81, 180; see also role-playing
dramatic art, 79, 100–1; see also role-playing
DRIEU LA ROCHELLE, Pierre, 153, 188
DE BARRY, Mme, 117
DUCHÂTEL, Gaspard Severin, 176
DUCHET, M., 171
DUCOS, Jean-François, 90, 96, 97, 101, 102, 103
DULAURE, Jacques, 78, 174
DUMAS, Jean, 177
DUNNE, Tom, ix
DURHAM, Mary, 184
DUSTER, Troy, 183
DUVAL, Amaury, 112–13, 123, 182
DUVERGIER, J.B., 181

EAGLETON, Terry, 140, 173
EDGERTON, Stanley Y., 180
EFRON, D., 166
EISENBERG, P., 166
ELIAS, Norbert, 7, 8, 9, 10, 11–13, 14–15, 16, 18, 23, 34, 70, 72, 73, 74, 128, 140, 142, 165, 166, 167
ELIZABETH, Mme, 121
embodiment, 34, 63, 100, 125, 157–9; women and, 125–7, 129, 132, 150–1, 159; see also Roland, Mme
*Émile, ou de l'éducation* (Rousseau), 140, 142, 143
*Encyclopédie*, 49, 67

energy, 102, 103, 121, 162, 179, 183
Epictetus, 95, 98
ELTON, R.A., 171
EULAU, Heinz, 173
EWALD, Fançois, 165
existentialism, 19

fascism, 2, 8, 14, 15; and aesthetic politics, 89
faction, 83
FALRET, J.P., 98, 178
family, 87, 125; ideology of, 87, 131, 141–3, 187
FARGE, Arlette, 169
fashion, 156–7
FAUCHÉRY, Pierre, 136, 137, 143, 186
FEATHERSTONE, M., 166
feminism, 2, 7, 9
feminization of culture, 150–1; see also novels
FÉRAUD, Jean-Bertrand, 16, 63
FERDINAND IV, King of Naples, 155
feudalism, 28, 29
FIGLIO, Karl M., 169
FLAHERTY, D.H., 172
FLESSELLES, Jacques de, 16, 63
folklore, French, 61–4
FOUCAULT, Michel, 4, 5, 6, 7, 9, 16–21, 23, 25, 26, 34, 44, 45, 66, 70, 125, 157, 165, 167, 169, 170
FRANCE, Anatole, 168
FRANKLIN, Benjamin, 72, 173
FRÉCINE, *député*, 177
French Revolution, 2, 3, 12, 21, 22, 27–39, 88, 125; desacralization, 159–61; and 'family drama', 155–6; histories of, 157; and *homo clausus*, 158; and middle class, 153–4; and modernity, 153–64; women and, 125–33, 154–6, 159; *see also homo clausus*
FREUD, Sigmund, 7, 13, 35, 64, 144, 166
FRIBOURG, André, 174
FURET, François, 22, 29–30, 32, 34, 37, 82, 100, 125, 126 157, 166, 167, 168, 169, 170, 174

GALANTE GARRONE, Alessandro, 171
GANCE, Abel, 168
GEERTZ, Clifford, 26, 33, 168, 169

# INDEX

GELFAND, Toby, 44, 169, 170
GELIS, J., 171
gender, 33; *see also* women; middle class
general will, 30, 33, 74–5, 83, 126, 159
GENSONNÉ, Armand, 95
GÉRARD, Alice, 168
*Gerusaleme Liberata* (Tasso), 138, 139
GILBERT, General, 91
GIRAUD, Marc-Antoine-Alexis, 114, 182
GIRAUD, Pierre-François-Félix, 114, 182
Girondins, 127, 130–1, 176, 179; representation of, 176
GOETHE, Johann Wolfgang von, 11, 12, 87
GOFFMAN, Erving, 166
GOLDBERG, Rita, 186
GOODEN, A., 174
GORDON, Linda, 165
GOUBERT, Jean-Pierre, 44, 169, 170, 171
GOUJARD, P., 169
GOULEMOT, J., 167, 177
GOULET, Jean, 180
GRANDCHAMP, Sophie, 175
Greenpeace, 23
GREER, Donald, 179
GREW, R., 169
GRIFFIN, Miriam, 172
GRILLI, Alberto, 172
GRIMAUX, Edouard, 177
GUÉRY, François, 167, 169
GUILHAUMOU, J., 168
guillotine, 106–23, 180, 182; and crowds, 112–16; and death, 160–1; history of, 107; and middle class, 117, 122–3, 160, 181
GUITTON, E., 172

HAIGH, E., 170
HAINES, B., 170
HALLER, Albrecht von, 54, 56, 170
HANNA, T., 166
HANSON, Duane, 24
HARTUNG, Fritz, 173
HASTRUP, Kirsten, 168

heads, 61, 63–4; and decapitation, 111, 119
health, 48, 58
HÉBERT, Jacques-René, 110, 124, 184
Hegelianism, 14
HEIDEGGER, Martin, 39, 160
HEINE, Heinrich, 15
HELLER, A., 176
HELLER, T.C., 172
HENNET, Leon, 184
HÉRAULT DE SECHELLES, Marie-Jean, 174
HERBERT, R.L., 172
Hercules, 162
HERMONT, Daniel, 169
*Histoire*, 168
*Histoire Magazine*, 168
HOBSON, M., 174
Homer, 72
*homo clausus*, 10, 11, 13, 14, 16, 18, 44, 48, 60, 67, 71, 82, 84, 156–8, 160, 161, 177
HORKHEIMER, Max, 164, 188
hospitals, 44–5
HOUCHARD, General Jean-Nicolas, 91
HUFTON, Olwen, 129, 184
HUGO, Victor, 168
HUNT, Lynn Avery, 22, 32, 33, 167, 168
hygiene, 47, 48, 51, 51, 60

iatro-medicine, 54–5
IMBERT, Jean, 180
imprisonment, 91, 100, 101; *see also* Roland, Mme; Stoicism; suicide
industrialization, 2; in France, 3
Inquisition, 161
intentionality, 36
irritability, 54

JACOB, Louis, 175
JAL, P., 176
JEWSON, N.D., 169
JORDANOVA, L.J., 170
*Julie ou la Nouvelle Heloïse* (Rousseau), 136, 137, 138, 139, 150, 151
JULIEN DE LA DRÔME, Mme, 175

KADANE, K.A., 187

# INDEX

KANTOROWICZ, Ernst H., 173
KAPLOW, Jeffrey, 181
KELLY, G.A., 179
KEOHANE, Nannerl O., 76, 172
KERMINA, Françoise, 168, 186
King's body, 4, 17, 75, 80, 125, 159, 160; *see also* sovereignty
KROEBER, A.L., 168
KROPOTKIN, Prince Peter, 28
KUSCINSKI, A., 177

LACAN, J., 149, 188
LACOMB, Rose, 85
LACRETELLE, Pierre-Louis, 108, 109, 115, 122, 181
LAFFEY, John F., 169
LAIRTULLIER, E., 175
LALLY-TOLLENDAL, Comte de, 110, 181
*La Princesse de Clèves* (Mme de Lafayette), 137, 138, 150
LA RÉVELLIÈRE-LÉPAUX, Louis-Marie de, 97, 175
LATOUR, Bruno, ix
LAUNAY, Michel, 177
LAVATER, Johann Kaspar, 146, 172
LAVOISIER, Antoine-Laurent, 90, 102, 175
LEBRUN, Charles, 160
LECLERC, *député*, 81, 180
LECLERC, Pauline, 128
LE FEBVRE DE BEAUVRY, 177
Legislative Assembly, 61
LE GOFF, J., 171
LEGOUVÉ, Gabriel-Marie-Jean-Baptiste, 175, 176
LEGOUVÉ, Ernest, 181
LE NAIN, Louis, 42
LENÔTRE, Georges, 181
*Les Aventures du chevalier de Faublas* (Louvet de Couvray), 139
LEVY, Darlene Gay, 184
L'HUILLIER, Louis-Marie, 90
liberalism, 4
LIPSIUS, Justus, 69–71, 78, 172
literacy, 62
LITTRÉ, Emile, 181
LIVESEY, Jim, ix
LOPEZ, C.A., 173
LOUIE, Richard, 179
LOUIS XIV, 44

LOUIS XVI, 108, 118, 130, 155, 160
LOUIS, Dr Antoine, 107, 109, 180, 181
Loustoucron, 61, 64
LOUVET DE COUVRAY, Jean-Baptiste, 79, 139, 174
LOUX, F., 171
LUCAS, Colin, 22, 167
Lucrece, 86, 126
LUXEMBURG, Rosa, 14

McMANNERS, John, 91, 177
MAINE DE BIRAN, F.R.G., 101
MALESHERBES, Guillaume-Chrétien, 99, 103, 179
MALLET DU PIN, Jacques, 124, 129, 183
MANDROU, Robert, 50, 170
MARAT, Jean-Paul, 28, 38, 64, 83, 106, 127, 174, 180
MARCEAU, Sergeant, *député*, 118
MARIE-ANTOINETTE, Queen of France, 121, 125, 127, 155
MARIE-CAROLINE, Queen of Naples, 155
MARIE-LOUISE, Queen of Spain, 155
MARX, Karl, 3, 15, 27, 34, 39, 76, 90, 154, 177
Marxism, 4, 27, 30–1, 34, 76, 155, 157
MATHIEZ, Albert, 28, 88, 184
MATSON, C., 174
MAUSS, Marcel, 9, 166
MAY, Gita, 130, 136, 186
MEAD, Margaret, 7, 150, 166, 167, 168
medical profession, 46
medicine, 44–67
Medusa, 63
MELCHIOR-BONNET, B., 168
MENDELSSOHN, Moses, 15
MENTELLE, Edmé, 148
MÉRICOURT, Théroigne de, 128
MERRIAM, Charles, 173
MICHELET, Jules, 28, 127, 128
middle class, 37, 38, 39, 40, 47, 66, 108; body image of, 158–64; and capital punishment, 108, 117, 120–3; definition of, 153–4; and French Revolution, 153, 157–9; gender and, 154–5; and

hegemony, 158; political culture of, 87, 102, 106, 153–4, 158; values of, 158; *see also* Bourdieu, P.; French Revolution
MILLER, Nancy K., 150, 188
mind-body problem, 19, 49
MITCHELL, Harvey, 170, 171
modernity, 37, 153–64
modernization, 33
MONTESQUIEU, C.L. de Secondat, 75, 76, 93, 177
Montpellier, 54, 56, 61
MORAVIA, Sergio, 170
MOREL, Marie-France, 60, 131, 170, 186
MORELLET, André, 107, 114
MORTIMER-TERNAUX, M., 171
MUCHEMBLED, Robert, 62, 171
mythology, 6, 103

NAPOLEON BONAPARTE, 73
nationalism, 40
National Socialism, 13, 14, 17
neo-conservatism, 23
nervous system, 53, 66
NEWTON, Isaac, 72
NIESTROJ, Brigitte, 187
NOAILLES, Marquise de, 182
non-naturals, 47, 48, 49, 50, 56
NORA, Pierre, 171, 173
novel, 136, 150; heroines of, 136, 137, 138–9, 150–1; and 'feminization', 140, 150; and identification with, 150–1; *see also* Fauchéry; Goethe; Richardson; Rousseau

objectivity, 66, 157, 158, 164
OELSNER, Charles Ernest, 111–13, 119, 180, 181, 182
OESTREICH, Gerhard, 69, 70, 71, 172, 173
O'LOUGHLIN, Michael, 172
ORR, Linda, 157, 168, 169
OSTERLOH, Karl-Heinz, 187
*otium*, 69, 72, 81
OUTRAM, D., 173, 176, 177, 184
OZOUF, Mona, 122, 173, 179, 183

PACHE, Jean-Nicolas, 127
PAINE, Tom, 1, 165

PALM D'ALDERS, Etta, 128
*Pamela* (Richardson), 139
PARKER, H.T., 69, 93, 172
parricide, 64
Parti Communiste Français, 29
pastoral, 42, 72, 87, 142, 187
patriarchy, 154, 155
PATRICK, Alison, 175
PAULSON, Ronald, 64, 155, 167, 171
peasants, 57–62, 67
PECCHIURA, P., 172
PENN, William, 72
Pericles, 80
PERROUD, Claude, 130, 172, 185, 186
PERTUÉ, Michel, 175
PETER, Jean-Pierre, 165
PETER, Edward, 167
PÉTION, Jérôme, 90, 177
PHILIPPE EGALITÉ, 79
physiology, 119
PICKSTONE, J.V., 170
PILASTRE, 81, 180
PIPONNIER, Françoise, 169
Plutarch, 79, 93, 94, 174
POCOCK, J.G.A., 175
POLHEMUS, Ted, 166
political culture, 22, 31–2, 33, 35, 36
political science, 31, 34
popular culture, 62
prison massacres, 63
privacy, 172
PROUTEAUX, M., 172, 173
PRUD'HOMME, Louis-Marie, 114

RABAUT SAINT-ETIENNE, Jean-Paul, 146; Mme, 179
RAMOND DE CARBONNIÈRES, Louis, 68
rationality, 53, 56, 58, 60, 61, 63, 64, 67, 158
reactivity, 84–5
regicide, 160
repression, bodily, 10, 12
republicanism, 85–7; and suicide, 104–5
REVEL, Jacques, 171
revisionism, 14
Revolution, *see* French Revolution
Revolutionary Tribunal, 90, 92, 116, 118, 177

# INDEX

RICHARDSON, Samuel, 72, 87, 137; see also *Pamela*; *Clarissa*; novels
RIOUFFE, Honoré, 78, 91, 93, 96, 98, 99, 104, 174, 175, 176
RIST, J.M., 178
ROBESPIERRE, Maximilien, 50, 68, 83, 96, 100, 106, 110, 121, 159, 160, 169, 175, 177, 180, 181
ROBIN, Régine, 22
*Robinson Crusoe* (Defoe), 68
ROCHE, Daniel, 74, 173
ROLAND, Eudore, 130, 141, 142–6, 149, 185, 188
ROLAND, Jean-Marie, 67, 83, 90, 130, 138, 146, 147, 175, 185, 187
ROLAND, Mme (Manon Phlipon), 28, 67, 85, 121, 124–5, 127, 129–51, 178, 179, 184–5, 186; and breast-feeding, 142–4; and daughter, 140–6, 185; and Girondins, 130–1; historiography of, 185; and imprisonment, 147–9; physicality and, 131–2; reading and, 132–3, 137–9, 150–1, 187; self-image of, 135–6, 150–1, 186; sexuality and, 133, 134, 147, 187; and Stoicism, 140–1, 148, 150–1; and suicide, 149; and retirement, 172; and writing, 129–30, 136, 188
role-playing, 73, 76, 77, 78–9, 81, 82–3, 100–1, 103
ROMME, Gilbert, 97, 100, 104
ROUCHER J.A., 178, 182
ROUSSELLE, Aline, 152, 165
ROUSSEAU, Jean-Jacques, 72, 74, 75, 76, 79, 87, 93, 144, 150, 151, 173; see also *Confessions*; *Emile*; *Julie ou la Nouvelle Heloïse*; *Contrat Social*
RUDÉ, George, 115, 169, 182
RUIZ, Alain, 180

SAINT-JUST, Louis, 68, 79, 174, 175
SAINT-SIMON, Claude-Henri, 170
SAINTE-BEUVE, C.A. de, 184, 186
SAMSON, Henri, 109–10, 118
sans-culottes, 98, 101, 102, 104, 116, 121, 122
SAPIR, Edward, 22
SCHAEFER, Jean Owens, 186

SCHAFFER, Simon, ix, 183
SCHARANSKY, Nathan, 23
SCHMITT, Carl, 13–15, 25, 26, 166–7
SCHWARTZ, B., 173
science, 154, 158; and gender, 154–5; and norms, 157–8
SEARLE, John, 33, 168
SECORD, Jim, ix
secularization, 72, 80; see also desacralization
SÉDILLOT, Jean, 183
SÉGUR, Louis, Comte de, 81, 175
SÉGUR, Joseph-Alexandre, 175, 176
self-consciousness, 84; women's, 128
Seneca, 70, 90, 93, 95, 98, 176
SENNETT, Richard, 167
sensibility, 54, 56, 66, 86, 106, 107, 117, 119–20, 122–3, 183
sensitivity, 54
*sensorium commune*, 113, 119
sentiment, 72
sexuality, 157; see also Foucault; Roland, Mme; women
SHAPIN, S., 183
SHORTER, Edward, 165, 187
SINGER, B.C.J., 167
SKLAR, Judith, ix
SKOCPOL, Theda, 31, 52, 166, 168
SMITH, Edwin Burrows, 174
SMITH-ROSENBERG, Carroll, 165
SOBOUL, Albert, 22, 29, 115, 122, 167, 168, 184
social sciences, 7
Société royale de médicine, 58
Socrates, 72, 78, 94, 113, 174
SOEMMERING, Christian, 111–13, 180, 181, 182
solitude, 79, 173
SOUBRANY, Pierre Amable, 90, 97, 177
soul, 49, 53, 55, 56, 66; see also *sensorium commune*
SOUVAN, Adélaïde Rosalis, 176
sovereignty, 8, 14–15, 49, 50, 72, 74, 76, 83, 126, 159, 173; see also autonomy; general will
SPACKS, Patricia, 140, 186
SPERBER, H., 166
SPIERENBURG, Pieter, 181

195

# INDEX

SPINOZA, Baruch, 15
state formation 2–4, 11, 14–15, 85–9; and French Revolution, 154–5
STAUM, M.S., 169, 170, 171
STENDHAL (Henri Beyle), 162
Stoicism, 49, 56, 66, 67, 68–89, 145, 156, 160, 177, 178; and death, 150; and execution, 117; and feminization, 140, 150; and heroic suicide, 91–3, 96, 97; and imprisonment, 97–100; and sensibility, 140; and women, 124, 140–1, 150–1; *see also* Roland, Mme
structuralism, 19, 20, 35, 36
subjectivity, 5, 14, 18, 33, 35, 66, 154, 157, 158
SUË, Eugène, 176, 181
SUË, Jean-Jacques, 84, 111–13, 175, 176, 180, 181, 182
suicide, 90–105, 123, 159, 160, 177; heroic suicide, 91–105, 123; legislation on, 91–2; and legitimation, 159; political solidarity and, 104; and republicanism, 104–5; and women, 149–50, 188; *see also* Roland, Mme
SUTTON, G., 170
SYDENHAM, Martin, 130–1, 175

TAINE, Hippolyte, 28, 115
TALMON, J.H., 35, 39, 168, 169
TANNER, T., 187
TARBELL, Ida M., 187
Tarquin, 86, 126
TASSO, 138, 139
TATIN, J.J., 173
TAYLOR, Ida Ashworth, 187
Terror, revolutionary, 81, 89, 103, 106, 110, 111, 120–3, 163
theatricality, 95, 96, 103, 123, 174; and punishment, 109; and suicide, 178; *see also* role-playing; dramatic art
THÉVENAZ, Pierre, 172
THIBAUDEAU, Antoine, 176
THOMAS, Ruth P., 188
THOMPSON, Leslie M., 166
THOMPSON, Stich, 171

TIMERMAN, Jacobo, 23, 167
Titus, Manlius Torquatus, 107
torture, 108
totalitarianism, 163–4; *see also* fascism
tragedy, 109, 114, 115, 116, 122, 123, 181
TRAHARD, Pierre, 175
TROUSSON, R., 174
TUETEY, Alexandre, 177
TURNER, B.S., 166, 167

VALAZÉ, Charles, 95
VALÉRY, Paul, 27, 168
VANPEL, R., 172
VERGNAUD, M., 175
VERGNIAUD, Pierre, 104
VIGEÉ-LEBRUN, Elizabeth, 186
virtue, 30, 72, 76, 77, 108, 119–20, 121, 122, 126; and women, 136, 137, 147, 155
visibility, 42–3, 44–5, 66; medical, 44–5
VOLNEY, Constantia, 51–3
VOLTAIRE, François Marie Arouet de, 72
VON BEUST, J.E., 172
VOVELLE, Michel, 123, 184

WAJDA, A., 168
WALDEN, Keith, 166
WALLON, H., 177
WALZER, Michael, 167, 173
WARNER, Marina, 183
WASHINGTON, George, 173
WEBER, Max, 3, 14, 38, 70, 166
WEINER, Dora B., 170
WILSON, Adrian, 187
women, 83–5, 101, 102, 103–4, 124–8; body-image, 125–6; and embodiment, 125–6, 132, 150, 159; and feminism, 128; and heroism, 84–5; historiography of, 127–8, 129, 184; and novels, 150–1; and republicanism, 85–7; and revolution, 154–6, 159; and sensibility, 86–7; sexuality of, 133, 136; and Stoicism, 103–4, 124; *see also* Roland, Mme
working class, 154–5, 162; and

body management, 179
WRIGHT, G., 180

YOUNG, Catherine, 187

ZANER, R.M., 167
ZIMMERMAN, G., 173